D1450960

Gospel Worship

Gospel Worship

or

The Right Manner of Sanctifying the Name of God in General

and particularly in these three great ordinances:

1. Hearing the Word

2. Receiving the Lord's Supper

3. Prayer

by JEREMIAH BURROUGHS

*Gospel preacher to two of the greatest congregations
in England: Stepney and Cripplegate*

Edited by Dr. Don Kistler

SOLI DEO GLORIA PUBLICATIONS
. . . for instruction in righteousness . . .

Soli Deo Gloria Publications
A division of Ligonier Ministries, Inc.
P.O. Box 547500, Orlando, FL 32854
(407) 333-4244/FAX 333-4233
www.ligonier.org

Gospel Worship was first published in 1648. This edition, in which grammar, spelling, and formatting changes have been made, is © 1990 by Soli Deo Gloria.

ISBN 1-877611-12-3

Sixth Printing 2006
Library of Congress Cataloging-in-publication Data

Burroughs, Jeremiah, 1599-1646.
  Gospel worship, or, The right manner of sanctifying the name of God :
in general, and particularly in these three great ordinances : 1. hearing
the Word, 2. receiving the Lord's Supper, 3. prayer / by Jeremiah
Burroughs ; edited by Don Kistler.
    p. cm.
  Originally published: 1990.
  ISBN 1-56769-068-8 (alk. paper)
    1. Public worship–Sermons. 2. Lord's Supper–Sermons. 3. Prayer–
Sermons. 4. Public worship–Congregational churches–Sermons. 5.
Congregational churches–Sermons. I. Title: Gospel worship. II. Title: Right
manner of sanctifying the name of God. III. Kistler, Don. IV. Title.

BV15.B875 2006
264–dc22

2005030869

Contents

The Life of

Jeremiah Burroughs

(1599-1646)

This very amiable divine was born in the year 1599. He was forced to leave the university, and afterwards the kingdom, on account of his nonconformity. After he later finished his studies at the university, he entered the ministerial work and was chosen colleague to Edmund Calamy at Bury St. Edmunds. In 1631 he became rector of Tivetshal in the county of Norfolk, but upon the publication of Bishop Wren's articles and injunctions, in 1636 he was suspended and deprived of his living. He sheltered himself for some time under the hospitable roof of the Earl of Warwick, but, on account of the intolerant and oppressive proceedings of the ecclesiastical rulers, the noble Earl, at length, found it was impossible to protect him any longer. Shortly after, to escape the fire and persecution, he fled to Holland and settled at Rotterdam, where he was chosen teacher to the congregational church of which Mr. William Bridge was the pastor.

Upon his arrival, he was cordially received by the church, and continued to be a zealous and faithful laborer for several years, gaining a very high reputation among the people. After the commencement of the civil war, when the power of the bishops was set aside, he returned to England, says Granger's *Biographical History*, "not to preach sedition, but peace, for which he earnestly prayed and labored."

Mr. Burroughs was a highly honored and esteemed person, and he soon became a most popular and admired preacher.

After his return, his popular talents and great worth presently excited public attention, and he was chosen preacher to the congregations of Stepney and Cripplegate, London, then accounted two of the largest congregations in England. Mr. Burroughs preached at Stepney at seven o'clock in the morning, and William Greenhill at three in the afternoon. These two persons, stigmatized by the historian Anthony Wood as notorious schismatics and independents, were called by Mr. Hugh Peters, one "the morning star," the other "the evening star of Stepney."

Mr. Burroughs was chosen to be one of the Westminster Assembly of Divines, and was one of the dissenting brethren, but a divine of great wisdom and moderation. He united with his brethren, Messrs. Thomas Goodwin, Philip Nye, William Bridge, and Sydrach Sympson, in publishing their own "Apologetical Narration" in defense of their own distinguishing sentiments. The authors of this work, who had been exiles for religion, to speak in their own language, "... consulted the Scriptures without any prejudice. They considered the Word of God as impartially as men of flesh and blood are likely to do, in any juncture of time; the place they went to, the condition they were in, and the company they were with, affording no temptation to any bias."

They asserted that every church or congregation has sufficient power within itself for the regulation of religious government, and is subject to no external authority whatever. The principles upon which they founded their church government were to confine themselves in everything to what the Scriptures prescribed, without paying any attention to the opinions or practices of men; nor to tie themselves down too strictly to their present resolutions, so as to leave no room for alterations upon a further acquaintance with divine truth. They steered a middle course between Presbyterianism and Brownism: the former they accounted too arbitrary, the latter too rigid, deviating from the spirit and simplicity of the gospel.

These are the great principles of the Independents of the present day.

Richard Baxter, who knew his great worth, said, "If all the Episcopalians had been like Archbishop Usher, all the Presbyterians like Stephen Marshall, and all the Independents like Jeremiah Burroughs, the breaches of the church would soon have been healed." The last subject on which Burroughs preached was his *Irenicum*, an attempt to heal the divisions among Christians. This title has been published by Soli Deo Gloria Publications. His incessant labors, and his grief for the distractions of the times, are said to have hastened his end. He died of tuberculosis on November 14, 1646, at the age of 47. The historian Granger says, "he was a man of learning, candor, and modesty, and of an exemplary and irreproachable life." Thomas Fuller has classed him among the learned writers of Emmanuel College, Cambridge. Williams' *Christian Preacher* says that his *Exposition of Hosea* is a pleasing specimen, to show how the popular preachers of his time applied the Scriptures in their expository discourses to the various cases of their hearers. He published several of his writings while he lived, and his friends sent forth many others after his death, most of which were highly esteemed by all pious Christians.

The Works of
Jeremiah Burroughs

(Adapted from Benjamin Brook's *Lives of the Puritans*, Volume 3, pages 18–25)

SERMON I

The Introduction

*"Then Moses said unto Aaron, it is what the Lord
spake saying, 'I will be sanctified in them that come nigh Me,
and before all the people I will be glorified.'
And Aaron held his peace."*

LEVITICUS 10:3

*T*hese words are the speech of Moses to Aaron, his
brother, endeavoring to quiet and comfort his
heart, which was (no question) exceedingly troubled by the great and sore affliction that was upon him in the
strange death of his two sons, Nadab and Abihu. The story is
this: after Aaron's sons were consecrated to the priestly office,
coming to attend their office the very first day after their consecration to offer incense to God, they ventured to offer incense
with strange fire, with other fire than God had appointed.
Upon that, the fire of God's wrath broke out upon them and
slew them both presently in that very sanctuary before all the
people. It was a solemn time, being the beginning of the solemn consecration of the priesthood. Upon this, the spirit of
Aaron could not but be exceedingly troubled to see his two
sons thus struck. Now Moses came to him and said, "This is
what the Lord spoke, 'I will be sanctified in them that draw
nigh Me, and before all the people I will be glorified.' " And
upon this, Aaron held his peace.

We read that once fire came down from heaven in a way

of mercy to consume the sacrifices, but now fire came down from heaven in a way of judgment, to consume the sacrificers, Nadab and Abihu. They were Aaron's sons, the sons of a godly man, the sons of the high priest. They were his eldest sons; for Aaron had other sons besides Nadab and Abihu. He also had Eleazer and Ithamar; but these were his eldest sons. They were two young men, struck in the very prime of their age. They were two who were newly consecrated in the priest's office, for so you find in the ninth chapter. They were two men of renown in the country and before all the people of Israel, two men whom God had greatly honored before, as you shall find in the beginning of Exodus 24.

Nadab and Abihu were men of great reputation and great renown whom God had honored in former times. When God called Moses and Aaron to come up to Him with the elders, He singled out Nadab and Abihu among the rest and named them. He said, "Come up unto the Lord, you and Aaron, Nadab and Abihu, and seventy of the elders of Israel." Moses and Aaron, and Nadab and Abihu alone are named, and then seventy of the elders in general; but Moses, Aaron, Nadab, and Abihu are specifically named, as if these were the four eminent men of renown among all the people of Israel. He named none of the seventy elders but these two, besides Moses and Aaron. Therefore, these two who were consumed by strange fire were renowned men and newly consecrated into their office.

QUESTION. What was their sin?
ANSWER. Their sin was in offering strange fire, for the text says that they offered strange fire that God had not commanded them. But had God ever forbidden it? Where do we find that God had ever forbidden them to offer strange fire, or appointed that they should offer only one kind of fire? There is no text of

Scripture that you can find from the beginning of Genesis to this place where God had said in so many words expressly, "You shall offer no fire but one kind of fire." And yet here they are consumed by fire from God for offering strange fire.

I find in Exodus 30:9 that they were forbidden to offer strange incense, but I do not find that they were forbidden to offer strange fire. In Leviticus 6:13, and divers verses in that chapter, we find that God had appointed that they should constantly keep the fire on the altar burning and never let it go out. It seems that it was God's intention that they should make use of that fire and that fire only. God would have them to pick out His meaning. God sent fire down from heaven upon the altar. In the latter end of the ninth chapter, God sent down fire from heaven and gave them a charge to keep that fire on the altar constantly and to never let it go out. So it seems that God would have them pick out His meaning, that because He had sent down fire from heaven upon the altar and gave them power to keep it constantly, God would have them understand therefore that what incense or sacrifice He would have them use should be only that fire and no other. It should be noted, though, that God never did say to them directly in these words, "You shall make use of this fire and no other," but God would have them to understand this. That's their sin, therefore, in offering strange fire.

Now fire came from the Lord and consumed them. Some think that this fire came from the altar, but surely it could not be any ordinary fire that consumed Nadab and Abihu at this time; for you find in the next verse that the bodies of Nadab and Abihu were not consumed by the fire. No, nor their clothes either. They were killed by the fire, and yet their clothes were whole. Therefore it was not an ordinary fire. It was some celestial fire that struck them and slayed them, for so the text says in verse 4: "Come near; carry away our brethren from before the sanctuary out of the camp; and so they went and carried them in their coats out of the camp." So their clothes and bodies were not consumed, yet they were killed by the fire. They were struck with a sudden death, and that in the presence of the Lord, such a death as God had never threatened in the Word before.

God had never threatened the priests and said, "If you offer strange fire, you shall be consumed by fire," but God smote them with death by fire. They did not have time to seek God, no, not so much (as we used to say) as to say, "Lord, have mercy on me." They had no time to promise amendment at all.

Now upon this heavy judgment, the heart of Aaron could not possibly be anything but very troubled; yea, and the spirit of Moses too, for Moses was their uncle. They could not but be exceedingly grieved. But Moses, being the brother of Aaron, and seeing that his spirit (no question) was exceedingly troubled, being under such a sad affliction, and that such a godly man as Aaron was should have such a sad judgment befall his children, Moses came and spoke comfortably to him and labored to support his spirit.

How did he do it? He did not come as you ordinarily used to visit your brethren: "Oh! You must be content with this!" No, but he came and applied the Word of God, and showed how God must be sanctified. And by that, he came to quiet the heart of his brother, Aaron. "This is that which the Lord has spoken," Moses said. He sought to stay the heart of his brother with that which God spoke.

QUESTION. But where do we find that God spoke this?
ANSWER. It's hard to find in any Scripture these words before this time; and therefore Augustine thinks it was only the word God had spoken, but not written. And so they had it from hand to hand by tradition as they did many other things, like the

prophecy of Enoch that the Apostle Jude speaks of. You do not find it written in the Book of God, and yet the apostle speaks of it; so that indeed it was from hand to hand. Yes, and we find it in the New Testament also. Paul speaks of a thing that Christ was to have said: "It is more blessed to give than to receive." You do not find it recorded in the gospels that Christ said so. So this is that which the Lord said, though it was not written from the beginning of Genesis to this very place. Otherwise, though it is not recorded in expressed terms, yet something is recorded to the same purpose and effect. It may seem to have reference to Exodus 29:43. There we have a Scripture which comes as near to it as any I know of, "... there I will meet with the children of Israel, and the tabernacle shall be sanctified by My glory." That's as much as saying, "I will be sanctified by those who come near Me. In those who come to worship Me in My tabernacle, I will be sanctified in all things that concern My worship. I will be sure to be sanctified there."

"I will be sanctified," that is, "I will be hallowed." It is the very same word that you have in the Lord's Prayer, "Hallowed be Thy name," only that's the Greek word and this is the Hebrew. But if you would translate this into Greek, you must translate it by the same that Christ spoke when He taught His disciples to pray, "Hallowed be Thy name." Hallowed and sanctified are all one. "Lord, let Thy name appear to be holy."

"I will be sanctified," that is, "I will have My name appear to be holy. I will make known unto My people, and to all the world, that I am a holy God." That's the meaning of "I will be sanctified." I will be known to all the world as a holy God.

"And before all the people I will be glorified." So it is in the latter part of the verse. It is as if God should say, "I account it to be My glory that I should be manifested to be holy before all the world."

"I will be sanctified," that is, "I will have My people to demean and carry themselves so as to hold forth their acknowledgment of My holiness, so that, by their behavior, I may appear to be a holy God. I will be sanctified by them, or otherwise, if they shall not in an active way sanctify My name, that is, if they shall not demean themselves so as to hold forth the glory of My holiness, then I will be sanctified upon them. I will demean and carry Myself towards them so that by My actions upon them I will make it appear what a holy God I am."

So God is sanctified in two ways. One is by the holiness of His people in their conduct towards Him, holding forth the glory of God's holiness. So you have it in 1 Peter 3:15: "Sanctify the Lord God in your hearts." The saints sanctify God in their hearts when they fear God as a holy God, and reverence Him and love Him as a holy God. They sanctify Him in their lives when their lives hold forth the glory of God's holiness. Then God is sanctified.

But then, if we do not do so, God sanctifies Himself in ways of judgment upon those who do not sanctify His name in ways of holiness. Thus you have it in Ezekiel 28:22: "And say, thus saith the Lord God, Behold I am against thee, O Sidon, and I will be glorified in the midst of thee, and they shall know that I am the Lord, when I shall have executed judgment in her, and shall be sanctified in her." This is all one with "I will be glorified in the midst of them." And in Ezekiel 38:16 and 23 you have verses to the same purpose: "And thou shalt come up against My people of Israel, as a cloud to cover the land; it shall be in the latter days: and I will bring thee against My land, that the heathen may know Me, when I shall be sanctified in thee, O Gog, before their eyes" (verse 16). "Thus will I magnify Myself, and I will be known in the eyes of many nations, and they shall know that I am the Lord" (verse 23). In the way of the execution of judgment, thus I will sanctify Myself, so I will be sanctified in those that draw nigh unto Me."

"In those that come nigh Me," that is, especially the priests who approach God (Ezekiel 42:13). They approach God especially, but it is meant generally of all those who deal in God's worship. "Whosoever shall come to Me, let them look to it. They must sanctify My name; they must so demean themselves in My worship as to hold forth My name to be holy. Otherwise, I will manifest Myself against them in the ways of judgment; for I will appear to be a holy God. I will have the glory of My holiness in one way or another from those who come near Me."

It is as if God should say, "Though it's otherwise with men, they indeed will be ready to favor those who are near them. But I will not do so."

Men will sooner pass by the offences of those near them than those who are not. Suppose that a stranger were to commit an offense. You would be severe towards him. But suppose that it were one of your own children or kinsmen; what would you do then? Do we not see that men will rather favor their own kindred than strangers, though the offense is the same? "But I will not do so," says God.

Suppose it is one of your own family. Will you not be ready to excuse them? Suppose it were your own child who should commit such an offense. Oh, what friends would you make to take him off of punishment? Though men would do so towards their own, yet be bitter and severe towards strangers, it will not be so with God. "Let those who are near to Me look to it. I will be sanctified by them. I will be sanctified in those who draw near to Me."

Now when Moses said that God would be sanctified in those who draw near Him, it was as if he had said, "Aaron, though I confess that the hand of God is heavy upon you this day, yet it is fitting for you to submit to God. It is fitting that God should be glorified, whatever becomes of you. You are dear to God, but God's name is dearer to Him than you are. Whatever the lives of your sons were, yet it is fitting that God should be honored and His name sanctified, whatever becomes of your sons or your comforts—therefore, let your heart be quieted. You have had a great loss and affliction upon you, but God has had glory. God has glorified Himself."

"How has God glorified Himself? Very much by this way, for God, by this way, has done an act to make all the people of the land fear Him, to cause them to worship Him with all reverence. All the people of the land, seeing such a judgment as this and hearing of it, will learn forever to fear and reverence this God. They will say, 'How shall we appear before this holy God? We need to take heed in His presence and worship Him according to the way that He would be worshipped.' " It is as if Moses had said, "This honor that God has by this means in the hearts of His people, you should account it a greater good than the lives of your children, whatever they are." This is the scope of Moses' speech to Aaron.

Now upon this, the text says, "Aaron held his peace." He was silenced. It may be that before this he was expressing himself in grief and sorrowing much in words; but now he was quiet and had nothing to say. He, by his silence, acknowledged that his children were dear to him, but that it was fitting that God should be glorified whatever becomes of his children. And therefore, Aaron held his peace.

But the word that is translated "held his peace" has more in it than mere silence, for the Hebrews have another word to signify mere silence of speech. This signifies a staying of the heart, so that it does not proceed in any trouble of spirit, a silence in the very heart. It is a staying of it, a staying of the motions of the heart.

I find the same word to be used in Scripture when Joshua said to the sun, "Stand still; stay thyself on Gibeon" (Joshua 10:12). It is the same word that is here translated, "and Aaron held his peace." That is, he was stayed from further vexing or troubling himself, from being disquieted. Whereas his heart was in a strong, violent motion, Moses' speech stopped him, and stopped his heart so as to make it stand still in a wonderful manner, as the sun did when Joshua spoke to it and it stood still. It is as if the Lord had said to his heart, "Aaron, your heart is in a mighty strong motion; but consider that I must be sanctified in those who draw near Me. So let all those motions of your heart be stopped and be quiet."

Thus you see the meaning and scope of the Scripture. In this Scripture you have these three special and notable points:

1. In worshipping God, there is a drawing nigh unto Him.
2. When we draw nigh to God, we should take heed to ourselves that we sanctify God's name.
3. If we do not sanctify God's name in our drawing nigh to Him, then certainly God will sanctify His own name upon us.

These are the three points that I intend to handle, and the second especially I intend to handle at length among you. I confess that upon another occasion, in one sermon, I have spoken out on these words; but now I intend not only in general to show you how you should sanctify God's name in worship, but likewise in the particular acts of worship, such as sanctifying His name in prayer, in receiving the Sacrament, in hearing the Word, in the several chief parts of worship how His name should be sanctified. In all these you draw nigh unto God. And for that end, I have pitched my thoughts upon this Scripture.

But before I come to these three great points, the principal points in the words read to you, I shall take up twenty observations that are scattered, as it were, that are of great use, and will help us further to make use of this Scripture in the other points that I shall come to afterwards and more largely.

1. In God's worship, there must be nothing tendered up to God but what He has commanded. Whatsoever we meddle with in the worship of God must be what we have a warrant for out of the Word of God. This speech of Moses' is upon the occasion of the judgment of God upon Aaron's sons for offering strange fire. They offered fire that God had not commanded. Hence I say that all things in God's worship must have a warrant out of God's Word. It must be commanded; it's not enough that it is not forbidden. I beseech you to observe it. It is not enough that a thing is not forbidden, and you cannot see what harm there is in it. But it must be commanded. I confess that in matters that are civil and natural this may be enough. If it is according to the rules of prudence and not forbidden in the Word, we may make use of this in civil and natural things. But when we come to matters of religion and the worship of God, we must either have a command, or something out of God's Word drawn from some command, wherein God manifests His will, either by a direct command, or by comparing one thing with another, or drawing consequences plainly from the words.

We must have a warrant for the worship of God. One would have thought that these priests were offering incense to the true God, so what harm was there in taking other fire? But there was no command for it, and therefore it was not accepted. It's true that there are some things in the worship of God that are natural and civil helps; and there we do not need to have a command. For instance, when we come to worship God the congregation meets. They must have a convenient place to keep the air and weather from them. Now this is only a natural help, and so far as I use the place of worship as a natural help, I need have no command. But if I put anything in a place beyond what it has in its own nature, there I must look for a command; for if I account one place more holy than another, or think that God should accept worship in one place rather than another, this is to raise it above what it is in its own nature.

So when any creature is raised in a religious way above what it has in it by nature, if I do not have Scripture to warrant me, I am therein superstitious. It is a very useful rule to help you. If any creature that you make use of in a way of religion beyond what it has in its own nature, if you do not have some warrant from the Word of God (whatever specious a show there may be in it), it is superstition.

There was a place that was holy, but it had an institution from God. As for garments, to use those that are decent, the light of reason is enough. But if I put anything upon them beyond what there is in them in their own nature, as has been done with a surplice, does that have any more decency in its own nature, or was it not only man's institution? Now when man shall put a religious respect upon a thing by virtue of his own institution, when he does not have a warrant from God, that is superstition! We must all be willing worshippers, but not will-worshippers.

We must come freely to worship God, but we must not worship God according to our own wills. Therefore, whatever we do in the worship of God, if we do not have a warrant for it, when this is said, "Who required this at your hands?" it will stop our mouths another day.

In Matthew 5:19 we read, "In vain do they worship Me, teaching for doctrine the commandments of men." It is a vain thing to worship God when there is nothing but a commandment of man for this worship. If you would worship God, you must have a commandment of God for the worship. And in Isaiah 29:13, there is a place to the same purpose that shows how the Lord is offended with any man who shall teach His fear by their own precepts: "Forasmuch as this people draw near Me with their mouth, and their lips do honor Me, but have removed their heart far from Me, and their fear towards Me is taught by the precepts of men."

Mark it. Now if this is so, may the Lord have mercy upon us in this thing. You have cause to be humbled, every one of you, I believe, in some degree of other; this congregation very much, and most other congregations that have had the fear of God taught them by the precepts of men.

How many things have there been in the worship of God that you can show no warrant for in the Word? A great many things are merely men's inventions. However, they are now cast out, because authority came and cast them out, and so you submitted to it. But that's not enough for you to submit to it because authority would have it so. You ought to be humbled before God for all your will-worship, for all your yielding to anything in the worship of God that was taught by the precepts of men.

You see how severe God was to Nadab and Abihu for just taking other fire than that which God had appointed, though there was no direct command against it. If the Lord has spared you and not manifested any displeasure upon you, you have cause to acknowledge God's mercy, and to be humbled for all your false worship. Certainly God expects this land to be humbled for its will-worship; otherwise we sow among thorns.

All the reformation that is among us is meaningless if there is not a humiliation for all our false worship. It is not enough that we now set up the true worship of God, but we must be humbled for our false worship. That's the first note: In the worship of God there must be nothing but what God commands.

2. In the matter of worship, God stands upon little things. Some things may seem to be very small and little to us, yet God stands much upon them in the matter of worship; for there is nothing wherein the prerogative of God more appears than in worship. Princes stand much upon their prerogatives. Now God has written the law of natural worship in our hearts. But there are other things in the worship of God that are not written in our hearts, that only depend upon the will of God revealed in His Word, which would not be duties except that they are revealed in His Word. And these are of such a nature that we can see no reason for them except that God would have them so. For example, there many kinds of ceremonies to manifest the honor to princes, that have no reason at all but merely because it is a civil institution so appointed. So God would have some ways of honoring Himself that the creature may not see a reason for but merely that it is the will of God to have them so.

God stands much upon little things, though men would think it a little matter whether they use this fire or that fire. Men will say, "Will not this burn as well as that?" But God stands on it. And so it was for the ark. Uzzah did but touch the ark when it was ready to fall. Now we would think it to be no great matter; but one touch of the ark cost him his life. There is not any one small thing in the worship of God but God stands mightily upon it.

In the matter of the Sabbath, that's His worship. For a poor man to gather a few sticks, what great matter is it? But God stands upon it. And so when the men of Beth-shemesh did but look upon the ark, it cost 50,070 men their lives. If it is a matter of a holy thing that concerns His worship, He would not have it abused in anything. Let us learn to make conscience of little things in the worship of God and not to think, "Oh, how particular these people are about these small things!" You do not understand the nature of divine worship if you are not particular about it. God is particular, and stands upon little things in the matter of His worship.

3. There are no privileges or dignities of men that can secure them from God's stroke. First, Moses, the man of God, was their uncle. Aaron, that great instrument of God's glory, was their father. They were men who were newly consecrated to the priest's office. They were renowned, men who God put much glory upon; yet if they will venture to offend God in this little thing, God's wrath breaks out upon them and kills them presently. Let us take heed, then, of venturing, and do not think that any services that we have done heretofore can bear us out. If the greatest cannot be borne with all their privileges, how dare we poor worms venture upon the displeasure of God? You who are a worthless creature, of no use at all in the world, do you dare provoke this God, when the Lord is so angry with men who are of great use and service as to let out His wrath upon them suddenly?

If you should see a prince not spare his favorite or his nobles who are about him, but upon one offense (that we think is but a little offense) the prince's anger should be so much against them as to cost them their lives, what cause is there for poor people to tremble then when they have done that which may incur the anger of their prince? You see that all outward privileges and greatness will not excuse a man from the stroke of God's justice. They should not excuse anyone from the stroke of man's justice. It's true that among men poor people go to prison if they offend; but if great men offend they escape.

But it is not so with God, for Nadab and Abihu were great and renowned men.

4. The more the dignity of men is, the more is their danger if they do not look to it. This note I gather from hence, that Nadab and Abihu were the two eldest sons of Aaron; and we find in Scripture that Eleazer and Ithamar, the two other sons of Aaron, escaped and were not thus consumed. Why? Because the two elder sons had the dignity and privilege to come and offer the incense, and, having greater dignity than the younger, but not being careful to behave themselves as they ought to do, the Lord smote them and the younger two escaped.

And so, many times, those who are in a meaner condition escape while those who are in a higher condition are struck. Let men who are in a higher condition look to themselves, for their danger is greater. And you who are in a meaner condition, do not envy those who are in a higher one, for you may be more safe in that mean condition which you are in than they are in theirs.

5. The beginnings of things of high concern sometimes meet with great difficulties and interruptions. This note I gather from hence, that Nadab and Abihu were struck at the very beginning of their priesthood. Suppose that there was a new public office erected in a commonwealth that concerned the public good of the kingdom; and in the very first erecting of the office, some hideous accident took place that rang throughout the whole kingdom, as if God from heaven had done something against them in that office.

Suppose that the first time the judges were to come to the bench, God struck them dead from heaven at the very bench. It would be a mighty matter to darken the glory and honor of that office. So one would think that it would have been a mighty matter to have darkened the glory and the honor of the priesthood. But God does not stand upon that. Many times the beginnings of great things are darkened by sad accidents; and therefore let us not be offended though we see some sad accidents fall out at the beginnings of great things, for though accidents fall out sadly at first, yet God may prosper it afterwards, as He did the priesthood.

6. Those who enter into public places, and especially such places as concern the worship of God, need to have the fear of God much upon them when they first enter into those places. This would be a very good point to preach to an audience of ministers. You see that the Lord smote Nadab and Abihu for this little miscarriage (as we would think) at their first consecration. But this note especially concerns ministers, and therefore I will pass over it.

7. God would have us all to pick out His mind from dark expressions in His Word. Though He does not express His will fully and in expressed terms, yet if there is anything in His Word whereby we may come to gather the mind of God, God expects that we should gather His mind out of His Word. If we do not, it's at our own peril.

OBJECTION. You will say, "How could they have known that it was God's mind that they should not offer any fire but that on the altar?"

ANSWER. They should have reasoned thus with themselves: "Has God let fire come down from heaven upon the altar, and has He commanded that it should be preserved on the altar for His service? Surely this must be God's mind, then, that we should make use of this fire rather than any other fire."

God expects that they should have reasoned thus; but because they did not pick out God's mind by reasoning after this manner, therefore the hand of God came out upon them. They offended, and it may be that it was through ignorance, but it was at their peril. If they were ignorant of the mind of God when it might be known, though it was only darkly revealed and had to be picked out from several places compared together, it was at their peril.

It is a point that we have a great need for, for such is the vain heart of man that if there is anything that God would have that is not suitable to his own ends, he will stand wrangling and objecting against it. "How does it appear? Can you bring expressed Scripture for it? Bring me expressed Scripture in words to prove it and then I will believe it." And so he will stand out until you bring so many words of Scripture that forbid such a thing or command such a duty.

Now, brethren, if you are of the temper that you will forbear nothing, nor set up anything but what you have directly expressed words of Scripture for, you may run at your own peril into woeful dangers, into woeful sins. Know that God has so revealed a great part of His mind as it is only to be known by gathering one thing from another. And God expects this from you, that if upon examination of Scripture one thing appears more likely to be His mind and will than another, you are bound to go that way which is more likely.

I have told you before that in matters of worship we must have warrant from the Word; but it does not follow that we must have a direct, expressed warrant for everything. As it is many times in some kind of picture, the great art is in the cast of the looks. You cannot say it's in the drawing of this line or the other line, but altogether. It is the cast of the looks that causes the beauty of the picture. So in the Scripture you cannot say that this one line or the other line proves it, but let them all be laid together and there will a kind of aspect of God's mind. We may see that this is the mind of God rather than the other, and we are bound to go that way.

Nadab and Abihu might have seen that they should rather

have taken fire off the altar than any other fire, but they presumed because they did not have expressed words. You can see that it was to their peril. Oh, take heed of standing out and wrangling against what is required because you do not have expressed words! The Lord has laid things so, and especially in the New Testament, for the ordering of the church in the New Testament. You do not have expressed commands for an abundance of things, but sometimes you have an example in some things, and not always a clear example, either. But compare one thing with another, and that which seems to be nearest the mind of God should be enough of a bond to tie us to go according to what the mind of God seems most probably to be in the Scripture. A humble heart will soon be convinced when another man is not.

We find clearly that such things as are most suitable to men's own ends, a little matter will serve to persuade men to it, though one might argue against it. I could easily show it, but I do not think it is so convenient in the pulpit to meddle with such things as these are. Those things that are suitable to men's own ends and ways they will close with, but other things that cross the flesh, that are most opposed to looseness and would bring men most under the government of Christ, those things men stand out against. They must have clear and expressed words, expressed and clear warrant out of the Word in so many terms, or otherwise by no means will they so much as yield to it. That's a point that, if God would but settle it upon our hearts, might be of very great use. A gracious heart will see the truth through a very little crevice. But it is marvelous to consider what a task it is to convince man of some part of God's will before he is humbled, and how easy it is to convince a man after he is humbled.

8. Sinners may meet with some judgments of God that were never threatened in His Word. God never threatened beforehand and said, "Whoever offers strange fire, I will consume them with fire from heaven." But they met with a judgment that was not threatened. Consider this: it may be that when we come and speak out of the Word and show you plainly how God threatens such and such sins, you are afraid then. But know that if you venture upon ways of sin, you may meet with dreadful judgments executed that were never yet threatened. Besides all those judgments that are threatened in the Book of God, you may meet with judgments unheard of, unexpected. As God's mercies go beyond what He has expressly revealed in His Word, "...for never was it heard since the beginning of the world what God has laid up for them that love Him," so God has judgments beyond what is in His Word.

Sometimes when the ministers of God open the threatenings that are in God's Word, you think that they are terrible; but know that God, in the treasury of His judgments, has more dreadful things than have ever been revealed in His Word. Therefore, learn to tremble not only at what is revealed in God's Word against your sin, but tremble at what there is in that infinite justice, power, and wisdom of God to find out and execute upon sinners. For you who are sinners, and especially if you are bold and presumptuous sinners, you may expect to meet with whatever evil an infinite wisdom is able to devise, and that an infinite power is able to bring upon you. You commit such and such a sin. Perhaps you do not know of any particular judgment that is threatened against it, but think thusly: "I who provoke God by my sins, what may I look for? It is more than I know to the contrary but that whatsoever the infinite wisdom of God is able to find out, and whatever misery I am capable of, that the Lord may bring upon me." Consider this and take heed of sin.

9. God is very quick with some in the ways of His judgment. It

may be that He may spare others for a long time, but concerning you He may say, "You shall not offend twice." If you will venture the first act, God may strike you with death. He did so here with Nadab and Abihu, for they were but newly consecrated. I find by the interpreters that they were to be in consecration for seven days, and this was the first day that they came to their place. And in the very first act that they did, God smote them. Let us tremble. The Lord is quick towards some and He is patient towards others; but do not presume that because He is patient to others He will be patient with you. He may take you in the very first act of your sin and be quick with you.

10. The holiness of a duty will never bear a man out in the miscarriages of a duty. This was a holy duty. These were the true priests of God who came to offer incense to the true God. It was right incense that they offered. There was only this one miscarriage: they did not have the same fire that God would have them have. For this miscarriage God came upon them, and all the good there was in the duty would not bear them out.

Consider this, you who perform many holy duties. Take heed of giving way to yourselves in any miscarriage. Do not think that because your duties are very good and holy, by doing them you may venture upon a mixture. Take heed of mixing any evil, any miscarriage in a holy thing. Though you have performed a thousand holy duties, yet that will not bear you out in the miscarriage of them.

11. The Lord is very terrible out of His holy places. The note is the same that you have in Psalm 68:35: "The Lord is terrible out of His holy places." When we have to deal with God, who can stand before this holy God? "Our God is a consuming fire." The Lord manifests Himself here most dreadfully to strike these two priests with fire, as in Ezekiel 9:6. "Begin at My sanctuary," says God. God is terrible, terrible towards those who shall dare to approach Him and yet are wicked or ungodly in

their approaching. He is terrible to those who are near to Him. God would have us all to tremble at His presence.

12. God's judgments are often very suitable to men's sins. Here they sinned by fire and they were consumed by fire. They offended by strange fire and God struck them by a strange fire. Oftentimes the judgments of God are very suitable to the sins of men. As here it is by fire, so another time we find it by water. Pharaoh sinned by drowning the infants of the people of Israel in the waters, and God drowned him in the sea. "If you will be drowning by water, you shall have water enough," said God. And so here, "If you will be meddling with strange fire, you shall have strange fire," said God.

God many times proportions judgments to sinners so that His righteousness might more appear. Those very creatures we sin with, many times God makes them, or others of the same kind, to be the executioners of His wrath. So it was with the Jews. They sold Christ for thirty pieces of silver, and thirty of them were sold for a penny afterwards. Consider the story of Adonibezek in the first of Judges, who was so cruel in such a way as to cut off the thumbs and toes of kings. Even so he was served in the like kind. It's ordinary for men who are of cruel, fiery spirits to meet with cruel, fiery spirits, too.

And I would apply it in this particular. You who are stout children with your parents, if God lets you live, you may meet with the very same in your children. And when you who are parents meet with stubborn children, you should reflect, "Does not God come righteously upon me?" And you who are servants, who are stout to your masters, when you come to have servants, they will be so to you. Perhaps you were unfaithful to your governors. When you come to have servants, it's a thousand to one that they will be so to you. Now you should strike your hand upon your heart and say, "It's just with God that it should be so, and that He should come upon me in my own kind."

13. They offered strange fire. Let's take heed, all of us, how we bring strange fire into God's service.

QUESTION. Bring strange fire into God's service, what is that? ANSWER. I find divers writers speaking about this. Ambrose said that lusts and covetousness are this strange fire. That which I would have you consider is this: Above all strange fire, take heed of the strange fire of passion and anger, and especially in the worship of God. At any time when you find your hearts heated and fired with anger, when you are about to worship God, remember this Scripture. Nadab and Abihu were consumed by God, with fire from God, for coming into God's presence with strange fire!

Perhaps your hearts have been burning hot with passion when you have been coming into God's presence. You are to pray with fervency, for so the Scripture says. We are indeed to be heated in prayer by the Holy Ghost in our hearts, but certainly not to come with the fire of passion and anger. "Lift up your hands without wrath and doubting." If you have been passionate, and your hearts have been heated that way, be sure to get your hearts cold before you go to prayer. And so when you come to hear the Word, if your hearts have been heated with passion, be sure you get them cold before you come to hear the Word. "Receive with meekness the engrafted Word that may save your souls."

And so when you come to the Lord's Supper, take heed of coming with wrath and malice, for then you come but to offer strange fire. It's a special consideration for ministers who come to preach. They should take heed of bringing strange fire into their pulpits, that is, of venturing their own passions. I have been convinced of this rule since I knew anything of preaching. That man who is appointed to reveal God's wrath needs to conceal his own. That's certainly a rule for all preachers, for the Lord sends His preachers to make known His wrath against men's sins; but the more they make known His wrath, the more they should conceal their own. And so by that means, when they come in the most open way to manifest God's wrath, the more their preaching would be accepted.

Now it's true that a carnal heart would be ready to think that when a preacher speaks out of true zeal to God, he will be ready to say that he is aiming at him. Take heed of that. I believe you have had but little occasion of such a temptation in this place. But however, this I know: it is the duty of the ministers of God to be sure to bring nothing but the fire of the Spirit of God, the fire that they have from the altar, their tongues being touched with one of these coals. They should not come with their own passions to further the righteousness of God. No, the wrath of man does not accomplish the righteousness of God.

(Preached November 16, 1645)

God Will Be Sanctified in Those Who Draw Near Him

"I will be sanctified in them that come nigh Me."

(LEVITICUS 10:3).

We began these words the last day, showed the scope of them, opened the meaning of them, and spoke of divers notes of observation that we gathered from this story of Nadab and Abihu, and of God's dealing with them. From the general story, there were many points of notable observation that were drawn. I'll add some few more now, and then come to the main doctrinal point in the text.

14. Many times, even dear saints of God meet with very sore and grievous afflictions in their children. The most eminent saints of God are not freed from very grievous afflictions even in their children. It was one of the sorest afflictions that almost any saint of God ever met with in his children, this affliction of Aaron at this time. These were two of his sons, renowned men in Israel, newly consecrated to the office of priesthood, and the very first day they came in to offer in their office they

were struck down before the people with fire from heaven and were consumed. Oh, what an affliction was it to Aaron their father, when he saw his sons destroyed in such a manner by God Himself!

Consider this, you who have children and are ready to murmur and complain of every little affliction that is upon you in respect to your children. If so be that your children are but a little sick, or if there is any miscarriage of them, you think it is a heavy hand of God. But especially if God takes away your children by death, then you mourn and will not be comforted. Yea, but though God has taken away your children by death, yea, perhaps it may be by a violent death, such as being drowned, or the like, yet they have not been stricken with fire from heaven by God, and they have not been of such public use.

These were renowned men, and taken away in their very sin, too. Your children may have gone upon their lawful employments and God has taken away their lives. There is no such cause of murmuring here. But God took away these children in their sins, and in a way as by fire from heaven. Thus God took away Aaron's children, and he was as dear to God as you are. And yet thus God deals with His saints: with Aaron in regard of his children, and with his elder children, and with two of them together. This example may be enough to still and quiet the hearts of men and women who are afflicted in respect to any calamity that befalls their children. You see what a hand of God is against the very children of Aaron.

15. God's judgments sometimes, though the effect of them is visible, yet they come in an invisible way. For you shall find, if you read on in this story, that they were smitten with fire from heaven; but it did not appear what fire for it did not so much as consume their clothes nor their bodies but went through all and struck them dead, and nobody could tell how. God's judgments come in a way that is invisible. If it had been in a

visible flame of fire, all would have seen it, and it would have burned their clothes or their bodies; but you shall find in the fifth verse that they were carried away from the sanctuary in their clothes. They were not burned.

16. Though the lives of men are dear and precious to God, yet they are not so precious as His glory. The glory of His name is a thousand thousand times more dear unto God than the lives of thousands and thousands of people. The lives of Nadab and Abihu must go so that God may be sanctified. If it comes to be that the lives of men and the sanctifying of God's name cross, the glory of God must pass on and must have its course, let the lives of men go which way they will.

We think much to have the lives of men taken away, but if we knew what the glory of God meant, and what infinite reason there is that God should be glorified, we would not think it so much that the lives of so many men should go for the glory of God. It is mercy that our lives have not gone many times for God's glory. How often might God have glorified Himself in taking away our lives? We have cause to bless Him that our lives have been preserved as long as they have.

17. The nearer any men are to God, the more need there is to take heed that they glorify Him, for they must expect to be spared the less if they sin against Him. Nadab and Abihu were the priests of God, and they came near to God, yet by their transgression. Though I told you that we do not find in any place of Scripture directly in words that this fire was forbidden, they should have gathered God's mind by consequence. And therefore, by the way, I only note that we must not think to urge upon men in all things strict commands in very words; but if it is commanded so as we may draw it by any consequence, it is a command. As now here for the negative, they did not have a negative prohibition in words, yet they had it by consequence. So for the affirmative, though we do not have the affirmative in expressed words, yet if we may have it by consequence, it

is an affirmative as well as the negative when we have it by consequence.

18. The nearer any come to God, if they sin against Him they must not expect to be spared. Do not think that God will spare you the more because you are a professing Christian or because you worship Him often. I suppose that you who are acquainted with Scripture know Amos 3:2: "You only have I known of all the families of the earth; therefore I will punish you for all your iniquities."

19. When a judgment is exemplary, then we should have recourse to the Word of God to see how God makes His Word good in that judgment. This is what Moses did: "This is that which the Lord has said." Do you see any remarkable hand of God in the execution of a judgment upon someone? Have recourse to God's Word and presently begin to think this: "What is there in God's Word against the sin that this man has been guilty of?" If you see a judgment of God upon a drunkard, remember the threats in the Word of God against drunkenness, and also the judgments of God upon unclean persons, swearers, Sabbath-breakers, liars, or any profane and ungodly persons. Have recourse to the judgments of God threatened in the Word against such, and so likewise concerning scorners and opposers of religion. Remember what is said in the Word of God against such, and so learn to sanctify God's name.

20. The greater honor that God intends to His name is making His name to be holy. "I will be sanctified in them that draw nigh Me, and before all the people I will be glorified." It is as if Moses should say in God's name, "I must and I will have glory from this people. And how? "By making My name appear to be holy. This is the glory that I stand upon above all other things, that My name may appear to be holy, that I may appear to be a holy God." I beseech you, brethren, to consider this. God stands upon nothing more than to appear to all the world to be a holy God. There's the glory of God's name in an

eminent way. God does not so much stand upon this, to appear to be a strong God, to appear to be a powerful God, to be a God of patience, or to be long-suffering. God does not so much stand to be an omniscient God, though all these attributes are dear to God—but that He may appear to be a holy God, that He stands upon.

Whatever glory of the name of God that God shall be content to have eclipsed in the world for a while, yet He is resolved that He shall have the glory of His holiness above all things. And, therefore, when the angels celebrate the glory of God, they do not say, "Lord Almighty, Almighty, Almighty," or "Lord Omniscient, Omniscient, Omniscient," but "Holy, holy, holy," those three together. The holiness of God therein appears to be the glory of God above all. God stands upon it that He will appear to be a holy God. Oh, that those who profess themselves to be servants of God would especially endeavor to hold forth God's holiness! You who are near to God, you who hope that you are God's children and make a profession of His name, labor to hold forth the glory of His holiness above all things in your holy lives and conversations, for God stands upon this, to have His name to be sanctified. "I will be sanctified," said God, "and I will be glorified." So He interprets the glory of His name by being sanctified.

It is as if God should say, "That's the glory that I look for, that My name may be extolled as holy." And therefore, the very first petition that Christ teaches us to pray in the Lord's Prayer is, "Hallowed be Thy name," which is all one with, "Sanctified be Thy name." Oh, let the name of God appear to be holy in the world! That's another note, that these two are joined together, "I'll be sanctified in those that draw nigh Me, and I will be glorified before the people."

21. It is the part of true friendship to help friends in their

distress and seek to comfort them from the Word. Though we ourselves are in afflictions, yet we should seek to comfort our friends who are in greater afflictions, and to comfort them by the Word of God; for so did Moses. Moses came to comfort Aaron and applied the Word, "This is that which the Lord said, 'I will be sanctified.' " Now mark it, there is no question that Moses was afflicted upon this heavy hand of God; for he was their uncle. But though it was heavy upon the uncle, yet it was heavier upon the father. And, therefore, though Moses was troubled, yet he knew that Aaron was more troubled, and therefore he went to Aaron and sought to comfort him, and he made use of the Word in comforting him.

Learn, then, to go and comfort your brethren, for Aaron was Moses' brother. Go and comfort them in their afflictions, and do not think that because you have some afflictions upon you that therefore you should not be a comfort to your brethren. Their affliction is greater than yours. And when you come to comfort, do not come in a mere carnal way and say, "Brother, you must be content." But you must come and apply something of the Word of God to comfort them and say, "This is that which the Lord has spoken." And to that end, you should labor to be exercised in the Word of God so that you may be able to go to your brethren and comfort them in any affliction. For there is no particular affliction but there is some part of the Word of God that is suitable to that particular affliction; and those who are well exercised in the Word of God can apply some word to every affliction. Indeed, this is an excellent friend; and such a friend is worth his weight in gold who can come to another friend in any affliction and evermore has something of the Word of God to apply to that affliction.

22. Aaron held his peace. And from there we may note that there is no better way to quiet a gracious heart under any afflictions than to say that God will fetch out His honor by it.

It may be grievous to me, but God fetches out His glory and honor by it. Applying the Word, and the consideration that God has His way to fetch out His glory in our afflictions, is the only way to quiet a gracious heart.

All these points might take up a great deal of time, but I will let them pass and come to the main point of all, "I will be sanctified in those that come nigh Me." There are these three points in these words:

- In the worship of God, men and women draw nigh to God.
- We ought to sanctify God's name in drawing nigh to Him.
- In worshipping God, there is a drawing nigh to God.

QUESTION. Is God not in every place?
ANSWER. Yes, certainly. We can never be in any place but we are nigh to God. God stands by us and looks upon us. It is not only when you are worshipping God that you are nigh to Him, but when you sin against Him, when you are swearing, profaning His name or His day, He stands and looks upon you. You are nigh to Him. And it may be said or written upon every place what was said of the city in the last words of the prophecy of Ezekiel 48:35, "The name of the city is Jehovah Shemma," that is, "the Lord is there." "In Him we live, and move, and have our being," therefore we are always nigh to Him. Yea, but though we are always nigh to God in regard of that essential presence of His, yet there is a more peculiar and special drawing nigh to God in the duties of His worship, and that the Scripture seems to hold forth unto you. First I'll show you how the Scripture holds it forth, and then in what respects the creature may be said to draw nigh to God in holy duties of worship, for it was here that they were coming to offer incense.

We draw nigh to God in holy duties. James 4:8: "Draw nigh to God," so that you may be nearer to God than you were, that is, by holy services and holy duties. Hence it is in Psalm 95:2: "Let us come before His presence with thanksgiving." So there is a more peculiar coming before God's presence when we come to worship Him than at other times. And verse 6: "Oh, come let us worship and bow down, let us kneel before the Lord our Maker." So Psalm 100:2: "Let us come before His presence with singing," for that's one part of the worship of God. But the Scripture is plain that there is a special coming before God when we are coming to worship Him; and in this respect the servants of God in Psalm 148:14 are said to be a people near to God. It is a very remarkable expression, and sets forth much the honor of the saints of God. There's the commendation of the excellent estate of the saints: "He also exalteth the horn of His people, the praise of all His saints, even the children of Israel, a people near unto Him." The saints of God, the children of Israel, the church of God, are said to be a people near unto God. Why near Him? Because they who worship God are much exercised in the worship of God. This is one respect of their coming so much before God in His worship, and therefore they are near to God.

QUESTION. Near Him? Why, in what respects may a man be said to draw nigh to God when he worships Him?
ANSWER. To that I answer, there are three respects in which a man, when he is worshipping God, may be said to draw nigh to God. First, because when we come to worship God, we come to tender up that homage and service unto Him that is due from us as creatures unto the Creator. That's the very end of worship. If you would know what it is to worship God, it is this: you come to tender up that homage and respect that is due

from the creature to the Creator. Now when a subject comes to tender up that homage to his prince, he comes toward him when he does it immediately. So we have no one to tender it up but by Jesus Christ. And when we tender it up, we must come ourselves too, for Christ does not take our service and tender it up to God if we are absent; but we must come with Christ, and Christ takes us by the hand and so tenders it up to the Father while we are in His presence. So we are said to come nigh to God in that respect because of the immediate tendering up of that worship of ours to God.

I call it immediate in respect of any creature, but in respect of Christ, indeed He is a Mediator to do it, but yet He does it in a spiritual way. And we have to do with no one but God through Christ in the way of tendering up our worship to Him. We may make use of an institution that God has appointed, but we do not tender up our worship to God through that; but in the use of the creature we do come to God, and our souls are to tender up that respect we owe to God immediately. Therefore in Leviticus 21:21, it is said of the priests in their sacrifices that when they were to come to worship God, "No man that hath a blemish of the seed of Aaron the Priest shall come nigh to offer the offerings of the Lord made by fire." So when any came to offer any offerings of the Lord made by fire, it appears that he came nigh to God. He came to bring a present to God, therefore he came nigh. So when we come to offer our spiritual sacrifices unto God, we come nigh to God to offer. It's the offering of a sacrifice to God. And that's the first thing, because the creature comes to bring a present to God; therefore he is said to draw nigh.

Second, the soul is said to draw nigh to God in holy duties because it presents itself before God in those ways that God uses to communicate His choice, precious, most excellent and glorious mercies to His people. I say, when we come to worship

God, we come to see ourselves before God in those ways that God uses to communicate the choice, most excellent, and glorious mercies that He has to communicate to His creature.

When we have to deal with things, like meat and drink and our outward businesses, we have to deal with God in them; but when we come to worship God, we come to present ourselves before Him in those things that He uses to let Himself out in a more special and glorious manner to the souls of His people. What's the reason that heaven is said to be the presence of God, and why are those who are in heaven said to live with God? Because there they behold the face of God, and are before Him in a special manner. Therefore, when Christ teaches us to pray, He teaches us to look up to heaven and to say, "Our Father, which art in heaven."

Now certainly the essential presence of God is on earth as truly and really as in heaven, and God is not so as to have one part in one place and another in another; but all God is in every place. But the reason God is said to be in heaven is because there the Lord makes known Himself in a more glorious manner than in any other place. Therefore heaven is the presence of God in a more special way. Now if the communication of God unto a creature is enough to make the presence of God more special, if this is enough to make the creature to live with God and to be before His face (because they are there where God most communicates Himself), then certainly when we come to worship God we come to be near God and with God, because the duties of His worship are those means that the Lord has appointed for letting Himself out in the glory of His goodness and mercy to His people. We may expect more communication of God's goodness through the duties of His worship than in any other way. And that's the second respect wherein you may be said to draw nigh to God in holy duties.

Third, you may be said to draw nigh to God because then we should (and, if we worship God as we ought, we do) act our faith and humility and all the graces of the Spirit. We act them, as it were, upon God when we come to worship Him. That's required in every duty of worship, that you should stir up the faculties of your souls and all the graces of the Spirit of God, and you should act them upon God when you are worshipping Him. It is not enough that you come with grace when you come to worship God, but there must be an acting of that grace upon God.

And so we find in Scripture that the acting of grace upon God is drawing near to Him. Therefore in Isaiah 29:13, the Lord complains, "This people draws near to Me with their lips, but their hearts are far from Me." It is as if God should say, "Indeed, they come and speak to Me, and therefore think they draw nigh to Me, but I expect that their hearts should be acting upon Me." That's the meaning. And in Zephaniah 3:2, God complains there that His people did not draw near to Him as they should. And it appears plainly that it was from this that their graces did not act so upon God as they ought. "She obeyed not the voice, she received not correction, she trusted not in the Lord, she drew not near to her God."

So that acting faith upon God is drawing nigh to God, and acting any grace upon God is drawing nigh to God. Now when is there a time for the acting of our graces upon God as when we come to worship God? And therefore in Isaiah 64:7, the Lord complains "that no man did stir up himself to take hold on Him." When we come to worship God, we should stir up ourselves to take hold of God. And thus you see in what respect the soul may be said to draw nigh to God when it comes to worship Him.

APPLICATION

USE 1. Learn what it is that you do when you come to worship God, and consider it every time you come to perform any act of worship. Truly this one thing would be of marvelous use, and it would help forward to the next point of sanctifying God's name. You are all convinced of this, that it is your duty to worship God. When you pray, you come to worship God. When you come to hear His Word, you come to worship Him. And when you receive the sacrament, you worship Him.

Now if I should come from one end of the congregation to the other and ask every one of you this question, "It is your duty to worship God, is it not?" you would all be ready to answer, "Yes!" And what do you do when you worship God? I fear that this second question would perplex many of you.

You will say, "We must pray to God and serve Him, hear His Word and go to the communion." Yes, but what do your souls do in this work of worshipping God? This should be the answer, and so you should think to yourselves and charge this upon your own hearts: "I am now going to worship God, either in prayer, Word, or sacraments. I am now going to tender up that homage that is due from the creature to the infinite Creator, so that I must so pray as I must manifest that high respect that I owe to God as my Creator." But to that I shall speak more afterward. For now, only remember that you go to tender up that homage that you owe unto God; and so every time you come to hear the Word, there is a profession that you come to tender up that respect and homage that you owe the infinite God. And so it is likewise when you come to receive the sacrament.

Second, remember that when you come to worship God you come to set yourself before the Lord in those ways in which God lets out the choicest of His mercies to His people.

You have many mercies from God in the enjoyment of the creature, but when you come to worship Him, you may expect the communication of His mercy in another way than through any creature in the world. The duties of His worship are the chief channels through which God lets out the choicest of His mercies to the hearts of His people. And when you are going to worship Him, you are going to present yourself before God. Indeed, there is a little glimmering of the light of God through other creatures to you, but the glorious beams of the light of God come through the duties of His worship.

And then, third, you are now going to act your soul upon God, so that if you have any ability to close with God, to act your soul upon Him, it must be put forth now at this time. You are, indeed, at all times to labor to enjoy communion with God. When you see the creatures, the sun, moon, and stars, you are to labor to lift up your heart to God, just as when you see the glory of God in the sea. And for your meat and drink, you are to bless God and to acknowledge God in all. But when you come to worship God, then all the strength of your soul is to be acted upon God in a more special manner. You must then, above all, labor to stir up whatsoever you have in your soul to act upon God. This is to worship God.

USE 2. If to worship God is to draw nigh to God, hence see the reasons why guilty consciences have little mind to the duties of God's worship. When a man or woman has given liberty to any licentious way and sinned against their consciences, if they have any light in their consciences, it is one of the most terrible things in the world to come to the duties of God's worship. They would rather do anything than come to holy duties such as prayer, and especially secret prayer. A man or woman who has an enlightened conscience and is under the guilt of sin finds that coming to God in holy duties is a very grievous burden to them. Why? Because to worship God is to draw nigh to God, and the guilt that is upon them has made the presence of God to be terrible to them; and therefore they would rather go into their company and be merry, eat, drink, sport, or anything rather than come into God's presence.

We know how it was with Adam when God appeared in the garden and called to him. He ran to hide himself. Why? Because he had guilt on him. Oh, the evil that the guilt of sin brings upon the soul! It makes the presence of God terrible. The presence of God should be more comfortable to us than our lives, but our sin makes God's presence grievous and terrible.

A child sometimes, when it has offended its father and is conscious of the offense that it has given its father, would rather be in the kitchen among the servants than to come into the hall or parlor where the father is because it has offended him. So it is with the guilty conscience when it is conscious of some haunting evil that it has given itself unto. It has no mind at all to come into the presence of the Father, but hangs far off.

My brethren, the very presence of God in the communion of the saints is terrible to a guilty conscience. Suppose you have traveled abroad and have been loose and wicked in your ways. I appeal to your conscience, when you come into the presence of some holy or gracious man or woman who lives closely with God, does it not daunt you? Now the presence of God in the very faces of His saints is terrible to a guilty conscience. How terrible is the presence of God in His ordinances then? Indeed, those men and women whose consciences are not enlightened, but are ignorant and dull, they can sin against God and go into His presence without any trouble. You have men swear and be drunk overnight and come to the sacrament the next day. What's the reason? Because there is no light in their consciences; their consciences are in darkness and they are besotted in their sin. But I speak now of one who has an enlightened conscience, the presence of God is terrible to such a one.

USE 3. Here's the reason why hypocrites meet with such vengeance from God as they do. We shall deal with this more especially afterwards; only take notice of it by the way. Hypocrites, above all men, may expect the most severe judgments of God upon them because they come so nigh God, for they come often to the duties of God's worship. Now they who will come so nigh God's presence, and come with base and ungodly hearts to cloak their villainy, of all in the world they must expect to have the most severe vengeance of God let down upon them. They who stand nearest the bullet must expect to have the strength of it to be most upon them. So when the wrath of God proceeds out upon sinners, wicked men who stand nearest Him have the greatest stroke of God's wrath—but more of that when I come to the third point, that God will be sanctified in those who draw near Him.

USE 4. If to worship God is to draw near to Him, then to neglect God's worship is to depart from Him. That must follow, and this is a dreadful thing. It is the sentence that will be at the last day of judgment, "Depart from Me." You who now are willing to depart from God, consider this. You who neglect worship, the worship of God in your families and in your closets, in the congregation and in the communion of saints, you have little minded or regarded worship of God, it may be, all your days. What have you been doing all this while? You have been departing from God all this while; and when your conscience shall be enlightened and awakened to see how far you are from God, how terrible will it be to you?

Remember this, you who have no mind to the duties of the worship of God, but love the commission of sin. You neglect God's worship. You were wont to worship Him in a constant way in your closets and families; but now you grow more loose, and so you grow more dead every day. You go off from God more and more. Surely, then, there can be no good in neglecting God's worship. And those who are loath to worship God because they cannot worship Him as they ought, from this point it appears plainly that there can be no good received by neglecting God's worship, for it is departing from God. Whatsoever plea there may be by any temptation to neglect God's worship, certainly there is danger in it; and, therefore, never listen to any such temptation that shall draw your hearts away from the duties of God's worship.

There is a generation of wantons in these times that makes little matter of continuing in the duties of God's worship. They were wont constantly to worship God and to attend upon the Word, but now it is nothing to them, and they are even ready to thank God that they do not make such conscience as they were wont to do in the duties of the worship of God.

It may be that they will say that heretofore some slavish terror carried them on in the duties of God's worship more than did the understanding of the freeness of the grace of God. But shall the understanding of the freedom of the grace of God carry you on less than your slavish terror did? Oh, blind and wanton spirit that does not know the ways of God, nor the freeness of the grace of God, nor the riches of it! Oh, what a dishonor are you to Jesus Christ, and to the freeness of His grace, that you can go up and down from day to day and never worship God! Did Jesus Christ come into the world to that end, to cause you to depart more from God? It is plain out of the Word that the duties of God's worship are those duties whereby the soul comes to draw nigh to God.

I beseech you, brethren, observe these men, whether there is that holiness in their lives, that spirituality, as there was wont to be. No, you shall find them to grow more loose by degrees, yes, sometimes to run into gross sins, grow many times to lying and deceiving, and to drunkenness and company-keeping, yea, to worse things by degrees.

Perhaps they are ready at first to say, "Is your servant a dead dog that I should do this?" But by departing from God, they grow dead to holy duties. We find by experience that the professors of religion do not have that holiness, heavenliness, and spirituality as they were wont to have in former times; and it is no wonder, for they do not keep as nigh to God as they were wont to do.

You who are seamen and travelers, sometimes you are near the sun, and then you are hot; but the farther from the sun you go, you grow to be colder and colder. And so those who neglect the worship of God go from the warm sun. They go from the light of God's countenance and from the presence of God, and so they grow cold and chilly. By degrees they grow to profaneness, and it is to be feared that many of them will grow to mere atheism.

USE 5. This is a use of exhortation, that we would be encouraged to worship God, and to be much in the worship of God. Hebrews 10:22: "Let us draw near." Who would not draw near to God? What a good thing is it to be in the presence of God! Is it not a sweet thing to be in His presence? We think it a sweet thing to be in the presence of godly men. Oh, that we might always live with such men and be near to them! That martyr, Doctor Taylor, rejoiced in this, that ever he came into prison to be acquainted with that angel of God, holy Master Bradford. And I remember some among the heathens who protest that they would rather be in prison with Calo than be in the greatest glory with some other. It is a blessed thing to be in the presence of God, to be with Him who is the God of our lives and the Fountain of all good. Let us draw nigh to God often. Let us know that it is a mercy that we draw nigh to God. We might have been banished from the presence of the Lord long before this time.

This is that which the happiness of the church is set out by in Revelation 22:4: "They shall see His face and His shall be in their foreheads." This is the privilege of the church. And that it is such a blessing to draw nigh to God you may see by Ephesians 2:18: "For through Him we both have an access by one Spirit unto the Father."

"Through Him," through Christ we have access by one Spirit unto God the Father; and now, Paul says, "Ye that were strangers and foreigners are made fellow citizens with the saints, and of the household of God." And then, "but now by Christ Jesus ye who sometimes were afar off are made nigh by the blood of Christ," and you have access through Christ. So our coming nigh to God is such a privilege as cost the blood of Christ; and will you not improve it? You were far off in your natural condition, but now you are nigh through His blood. Let this text warm your hearts this morning, that you who were far off have been made nigh by the blood of Christ, made nigh to God. It will be a means to forever draw your hearts to all those ways whereby you may draw nearest to God.

And by drawing nigh to God often, you will come to increase your graces abundantly. How will your graces act? The presence of God will draw forth the acts of grace as the presence of the fire draws forth out heat. So the presence of God will draw forth our graces.

And by this means we come to live most holy lives. We read

that Moses was upon the mountain forty days with God; and when he came down his face so shone that the people were not able to bear it. What's the reason? It was because he was so near to God. Would you have your faces shine in a holy conversation before men? Converse much with God; be often with God; be near to Him, and that will make you shine as lights in the midst of a crooked and perverse generation. We find it so with some who converse much with God; there is a shine upon their very countenances.

Further, it is a special sign of our adoption to love to be near God. What should a child love most but to be in the presence of his father? Would you know whether you have received the Spirit of adoption or not? I can hardly give you any one sign so clear as to love to go into God's presence. As David said, "I was glad when they said, 'Come let us go up unto the house of the Lord.'" You shall have many who love to be in God's presence so that they think on it overnight and long for the time when it comes. I am never better than when I am with God. I think when I get into God's presence, either in prayer or any duty of God's worship, I find my heart warmed and quickened. They are ready to say with Peter, "Master, it is good being here."

And that's another thing; it is that which will put us in mind of the life of heaven. The only thing in heaven is to be in the presence of God. Why, the more you are near to God in the duties of worship, the more you are in heaven. And do you not pray that the will of God may be done in earth as it is in heaven? Now the saints and angels are always before God worshipping Him. Then be as much as you can in the presence of God. If you would be in heaven, be in the presence of God. Many of the saints find it so.

It is not so with carnal hearts; they are weary immediately. When they are in prayer or hearing the Word, it is not so with them. Yes, that's because they do not have the presence of God. In Malachi 1, what weariness is there? You can be gaming until one o'clock at night, and, though you should lose your supper or the work of your family, it is not tedious to you to be exercised in those things that please the flesh. But when you come to worship God, how quickly are you tired? Now what will you do in heaven, where there is nothing else to do for all eternity but to worship God?

Then it must be delightful to God that you should come near Him. There is nothing in the world more pleasing to God than to have His saints come into His presence. What delights a father more than to have his children about him? Never did any father or mother love to have their children by them as God loves to have His children come nigh Him and be with Him. The truth is, one great reason why God suffers you to fall into afflictions so much is that you may come running to Him. How does the child come running to the father or mother when it is afraid? Why, the Lord is willing to permit men to do you wrong so that you may run to Him, so that He might have more of your presence. You who are such poor creatures, yet hear this day that there is nothing in the world in which God takes more pleasure (next to the presence of His own Son, Jesus Christ, and His saints and angels that He has with Him in heaven) than to have His saints come near Him, to have them always to be under His wing.

And then, by coming into God's presence in His worship, there will grow a sweet and blessed familiarity between God and your soul, for you will be speaking to God and God will be speaking to you too. We know many times that dear friends who are very nearly linked together grow estranged from one another if they are absent from each other for a long time. And so by degrees their friendship is deadened. But when they are together every day, and there is an intercourse of love and friendship, then their friendship is kept active and quick. But if they are absent long, indeed if they are absent in another country where they cannot come together, they are sure that it is not through any neglect. This will not dampen their friendship. But when they are near to each other and do not come to visit, then they think it is out of neglect, and they become estranged.

So it is with the soul. If there were no possibility of coming into God's presence, then it would not hinder the sweetness of the love of God to us. But when we have those duties of worship wherein we may draw nigh to God, if we neglect them, our familiarity with God will be quickly lost. "Acquaint thyself with God and be at peace." God is willing to be acquainted with His servants. The Lord loves to be familiar with the poorest of His saints; and will you not maintain that sweet familiarity with God? These two benefits will follow upon your familiarity with God.

First, those who are most familiar with God are most potent with God. A stranger cannot prevail in any petition like a familiar friend can. Thus, my brethren, when strangers come into God's presence, God does not regard them as much; but when His familiar ones come into His presence, the saints of God who keep close with Him in constant communion and converse in the duties of His worship, God takes them as His familiar friends, and they will prevail with God.

Second, by this means the terror of death will be taken away. There is no such way to take off the terror of the thoughts of death as by keeping a familiarity with God. Death, then, is joy to those who converse with Him. When that reverend divine, now with God, Dr. [John] Preston, was about to die, he had this speech, "I shall but change my place, I shall not change my company." Whereas it is otherwise if you grow estranged from God. When death comes, it will look upon you with a terrible face; for then you have to deal with God. You are then to go into the presence of the infinite, dreadful God into whose presence you never had any mind to go before. Death then says, "I must now carry you into the presence of God." As your body returns to the dust, so your soul must return to God who gave it, that is, to receive its eternal doom.

But a saint may ask, "Why must my body return to dust, and my soul to God who gave it? It is He with whom I have been every day. I can say as He said, 'My soul, go forth, go forth; why are you unwilling to go forth to Him that you have conversed with all your days?'"

What safety there is in being near to God, especially in these dangerous times? In the times wherein we live, it is safe to be near to God. In Psalm 22:11, "Be not far from me, for trouble is near," said David. Lord, trouble is near me; do not be far from me. It's a blessed thing to have God near us when trouble is near us. Trouble is near many of you. Perhaps there is not a span's breadth between death and us. What a blessed thing, then, it is to have God to be near us.

When the poor chick sees the hawk come to seize it, it is likely to be surprised. If the hen is near, the chick runs to the hen who covers it and keeps it safe. So it should be with us, for Christ said of Jerusalem, "How often would I have gathered thee as a hen gathereth her chicklings?" There is a company of hawks abroad in the world, and we are poor, shiftless creatures. Now, how happy are we, then, if we can run under the shadow of God's wings? There is a kind of shadow in the presence of God in the enjoyment of the creature; but the shadow of God that we have in His worship is as the shadow of His wing. There is the shadow of a tree, and that may help from some kind of trouble, but there is another manner of shadow under the shadow of the wing of the hen, because that nourishes the chick. Then men of the world have the shadow of the tree, as it were, God's general providence, which is over all creatures; but the saints of God who draw nigh to God have the shadow of God's wing, like the shadow of the hen's wing to the chick, that comforts it and safeguards it. Let us, by the duties of worship, thus draw nigh to God and keep nigh unto Him.

(Preached November 30, 1645)

The Importance
of Preparing for Worship

"I will be sanctified in them that come nigh Me."

LEVITICUS 10:3

I will only add one particular more to what we said the last day and then proceed. If in the duties of worship we are nigh to God, then hence appears the great honor that God puts upon His servants who worship Him. Certainly the worshippers of God have great honor put upon them because the Lord permits them to draw nigh unto Him. They are such as are precious and honorable in His eyes. I will not enlarge myself in this, but will give you three Scriptures that show the great honor and respect God puts upon those whom He admits to come and worship Him.

The first Scripture is Deuteronomy 4:17. There Moses is speaking of the people of Israel, and the great respect God showed to them more than others. He says, "What nation is there so great, who hath God so nigh unto them, as the Lord our God is in all things that we call upon Him for?" How does it appear that the nation of Israel is a greater nation than the other nations are? That they "hath God so nigh unto them in

47

in Psalm 4:3: "The Lord hath set apart him that is godly for Himself." You are separated from the world. To what end? It is that you might be near to Him. This is your privilege, and you should account it your great honor. You do not have that honor and respect in the world as others have, but you are one of God's separate ones, you who are near to Him.

A third Scripture is Psalm 73:28. There you may see how the prophet David highly esteemed the great honor that the Lord put upon him in his being near to God: "But it is good for me to draw near to God." Mark how he speaks: "But it is good for me." Why? Verse 27: "For lo, they that are far from Thee shall perish. Thou hast destroyed all them that go a-whoring from Thee." It is as if he had said, "There are some who seemed to be near to Thee heretofore, who were as the wife to the husband, but they have gone a-whoring from Thee. Base hypocrites, base apostates, they have gone a-whoring from Thee. Their hearts are carnal; they did not find that contentment and satisfaction in Thy worship as Thy saints do. Therefore, they have gone a-whoring from Thee; but it is good for me to draw near to Thee."

It is an excellent Scripture. Do you see any young ones or others who were very forward not many years ago, and would speak of good things and seem to rejoice in the Word, but now they are gone a-whoring? They have departed from God and His ways, and the pleasures of the flesh have taken their hearts. "Thou wilt destroy them that go a-whoring from Thee," said David. So you should think to yourself, "Oh, how miserable is the condition of those who once were forward in the profession of religion, and have now gone a-whoring from God. But it is good for me to draw near to God. They are gone from Thee, and Thou wilt destroy them; but it is good for me to draw near to Thee."

all things that they call upon Him for."

Herein any man, woman, or nation may be said to be great, that is, greatly honored by the Lord God, in that they have the Lord nigh unto them and they are nigh unto Him. Here's the greatness of a nation. You would think that if one would describe the greatness of a nation it would be in their great wealth, their great trading and traffic that they have, and the fertile place in which they live. No, this is not the greatness of a nation, but "what nation is there so great, that hath the Lord God so nigh unto them?" There's the greatness of a nation, and so a spiritual heart would count greatness to consist in having God to be nigh unto it.

The second Scripture is Numbers 16:19. There we have Moses speaking unto the sons of Korah, rebuking them for their sin. He brings to them this aggravation of the greatness of their sin saying, "Seemeth it but a small thing unto you that the God of Israel hath separated you from the congregation of Israel to bring you near to Himself?" That is, is it a small thing to you that you should come to worship Him? Is not this honor enough? It is as if Moses had said, "Why do you contend for any more honor? The Lord has separated you to bring you near to Himself!"

OBJECTION. "This was spoken of the priests," you will say.
ANSWER. But it may be said of every gracious soul, for Christ has made every believer a king, priest, and prophet unto Himself. Now there is no believer but Jesus Christ has separated him or her from the rest of the world to be near to God. This is the dignity that God has put upon you, that you are separated by His grace to be one near to Him, whereas others of the world depart from Him; they continually depart more and more. But the Lord, by His grace, has set you apart for Himself, as it says

"I bless myself in drawing near to Thee, Lord,. I bless the time that ever I did draw near to Thee, and I bless those ways wherein my soul has drawn near to Thee."

Such as worship God rightly, and delight in the worship of God, are such as have a great honor put upon them. They draw nigh to God. And thus I have finished the first point.

The second point is that which will hold us for some time, and that is the sanctifying of God's name in our drawing near to God.

When we worship God we draw nigh to Him, but let us take heed how we draw nigh. Hebrews 10:22: "Let us draw near with a true heart." And Ecclesiastes 5:1: "Look to thy feet when thou comest into the house of God." Now for the sanctifying of God's name in drawing nigh to Him, I shall endeavor to open it, first, in showing you wherein the sanctification of God's name consists, or what we should do that we might sanctify the name of God in drawing nigh to Him; and, second, the reason why God will have His name to be sanctified in those who draw nigh to Him.

How we should sanctify the name of God in drawing nigh to Him is under these two headings:

First, there must be a due preparation unto the worship of God that we exercise ourselves in at any time.

Second, there must be a right behavior of our souls in it. In these two things consists the sanctifying of God's name in His worship. Now, under these two headings all that I shall speak about the opening of the sanctifying of God's name will be contained. At this time I shall only speak of the first.

THE DUE PREPARATION OF THE SOUL UNTO THE DUTIES OF GOD'S WORSHIP

Therein consists a special part of the sanctifying of God's name in drawing nigh to Him. We find in Scripture that preparation for worship is called "sanctifying ourselves." And, finding this in Scripture, it hinted me upon this heading to speak of the preparation unto worship in sanctifying God's name because I find in Scripture sanctifying ourselves for worship and preparing ourselves for worship are all one. I'll give you these two texts.

In 1 Samuel 16:5 you find that Samuel, when he was sent by God to anoint David in Bethlehem, said, "I am come to sacrifice unto the Lord; sanctify yourselves and come with me to the sacrifice." The elders asked him, "Do you come peaceably?" Samuel answered, "Yes." What then? "Sanctify yourselves and come with me to the sacrifice."

That's all one. It is as if he had said, "Prepare yourselves and come with me to the sacrifice."

And so in Job 1:5 you find that the holy man Job, when his sons had been feasting, was somewhat afraid lest there should be some miscarriage, and lest they had sinned against God in their feasting. As it is very hard to give liberty to please the flesh and not sin, not to transgress bounds, therefore Job, though he did not hear of any notorious abuse of their feasting, was still afraid lest they should sin. He knew how dangerous it was to have so much satisfaction to the flesh and not to transgress bounds. Therefore it was said, "He sent to his sons and sanctified them. It was so, when the days of the feasting were gone about, that Job sent and sanctified them."

Job sent unto them to prepare them to offer sacrifice, to prepare them for the worship of God. The Scripture holds this forth, then, that to prepare for worship is to sanctify for worship. And so it is one special thing that is required in our sanctifying of God, in our drawing nigh to God, to make a due preparation for His holy worship.

Now for the orderly handling of things, I shall, first, show you that we must prepare for the worship of God. Second, I shall show you wherein this preparation for the worship of God consists. Third, I shall show the excellency that there is in this, or what great good there is in preparation for God's worship. Fourth, I shall answer a case of conscience or two. Fifth, I will show you what the behavior of the soul is in sanctifying God's name. And, sixth, I shall show you the reasons why God will be sanctified in the duties of His worship.

There must be preparation for the worship of God. The God whom we come to worship is a great and glorious God, and, having to deal with such an infinite, glorious, dreadful Majesty, it is fitting that we should make preparation when we come nigh unto Him. Therefore, in Exodus 19:10, when God came among the people to give them His Law, He required that they should be sanctified today and tomorrow, and that they should wash their clothes and be ready against the third day, for the third day the Lord would come down upon Mount Sinai in the sight of the people. God did not stand so much upon their clothes, but it was an inward washing.

Now, my brethren, if when God came to give the Law they were so to prepare, then certainly when we are come to worship God in the way of the gospel we are to prepare as well as they, because God is coming. For what is observable is why they were for two straight days to make such preparation. The argument is because of the presence of God. "The Lord said to Moses, 'Go and sanctify the people today and tomorrow, and let them wash their clothes and be ready against the third day.' " Why?

"For the Lord will come down in the sight of all the people upon Mount Sinai." The Lord will come down the third day, and therefore let them be sanctified.

So when you go to worship God, you expect, or should expect, that God will come to you, and that your heart should be drawn to God. And, therefore, you should make some preparation. (As for the time of preparation, we shall speak to it afterward when we come to the cases of conscience about preparation for worship.) And so, in 1 Chronicles 22:5–14, David makes preparation for the house of God because it was the house of God he had to build. Though he could not do it himself in his own time, yet being the house of God, what great preparation was made by David! The moral is this, that the house of God, being a type of the church and the worship of God, as well as of Christ, it shows that there should be much preparation when we have to deal with God in His ordinances.

As God whom we draw nigh to is great, so the duties of God's worship are great duties. They are the greatest things that concern us in this world; and it is a sign of a very carnal heart to slight the duties of God's worship, to account them as little matters. Carnal hearts ordinarily think of the things that concern their businesses in the world as being great matters. "Oh, I may not neglect this. I may not neglect that. I may not neglect such a business. I may not neglect to visit or gratify such a friend. But as for the worship of God, it is good indeed, but whether it is done or not is no great matter." Therefore, they can put off prayer. If they have any business, the time of prayer must pay for it. They can put that off upon any slight occasion; they do not account the duties of God's worship as great matters.

My brethren, I beseech you, learn this lesson this morning. Learn to account the duties of God's worship as great matters.

They are the greatest things that concern you here in this world, for they are the homage that you tender up to the high God, as you heard, and those things wherein God communicates Himself in His choice mercies.

Now, these being such great matters, there is cause that we should prepare for them. For that one thing of prayer, said Luther, is a great work and a difficult work, and therefore there needs to be preparation for it. Business of great consequence we make preparation for. Indeed, if a business is a slight business, we can fall upon it suddenly. You do not make preparation to go in a boat on the Thames; but to go on a voyage you would make great preparation. Now if men and women would but understand the duties of God's worship to be great, they would see a necessity to make a preparation.

Many men, for want of preparation to duties, lose a great part of the time. When they come to perform a duty of worship in prayer, they spend half the time that is convenient to be spent in prayer before they begin to pray. And so in hearing the Word, they are a long time before they can settle themselves to attend to the Word, or in any other kind of worship. I say that a great deal of time in the worship is ordinarily spent before we can get our hearts to close with the worship. Now that is a sore and a great evil, to lose any part of the time of worship.

Christians, I beseech you to account highly your time of worship. You have been so long at prayer, yes, but how much of it has been lost because you have not prepared beforehand for it? Perhaps you kneeled upon your knees, but you were a long time before you could get your hearts warm at your work. Why, you should have been warm before you came!

It is so, oftentimes, with many men when they meet together and there is no preparation for their business. They come together and are a long time before they can buckle to the business for which they came because there was no preparation. But if preparation is made, then every man knows beforehand what his work is. They can fall to it, and then dispatch as much in one hour as others do in two or three, but of that we shall speak more afterwards.

There must be preparation because our hearts are naturally exceedingly unprepared for every good work. We are all naturally reprobate to every good work. The duties of God's worship are high and spiritual and holy things; but by nature our hearts grovel in the dirt, and we are carnal, sensual, drossy, dead, slight, sottish, and vain, altogether unfit to come into the presence of God. Oh, that we were apprehensive and sensible of the unfitness of our hearts to come into God's presence! Perhaps because you do not know God, you can rush into His presence without any more ado; but if you knew yourself and God, you could not but see yourself altogether unfit for His presence, so as to wonder that the Lord should not spurn you out of His presence every time you come unto Him. There needs to be, then, preparation because we are so unfit to come into His presence.

There needs to be preparation because of the great hindrances of the worship of God. This business and the other business would hinder. The entanglements would hinder; the temptations of the devil would hinder. Sometimes the indispositions of our bodies mightily hinder, and the stirrings of the passions of our minds hinder. If there is any business that goes amiss in the family and anything goes cross, how are we put off the hinges and made unfit for holy duties! There needs to be preparation, therefore, because there are so many hindrances in the way. Many of you will complain that you are so much hindered, but do you do what you can to make preparation beforehand? Do the hindrances that you complain of make you so much more careful to make due preparation for holy duties?

We find that the heathens themselves, when they worshipped their idol gods, would make some preparation such as was suitable to those gods that they worshipped. Therefore, they would wash their flesh and purge themselves; but though their preparation was very poor, yet they taught us this much, that they were convinced in their consciences that when God was to be worshipped, people should be prepared.

We find that the Scripture makes the uprightness of the heart to consist much in preparation for worship, and makes the falseness of the heart to consist in this, that men do not prepare. Perhaps you have not thought much of this, but yet it is of excellent use to you. We shall find that the Scripture makes the very uprightness of the heart to consist in the preparation for duty, and the falseness of a man's heart to consist in this: he does not make conscience to prepare his heart for God and His worship. And this I will show unto you very plainly and clearly.

Take these two examples. The first is Rehoboam, and the second is Jehoshaphat, one a wicked man whose heart was false, and the other a godly man whose heart was right with God. The falseness of the heart of the one is in 2 Chronicles 12:14. There you have what God's thoughts of Rehoboam were in the verses before; but now He brings the reason of His sentence upon him, and, says the text, "he did evil, because he prepared not his heart to seek the Lord."

There were many good things that Rehoboam did. I might show you some things, such as how he obeyed the prophet of God when he was seeking to revenge himself upon those who rended themselves from his obedience. The Lord did but send His prophet, and though he had an army ready to revenge himself upon those who rended themselves from under his government in a way of rebellion, and though he obeyed the word of the Lord, but for all that he did evil in the sight of the Lord. God looked upon him as a man who had no uprightness in him. Why? He did not prepare his heart to seek the Lord. Said God, "I look upon all that Rehoboam did as nothing. I look upon his ways as evil, and upon he, himself, as a wicked man." Why? "Because he did not prepare his heart to seek the Lord. If his heart had been upright with Me, he would have prepared his heart to seek Me."

I beseech you now to lay this text to your hearts. Do you prepare your hearts to seek God? When you go to prayer, can you say that you take pains in preparing your heart for it? Do you prepare your heart to hear the Word? Do you prepare your heart to receive the sacrament?

Now Jehoshaphat was a godly man. In 2 Chronicles 19:3 you may see what the Lord said of Jehoshaphat, who was godly, "Nevertheless, there are good things found in thee, in that thou hast taken away the groves out of the land, and hast prepared thine heart to seek God." Jehoshaphat was found guilty in joining himself to wicked men too much. The prophet came to him and said, "Would you help the ungodly and love them who hate the Lord? Therefore is wrath upon thee from before the Lord." Jehoshaphat here, we see, was very faulty in joining with those who were wicked, and is rebuked by the prophet from the Lord. "What? Will you join with the wicked? The wrath of God is upon you."

But for all that, observe this. At that time when the Lord is most displeased against Jehoshaphat, and sends His prophet in His name to pronounce that the wrath of God is out against him, for all this, God cannot but take notice of this, that he had an upright heart, though he failed in that particular. "Yet there is some good found in thee, in that thou hast prepared thy heart to seek God." It is as if God were to say, "Indeed, through some sudden temptations you are drawn aside in this particular act, yes, but it has been your care to prepare your heart to seek Me, and, in that regard I look upon you as having an upright heart."

And thus you see how much the Scripture puts upon preparing the heart to seek God. And so in 1 Samuel 7:3, you find that the Scripture makes the uprightness of the heart to consist in this: "And Samuel spake unto all the house of Israel saying, 'If ye do return unto the Lord with all your hearts (what then?), then put away the strange gods, and Ashtaroth from among you, and prepare your hearts unto the Lord and serve Him only.' "

It is as if Samuel had said, "If you will return indeed to the Lord, if indeed your hearts are upright (according to what you seem to profess in turning to God), then prepare your hearts to seek the Lord."

You do not, in truth, turn to God unless you make conscience to prepare your hearts. Therefore, you who never knew what it was to make conscience to prepare your hearts for holy duties, know that you have not turned with all your heart unto the Lord. There has not been the true turning of your hearts unto the Lord. Thus you see that much lies upon preparation for the duties of God's worship.

"Well," you may say, "seeing that so much lies in it, I pray, open to us wherein it consists."

PREPARATION FOR WORSHIP CONSISTS IN THESE FIVE THINGS:

First, in possessing the heart with the right apprehension of that God before whom we come to tender our duties. We make conscience to prepare our hearts when we labor upon our going to worship God to get our hearts possessed beforehand with right apprehensions of the majesty of that God whom we are going to worship, and of the greatness and weight of the duty that we are setting about, the nature of it, the manner how it is to be performed, the rule by which we are to be guided, and the end at which we are to aim.

Meditation is a good preparation for holy duties. And these are the general headings of our meditation for our preparation to duty: what God He is with whom we have to deal. Meditate on God's attributes; and then meditate on the weight of our duties, the nature of them, the rule of them, and the end of them. Get your hearts possessed with meditations of this nature, and in this, as a special thing, your preparation for holy duties consists.

The second thing in which the preparation to a duty consists in is taking the heart off from every sinful way (the endeavor, at least). If there is iniquity in your hand or heart, labor to put it out. When you come into God's presence, do not bring into the presence of God the love of any sin in your heart, but labor to put it from your heart. In 2 Chronicles 29:5, we find that is required for preparation. The text says that Hezekiah said unto them, "Hear me, ye Levites, sanctify now yourselves, and sanctify the house of the Lord God of your fathers, and carry forth the filthiness out of the holy place." It is a sanctifying thing to carry forth the filthiness out of that thing we would sanctify. So sanctifying our hearts is done by carrying forth the filthiness out of our hearts so as to be fit for a duty. And in Job 11:13–14 we read: "If thou prepare thine heart, and stretch out thine hand towards Him," what then? "If iniquity be in thine hand, put it far away, and let not wickedness dwell in thy tabernacles." These two must be together.

A third thing is this: the preparation of the heart is the disentangling of the heart from the world and from all occasions and businesses in the world. I am to worship God, but how is my heart ensnared and entangled in this and the other business? Now when I come to worship God, I must lay aside all; for the preparation of the heart is the separating of it for such a work. That's the nature of sanctification, separating something from a common use. I am to worship God. Now I must labor to separate my heart from a common use. At other times God gives me liberty to let out my heart to common uses, but when I come to worship Him I must separate my heart from all common uses so that my heart may be wholly for God.

When Cicil, who was Lord Treasurer, went to read, he would lay his gown off and say, "Lie there, Lord Cicil." So when we go to duty we should say, "Lie there, world." And by laying aside the world, I mean laying aside all household affairs, or affairs in trading, and so forth. I must be as one who has nothing to do in the world for that time. It is true that the time cannot be said to be holy for this, as the time of the Sabbath day is holy.

QUESTION. "Why may not any time be said to be holy that I spend in holy duties?"
ANSWER. No, that is not enough to make time holy, for the time that God makes holy is not holy because of the duties that I perform during that time, but the duties that I perform then are more acceptable because they are done during this time. And so that makes a place holy, not because it is appointed for holy duties and uses, but because it is so appointed by God, and performing a duty in that place is more acceptable to God than in another place. But now, though we cannot make our time holy in that second sense, yet in the first, it is time set apart for a holy use, and, in that regard, it is holy.

And so we should look upon it as not to have our outward business to devour that time that is holy in that regard. When

Tobiah and Sanballet sent to Nehemiah to come and confer with them, he said, "No, I cannot go, for the work is great that I have to do." So we must not entangle ourselves and meddle with other things when we are to come to worship God, for our work is great.

The fourth thing for preparation is to watch and to pray. We should watch over our hearts lest they be made unfit for duties. So we should prepare for prayer all day long in this sense. That is, we should watch over our hearts so that they are not let out so far as will hinder us in prayer when we come to do it. I remember Tertullian said that the Christians supped as if they were about to pray. So when you are with company, you should watch unto prayer. Oh, that you did so. You cannot but be conscious of the fact that oftentimes when you have been with company your hearts have been out of tune and frame, so that you have been in no way fit for prayer. When you come home, your house and family finds it so. You who take such delight in company and sitting up late, I appeal to your consciences whether you can come home and find yourselves to be fit in either your family or closet to go and open your hearts to God.

This is one note, by the way, whereby you may come to know whether you have been immoderate in company at any time. God does not give men liberty, be busy in any outward occasions in the world so as to make them unfit for His service. Preparation consists in watching over your hearts so that you may not be made unfit for any holy duty when God calls you to it, but that you may be ready even to every good work.

Fifth, preparation consists in the readiness of the faculties of the soul and the graces of the Spirit of God to act and set upon a holy duty. When a man or woman finds the faculties of their soul and the graces that are in them to be ready to act as soon as they fall upon a duty, they will be like a company of bell ringers. When they have made all preparation for raising the bells, then the instant they begin to pull all the bells go in that tune according to their skill. And so it should be with our hearts, the faculties of our souls and graces. Though now we are not upon a duty, yet we should be so ready that upon a pull, as it were, all the faculties of our souls and graces of God's Spirit should work in a melodious way.

There are those who keep their hearts so prepared that the very first moment they set about the duty of worship, all faculties and graces begin to act and stir and are working towards God like a fire. When all the matter is already laid out, immediately it comes to be kindled and flame out; and thus it should be with our hearts. So now you see wherein the preparation of our hearts for duty consists.

The next thing I wish to address is the excellence of this preparation. And that may, in way of application to you, make you to be in love with preparation for holy duties. There is an abundance of good in it.

First, by this means we come to make every duty of worship easy to us. Things are difficult when we come upon them unprepared. If you have a friend come to dinner or supper suddenly, and you have nothing prepared, there would be a great deal of stir in the house. But if you have everything prepared, it would be carried on in an easy way. The reason why people complain so much of difficulty in duty is because their hearts are not prepared. Indeed, we naturally have many things to keep us from God; but when the heart is prepared for a holy duty it goes easily to God, even into the infinite ocean of all mercy and goodness. It is like a ship that goes off to be launched when you have made preparation for it; and the heart can go with a holy boldness to God when you have made preparation for holy duties.

In Job 11, the place that I quoted before for the work of

preparation, consider a verse or two farther and you shall find what an abundance of good comes from keeping the heart prepared in things that are good. Verse 13: "If thou prepare thine heart." Verse 15: "Then shalt thou lift up thy face without spot, yea, thou shalt be steadfast and shall not fear." When the heart is prepared for that which is good when it comes into the presence of God, it is able to lift itself up without fear in a steadfast, comfortable way, and this will justify the cost of any labor.

Second, if the heart is prepared, it will do a great deal in a little time. In 2 Chronicles 2:36 it says that "Hezekiah rejoiced, and all the people, that God had prepared the people, for the thing was done suddenly." The thing came off freely and suddenly when they were prepared. Hezekiah rejoiced and blessed God for such a mercy as this was. It is a great mercy to have the hearts of people prepared unto a good work. And so in 2 Chronicles 27:6 the text says, "Jotham became mighty because he prepared his ways before the Lord his God." Jotham grew mighty by this; and so certainly the way to grow to be very strong and mighty, to be able to do a great deal in a little time, is to make preparation.

There may be as much work done in one hour as in ten times as much time when the heart is not prepared for it. In Ezra 7:10, you find that the reason given why Ezra had such good success in his journey was because he had prepared his heart. Make preparation for holy duties and you shall have success in holy duties. There is a notable Scripture for that in Psalm 10:17, where the Holy Ghost says that God prepares the heart. And what then? When God prepares the heart, He causes His ear to hear. There was never a prayer made wherein the heart was prepared for it but that prayer was heard. They both go together. "Lord, Thou wilt prepare their heart, and Thou wilt cause Thine ear to hear." If God has prepared your heart, you will be sure to be heard then. Is it not worth a world to know that you are accepted by God in every duty of worship that you offer up to Him? This one Scripture, Psalm 10:17, will show it. Oh, the excellency that there is in preparation for duty!

There is one more thing that is very observable and that is this: where the heart is prepared for duties, there the Lord will pass by weaknesses and imperfections in duties. When you come to perform holy duties, you are troubled and ask yourself, "Will the Lord have regard to such a duty as this is?" You may have certain assurance that the Lord will have regard if you can make this point good to your own soul, that it was your care to make preparation for this duty. Can you say, "Lord, I have endeavored and done what I could to fit my heart for duty. But, O Lord, I find when I am at it that there are wonderful distractions, much deadness and vanity. What shall I do?"

Why, can you make good the former and appeal to God that indeed it was your care to make preparation? I'll give you one Scripture to quiet your heart in this, that the weakness of the duty shall be pardoned and passed by where there is care to prepare beforehand. The Scripture is 2 Chronicles 30:18–19: "But Hezekiah prayed for them saying, 'The good pardon every one.' " Which ones? "Every one that prepareth his heart to seek the Lord God of his fathers, though he be not cleansed according to the purification of the sanctuary."

It is as if he should say, "O Lord, there are many things amiss in this people. They are not, in many regards, purified according to the order Thou has set. But, Lord, if Thou seest any heart prepared to seek Thee, though they fail in such particulars, Lord, heal them and pardon them." Did God hearken to his prayer? Mark the following words, "And the Lord hearkened to Hezekiah and healed the people."

"No," said God, "I will not stand so much upon the purification of the sanctuary if they have prepared their hearts to seek Me." Take this Scripture; know that it is written for your instruction, and you may make use of it to your own soul this day. If you can appeal to God that you are careful to prepare your heart as you desire, the Lord will pardon you and heal you. Make conscience of preparation for holy duties.

Further, by being careful to make preparation for duties, within some little time you will bring your heart to such a frame as it will always be ready for duty without much ado. Indeed, at first it is somewhat hard.

You will say, "Are we bound to spend some time beforehand each time we go to prayer, or every time we go to the Word?" That would have been one of the cases of conscience, but I cannot come to answer that. But I may say this, be careful to prepare for duties, you who are young beginners, or you who have made profession a longer time, but have yet not had the weight of this duty upon your spirits. Now be careful for a while to prepare for every duty of God's worship to which He calls you, and, I say, within a little time you may bring your heart into such a temper that you may be ready at all times to perform holy duties because you shall be able to come to that temper and frame to which the apostle exhorts us, "Pray continually."

Indeed, so it should be with us. We should always be prepared either for prayer, hearing the Word, or receiving sacraments. Now because sacraments are so rare, those who have any enlightened conscience think that they dare not but prepare for sacraments; but you should always be in preparation for the receiving of the sacraments, as the primitive Christians were. And those who have been acquainted with this point of preparing for duties have come to such a frame of spirit that there is not as much time required of them as others, for they are in a constant fitness—so that there is not an instant of time in the whole day but, if God called them to prayer, they could immediately fall down upon their knees and pray so as to sanctify God's name in prayer.

That would be an excellent temper, indeed, if you could find it so that you walk so spiritually and holy before God that there could never be a quarter of an hour from morning to night, nor from the beginning of the week to the end, but if you were called to pray or to receive the sacrament, you had your heart fitted so that you could come into God's presence with a prepared heart and would be able to sanctify God's name in that duty. Acquaint yourselves with this work of preparation, and so you may have hearts fitted to come into God's presence at any time.

(Preached December 7, 1645)

Two Cases of Conscience

"I will be sanctified in them that come nigh Me."

LEVITICUS 10:3

We now proceed to what remains. There are only two cases of conscience to be resolved for the perfecting of this point, and then we proceed to other things.

CASE 1. Are we always bound to set some time apart for preparation to the duty that we are about to perform?

We must distinguish between persons. There are some who are exercised in the way of godliness and keep their hearts close with God in ways of holiness. Now for them it may be supposed that through their exercise in the ways of godliness and keeping their hearts constant with God in communion with Him, walking with God closely, that they are at all times, "prepared unto every good work," and are fitted to fulfill that command of the apostle to "pray continually." That is, in the disposition of their hearts, they are fit to pray any time. There is no day in the week nor hour in the day but they (if God calls them to it) could fall down in solemn prayer. And indeed, this is an excellent condition, and a good evidence of the heart's walking close with God, that there is no time but they are fit to pray and fit for any ordinance, yes, to receive the Sacrament of the Lord's Supper.

It is possible to keep the heart so close to God as to be fit for prayer, for the hearing of the Word, and for receiving the Sacrament every day, or any hour in the day; but this needs a very close walking with God and communion with God, and, the truth is, this is very rare. Most men let out their hearts so much to other things, as their consciences cannot but tell them, that if God called them to prayer at such a time in the day, they would be altogether unfit for it. But it is not so with those who walk closely with God, even though they are in the world.

You will say, "If a man has business in the world, how can this be?"

Yes, though they have business in the world, yet they can carry the heavenliness of their hearts along with them. "Our conversation is in heaven," said the apostle in Philippians 3. Now the word that is translated "conversation" is a word that signifies our city business. Our trading is in heaven. When we go to the city, the exchange, or any business, yet our trading is always in heaven.

But there are other sorts of people who need at all times to look to their hearts in way of preparation, such as those who first set upon the duties of religion. Young beginners who begin at first to set their faces towards heaven to worship God need to look to their hearts. They should spend some time in preparation when they come to holy duties. The truth is that when the conscience of a man or woman is at first enlightened and awakened, they will be very careful in preparing for holy duties. The fear of God is upon their spirits at first, and it should not be less afterwards. The constancy of God's fear should bring their hearts to such a holy temper as to make them fit for holy duties always.

Those men and women who at any time sin against conscience shall commit such sins as will, in a way, lay waste their conscience; those sins shall break the peace between God and their souls. They need to spend some time in preparation for holy duties. They cannot come into the presence of God to enjoy communion with God but they need beforehand to be very serious in the examination of their hearts, to endeavor to work their hearts into mourning for their sin, and to labor to possess their souls with the presence of God even before they come. These two sorts of people—such as have not been acquainted with the ways of godliness, or such as have broken their peace with God by some evil carriage towards God in some vile way—it is required of them to be more solemn in the work of preparation.

CASE 2. The second case is indeed the main one. Suppose we come to duties and begin to examine our hearts, and begin to think to ourselves whether or not we are prepared for holy duties. And suppose that we do not find our hearts prepared according to what we desire. May we then let the duty go for that time and forbear the performance of it, such as prayer, receiving the Sacrament, coming to the Word, or any other holy duty?

The reason for this doubt is because when any man or woman is conscientious, they think with themselves that they must sanctify God's name in holy duties. Now if they cannot find their hearts in a disposition to sanctify the name of God in holy duties, they are ready to think thus: "Would it not be better to neglect this duty and lay it aside for the present? Will God accept a duty when I perform it and am not fit for it?"

ANSWER. This is a temptation that sometimes carnal hearts have, and they are ready to take this temptation, and are willing

to neglect the duty upon such a thought as this, that they are
not prepared. The truth is, they are more glad to let the duty
fall than they are sorry for want of preparation of their hearts
for the duty. I beseech you to consider this, whether you have
not found it so that sometimes, when you have not been fit
to perform a holy duty, there has not been a more secret
willingness of the heart to let the duty go than a sorrow of the
heart because you are not fit for the duty.

This is a very evil sign that the heart is very much distempered.
Those who are godly indeed find that, when they find their
hearts unprepared for the duty, it is the trouble of their souls.
It is that which goes near to their hearts. When they think with
themselves that they are now likely to lose a duty of the worship
of God, they are now likely to lose their communion with God
in a holy duty, they even look upon themselves in an evil case
in regard to this; and it makes them watchful for time to come
to take heed of those things that have put them upon such an
"unpreparation" as they find their hearts to be in at this time.
Now if it is so with you, it is a good sign that your heart may be
upright with God, though through infirmity it comes at such a
time as to be unprepared for the duty.

QUESTION. "Yet suppose that I find I am not prepared and
I am grieved and troubled for it (for that must be premised);
would I be better to leave the duty for this time than to fall
upon it in such an unprepared manner as this is?"
ANSWER. I would answer, first that the omission of a duty,
or the laying aside of a duty, will never fit the soul for a duty
afterwards. It is no way to make your soul more fit afterwards
because you have laid it aside for the present. Do but observe
your own hearts that way and you will find this by experience.
At some point you have been busy in a duty of the world, and

occasions have hindered you so that your heart is out of temper and frame for a duty and you lay it aside. Now are you more fit the next day? If you neglect duty in the morning upon any business, are you more fit to perform duty at night because of it? You will not find it to be so.

The forbearing of a duty now will not make the soul more fit for a duty afterwards. Therefore, it is not wisdom to forbear a duty for lack of preparation, because the forbearance will never help to further preparation, but will make the soul more unfit for duty. It is an excellent speech that Luther had concerning himself, "I have learned this by experience, that the more often I omit duty, the more often I make myself the more unfit for duty, and the more cause I have to abhor myself." It is not the deferring that makes you the more fit.

Therefore, consider that this is but a temptation, and that is the second thing that I would propound to those that shall omit a duty because they are not prepared. This is but a temptation to keep you from it, to tell you that you are not prepared. And if you shall forbear it because you are not prepared, in this thing you gratify the devil; and the devil has what he would have, and so would be encouraged to tempt you at another time because he has now what he would have in causing you to forbear the duty.

He first labors to make you unfit for it. Then he tempts you to forbear it because you are unfit. This is the subtlety of the devil. From whence is it that you are unfit but from the temptation of the devil? Luther was a man who had as much converse with God as any in his days, and a man who had as much to draw his heart away, as many temptations and as many businesses as any; for indeed the great cause of Christ in all the Christian world in a great measure under God lay upon his shoulders, and yet he said, "If anyone thinks that prayer must be deferred till the soul is purified from impure cognitions, he does nothing other than help the devil, who is powerful enough." He thinks to be wise in deferring the duty because he is not fit and because he has many ill thoughts and troubles in spirit, but he does nothing else, Luther said, but gratify the devil, who is strong enough without this. Oh, let us take heed of gratifying the devil in his temptations! Therefore, remember that it is a temptation for you to omit a duty merely because you are not prepared for the duty.

The third answer I have for this question is this: If anyone performed a duty of worship in that sincerity and strength that he is able to do, though he is not as prepared as he ought, yet it is better to do it than to neglect it. It is true that some perform a duty in a mere formal way to satisfy their consciences, or to cloak and cover their sins and the like. Perhaps they may so perform it as it might be better to be unperformed than to perform it as they do; but if you endeavor to the utmost of your strength to do it, though you are not as prepared as you desire, yet it is better to do it than to omit doing it. And you will find it so, for one duty prepares for another.

Though it is not done as I desire it should be done, yet doing it as well as I can at this time will help me to do it better at another time—that is certain. As one sin prepares the heart for another sin, so one duty prepares the heart for another. Suppose that a man commits a sin and has an enlightened conscience that hinders him from committing his sin with that full strength with which he would do it. Many a man has a mind to sin, but through the enlightening of his conscience he cannot sin with that delight as he would because his conscience flies in his face and interrupts him. Yet for all this, through the strength of his corruption, he will break through to that sin. Now though at first they cannot commit that sin with the same delight and freedom as they do at other times, yet if their corruptions are so strong as to break through the light of their consciences, the next time they come to commit that sin they will commit it with a great deal more ease and freedom.

This is evident by experience. There is none of you but if you will observe your hearts will find this. A temptation comes to you to sin. Now you cannot do it with as much freedom as you would, but yet you break through it. If such is the case, you will find that the next time you will commit it with more freedom. And so one sin will prepare for another. It may be that you have some trouble of conscience at first, but the next time you will have less trouble, until at last you can commit it freely without any trouble of conscience at all.

As it is in sin, so it is in godliness many times in some degree. At first you have a motion to a holy duty, but through the stirrings of your corruptions you are not fit for it. Now, if you will just break through that difficulty, the next time you will be more fit, and the next time after that you will be more fit, and so still more and more fit, just as it is in sin. If a man, when he has some trouble of conscience, would just listen to his conscience and not commit that sin, his conscience would grow stronger and stronger upon him and would strengthen him against that sin. So if any man or woman listens to the temptation to defer duty, and puts it off because they are not prepared, why, after that the temptation will grow stronger. Therefore, set upon the duty, and the performance of one duty will prepare for another.

In the fourth place, while men and women are struggling with their souls and the corruption of their hearts and do not fall upon seeking God, by their very struggling to prepare themselves, many times, they ensnare themselves. It may be that you have thoughts of atheism or some other wickedness. The very struggling with those thoughts may ensnare your heart. Now the better way would be to fall upon prayer, and to cry to God to help you against them. For while you are struggling and striving with those thoughts, you are striving with the corruption of your heart and with the devil all alone; but now, when you fall to the duty, you call in the help of God and of Jesus Christ, and that is a great deal better. While you are musing, plodding, and troubling your heart that way, you are struggling alone; but when you fall upon the duty, then you call in help from God, and so you are more able to the performance of the duty than you were before. And therefore, it is the best way to fall upon a duty. Though you cannot find your heart prepared as you desire, the very falling upon it will fit you for it. So much for the answer to those two cases of conscience.

Now then, we are to proceed further in opening the sanctifying of God's name in holy duties. So much for the preparation of the heart.

QUESTION. But when the heart comes to the duty, in what manner should the duty be performed so that the name of God may be sanctified in the duty? Or what is the behavior of the soul in sanctifying God's name when it is in the very act of duty?
ANSWER. Generally, when I labor to perform duties so that God may have such glory from the duty as is fit for a God to have in some measure, then I sanctify God's name.

You will say that this is a very hard thing, to perform a duty so that we should give God the glory that is fit for a God to have. Certainly this is not done by every manner of performance of a duty of worship; yet you shall hear this opened to you, and I hope you shall have it made very plain before you.

First, therefore, I shall show you that when we are to perform a duty of worship, we should set ourselves to glorify

God as a God, that is, to do it in that manner so that God may have the glory that is fitting for a God to have. In the duty of praise, Psalm 66:2 says that we are to "make His praise glorious," that is, to do it so as to lift up His name in it, and so that God may be glorious in your praise. In Romans 1:21, the apostle, speaking of the heathens, rebukes them. For what? It was for this: "because that when they knew not God, they glorified Him not as God, neither were thankful." Now this is spoken especially of the worship of God, for he says afterward in verse 23 "that they changed the glory of the incorruptible God into an image made like to corruptible men."

So that it's spoken of the worship of God that "they glorified not God as God." So, then, to sanctify God's name is to glorify God as God; and, therefore, our Savior, in John 4, when He spoke to the woman of Samaria told her that God is a Spirit and must be worshipped in spirit and truth. That is, we must labor to suit our worship to what there is in God so that our worship may be proportionable in some measure to the nature of God Himself. And therefore, God being a Spirit, His worship must be a divine worship.

I have read of some of the heathens who worshipped the sun as a god, and they would offer to the sun something suitable. Therefore, because they so admire the swiftness of the motion of the sun, they would not offer a snail to the sun but a flying horse, a horse with wings. Now a horse is one of the swiftest creatures, and the strongest creature to continue in motion for a long time together; so they added wings to the horse, thinking that to be a suitable sacrifice to the sun.

So when we come to worship God, that is, to sanctify His name, we must behave ourselves so as to give Him the glory that is fitting for a God to have. In those three particulars that I opened to you, I showed you wherein we draw nigh to God.

This was one, I told you, that when we come to worship God we must come to offer up some present to God. Now, then, we must tender up such a present as is suitable to God's excellency.

If a man should come to give a poor man a present, it would be taken well even if it were not worth twelve pence. But if you were to tender up a present to a prince or monarch, an emperor, then you must tender up a present that is fitting for the quality of the person. Therefore, in Malachi 1:8, when the Lord rebukes them for their sacrifices that were such poor things, He says that they should go and offer this to your governor and see whether he will accept it or not. So certainly, that which may be accepted by a lowly man would be accounted a scorn if you should offer it up to a prince or emperor.

Now when we come to worship God, we must consider that we are to tender up service to God, who is the great King of kings and Lord of lords.

QUESTION. But you will say, "Is it possible for any creature, when it comes to tender up its worship to God, to tender up that which is fitting for a God to have? This may be a discouragement unto prayer or any other duty of worship rather than an encouragement."

ANSWER. Though we may be very poor and lowly, yet it does not hinder us, but we may tender up that to God which God will acknowledge to be suitable to His infinite excellency.

As first, if we tender up to God all that we have, though we are never so poor and mean, yet if God has the strength of our souls, God accepts it. For we are to know that God does not stand in need of what we have or of what we do, but that we might show our respect to Him. Therefore, if we give all that we have, God accepts it. If a child puts forth all the strength that it has to do a business that the father bids him, whether the business is done or not, the father looks upon it and accepts it as suitable to the child's strength; and it shows the respect that the child has for his father.

The story is told of an emperor that when a poor man had nothing to offer him but a little water that he had taken up with his hand, the emperor accepted it because the man had nothing else. So that is what God looks for, that the creature should lift Him above all. If, therefore, when you come to worship God, God has more of your heart than any creature in the world has, God accepts that. Can you say when you go to worship God, "Lord, it is true, there is much weakness in my spirit, but Thou that knowest all things know that Thou hast more of my heart than ever any creature in the world has."

This is suitable to God. God will account this (in the Covenant of Grace) to be a present suitable to Himself. Under the Law, when they offered for the building of the temple, everyone could not offer gold and silver and precious stones, but some came and offered badger skins, and some women spun and offered goat's hair to the building of the temple, and so God accepted that as being the most they could do.

When we not only offer unto God the most we can, but when we add to this the grief of our souls that we can do no more; when the soul shall strive to the uttermost it can and when it has done all, it says, "I am an unprofitable servant. Oh, that I could do more!"—this is suitable to God.

Though the people of God are weak, yet the weakest servant of God is able to offer up to God something that is suitable to the infinite majesty of God upon this ground: because there is a kind of impression of God's infiniteness in those services that a gracious heart tenders unto God, and therefore it is suitable to God.

QUESTION. But God is an infinite, glorious God. He is infinite, that's certain, but how is it that the duty of worship that a gracious heart tenders unto God has an impression of God's infiniteness upon it?

ANSWER. If that can be made out, then, indeed, we may be encouraged to worship God. Thus, that which a gracious heart tenders up to God has an impression of His infiniteness in this regard, because as God has no limits to His being, so a gracious heart, when it comes to worship God, will not propound any limit or bounds, but, in the desires of it, would fain be enlarged infinitely if it could. If it were possible for a creature to be enlarged to God infinitely, it would be.

Herein lies, I believe, the main difference between the most glorious hypocrite in the world and one who has true grace, yea, who has but the least degree of grace. The most glorious hypocrite in the world who, it may be, for the outward act does more than one who has true grace, yet such a one limits himself—that is, so much as may serve for such and such ends of his, so much as may serve his turn, either to satisfy his conscience or to get credit and esteem, to be accounted eminent in such a way—that much he does, but his duty is always limited within such bounds. And if he could conceive that he might go to heaven, and that he might have as much credit and honor and as much peace of conscience with doing less, he would do less. But now one who has grace, though but little, though but the least dram of grace, goes farther.

"Indeed," says he, "though through the little grace that I have I cannot do what another can do, yet this enlarges my heart so that I would have no bounds set in what I do for God, but I would have it enlarged to the uttermost latitude, if it were possible, beyond whatever has yet been done for God in the world. And the more I do, the more I desire to do."

That's now a kind of infiniteness that there is in the heart where grace comes. I say, grace enlarges the heart to a kind of infiniteness so that the more it does, the more it would do. There is no hypocrite in the world but will have periods where he will rise thus and thus and thus high. Ordinarily you shall find that if he lives in some company, there he is high; but if he lives in other company, there he is lower.

Now there is nothing that limits a gracious heart but to all eternity it would work and work more and more for God. Here is a worship that is in some way suitable to the infinite excellency that there is in God. Here's a kind of proportion (if I may so speak) even between the creature and God Himself in this thing, but it is the grace of God in the creature. Here is the image of God indeed, because grace so enlarges the heart even to an infiniteness, as it were, for God. And thus you see in general what it is to sanctify God's name, to tender up to God that which is in some way suitable to the glory of the infinite God.

There is a second thing, that then I sanctify God's name when I come so to worship God as my heart works and follows after God as a God. So it becomes the soul of a creature to follow the infinite Creator and to work after the infinite Creator. So David said in Psalm 63:5, "My soul followeth hard after Thee, O God and (mark, it's a very sweet Scripture) Thy right hand upholdeth me." Those whose hearts follow hard after the Lord have the right hand of God upholding them. It's a mighty encouragement to put both the heart to the uttermost, because when you do the right hand of God upholds you. So your heart must follow after God more than it followed after any creature.

When I come to draw nigh to God, I come to present myself for the communication of the choicest of His mercies. So then I sanctify God's name when I labor to prepare and open my heart for God for the choicest mercies that God has to bestow upon His creature, when there is such a temper of heart that my conscience tells me it is suitable to that which is fitting for a soul to have that expects to receive the choicest mercies from God; but that we spoke of already in the opening of our drawing nigh to God.

Now we come more particularly to this, to open the sanctifying of God's name. We will examine, first, in what particulars the behavior of the heart may be discovered to be suitable to God in respect of God's greatness and glory, and, second, what the behavior of the heart should be as suitable to the various attributes of God.

It will cost us some time to open the particular things in the behavior of the heart in reference to the greatness and majesty of God. Considered more generally, as in Psalm 48:1, "Great is the Lord, and greatly to be praised." And also in Malachi 1:14, "Cursed be the deceiver which hath in his flock a male, and voweth, and sacrificeth unto the Lord a corrupt thing." Why? " 'For I am a great King,' saith the Lord." And therefore, cursed, is he who does not offer a sacrifice suitable to God's greatness. And in 2 Chronicles 2:5 we find that Solomon, when he was preparing for the temple, would build a great temple. Why? Because God was a great God for whom he was building it. So the worship of God must be suitable to His greatness.

QUESTION. "In what particulars does the behavior of the soul consist that is very suitable to the greatness of God in general?" ANSWER. There are many things in this.

First, you must be careful to bring a sanctified heart. You cannot tender up worship suitable to His greatness unless you bring a sanctified heart with you. There must be holiness in the heart. Under the Law, you know, if anyone came to offer a sacrifice in his uncleanness, he was to be cut off. And so it must be here. We must look to it that we do not offer to God in our uncleanness. "Wash you and make you clean" (Isaiah 1:16), and then, "Come, let us reason together." There is no coming to God without washing and making clean. Psalm 93:5: "Holiness becometh Thy house, O Lord, forever." Holiness becomes the presence of God forever. We must look to get a sanctified heart.

Sanctification consists in these two parts, mortification and vivification. There must be a mortifying of the lusts of the heart. We read in the Law that every sacrifice was to be salted. That signified the mortification of our hearts when we come to offer up ourselves as a sacrifice to God. The salt ate out the raw humors and kept the flesh from putrefying. So does the grace of God in mortifying our lusts. In Hebrews 9:14, you have a notable Scripture for the cleansing of our hearts when we come to offer any sacrifice to God. "How much more shall the blood of Christ who through the eternal Spirit offered Himself without spot to God." So you cannot serve the living God until your consciences are purged from dead works. And how do your consciences come to be purged from dead works? It is through the blood of Christ, who through the eternal Spirit offered Himself without spot to God. He must purge your consciences.

So here's the way of sanctifying God's name, by applying Jesus Christ, who was offered to God without spot, so that our consciences might be purged from dead works, so that we might be purged from that natural filthiness and uncleanness in which we all were. For the whole world lies in filth as carrion lies in its slime. Now if we would worship God so as to sanctify Him, we must apply Christ to our souls and get our consciences purged from dead works, and have the Spirit of Christ in us to quicken our hearts in the ways of holiness. To have the image of Jesus Christ in us, whereby we may be holy according to our proportion even as He Himself is holy, this is the sanctifying of the heart.

There must be a habitual sanctification and an actual sanctification of the heart. A habitual, that is, that the heart must be changed through the work of regeneration. There must be a regeneration in the heart. There must be divine principles of the graces of the Spirit of God in the heart.

QUESTION. "But may not an unregenerate man pray?"
ANSWER. It is true, it is his duty to pray. "Pour forth Thy wrath upon the heathen, and upon the families that call not upon Thy name." But it's as true that they cannot sanctify God's name in doing it. But if we would sanctify God's name in it, there must be a habitual holiness in the heart, for everything acts according to its principles. In nature it is so, and so does the heart when it comes to worship God. It acts according to the principles that it has.

And there must not only be habitual sanctification, but actual sanctification as well. In Exodus 19:10–11, you see what ado there was to fit them for the hearing of the Law, because "God was to come among them." God is to come among us, and we are to come to God when we are to perform holy duties. Therefore it is not enough to have grace, but there must be an improving of grace. There must be an acting of grace not only when you come to receive the Sacrament, but every time you pray and hear there must be an acting of grace, a purging out of your corruptions.

So that one cannot sanctify God's name in holy duties unless he comes so far as to be able to say, "Lord, Thou that knowest all things knowest that there is nothing that Thou revealest to be contrary to Thy will but my heart is against it." That's the least. You cannot have any peace of conscience in drawing nigh to God until you come this far, to have the heart to work thus against sin, and to set upon every good that God reveals to be His mind. You know when a man of quality comes to your house what a stir there is, not only in sweeping, but in making all things as clean and tidy and shining as possibly can be. Thus it should be when you come to God.

And the reason why there must be this sanctifying of the heart is, first, because the Lord first accepts the person before He accepts the action. Men, indeed, accept the persons of men because they do good actions; but God accepts the actions of men because their persons are good. If we see a man do good, then we love him and accept the person of the man; but God will first accept the person before the action, as the Lord accepted Abel first and then accepted his offering. So you must look to have your persons first accepted by God before any duty can be accepted.

You think that though you are wicked and sinful, yet if you amend your life, God will accept you. You go that way to work; but certainly that is the wrong way. You must first look after the means of acceptance of your persons, which is through the righteousness of Jesus Christ and through the sanctification of His Spirit whereby you come to have His image and life, and so are accepted. And then all that proceeds from you comes to be accepted.

There is not any action that comes from you that comes to be accepted to eternal life until your persons are accepted by God, and, therefore, there must be a sanctifying of the heart before there can be a sanctifying of the name of God in the duties of His worship. Therefore, when you come to perform any duties of God's worship, you should consider this," Is my heart sanctified? I must sanctify God's name, and how can I do that unless my heart is sanctified?"

Secondly, our hearts must be sanctified because the Lord looks more to the principle from whence a thing comes than at the thing itself. Were our hearts as right as they should be, then we would not so much regard what all the good things that come to us from God are as much as what the principle is from whence they came—that is, whether what we enjoy from God is from the love of God in Jesus Christ or not, whether it is from the general bounty and patience of God or from the special love of God in Jesus Christ. Our hearts would regard that most if we were spiritual.

Now then, as a godly man is not satisfied with enjoying any good thing from God unless he knows it comes from a principle of love to him in Jesus Christ, so God is not pleased with anything that comes from us unless He knows that it comes from a principle of love, grace, and holiness in our hearts.

Third, according as the heart is, so will the service be. Certainly if the heart is unclean, the duty will be unclean. Perhaps the words may be fine and brave, but if there is an unclean heart, the duty will be unclean. Suppose a man with the plague makes a brave oration. His breath is still infectious. So it is in our services with God. If our hearts within us have the plague, then certainly the breath that comes from us, all our duties, will be unclean. And, therefore, that is the first thing that we are to look for in the sanctifying of God's name in holy duties. Look to have your heart sanctified, and consider from what principle it comes. It is for lack of this that thousands of our duties are cast aside and God never regards them. But this is the first particular, there are many more to speak of.

(Preached December 14, 1645)

Sanctifying the Name of God in Holy Duties

"I will be sanctified in them that come nigh Me."

LEVITICUS 10:3

The third thing, therefore, for the behavior of the soul in sanctifying God's name in worship is this: when we come to worship God, if we would sanctify God's name, we must have high thoughts of God. We must look upon God as He is upon His throne, in majesty and glory. In Isaiah 6:1–2 you find that the prophet saw the Lord upon His throne. It is an excellent thing when all who come to worship God, every time they come to worship Him, have their eyes darted up to heaven and behold the Lord God sitting in His glory upon His throne.

So you find it in Revelation 4. The twenty-four elders who worshipped God saw Him upon His throne in His glory and so they worshipped Him. They worshipped God to purpose when they saw the Lord in that majesty as He was. We should at all times have high thoughts of God. Take heed of having low thoughts and apprehensions of the infinite majesty of God at any time, but especially when you are to worship the great

God. Then look upon the Lord in that infinite distance that there is between Him and you, yea, that infinite distance there is between Him and all the creatures in the world.

Look upon the Lord as lifted up in glory, not only above all creatures, but above all excellencies that all angels and men in heaven and earth are able to imagine. Look upon the Lord as having all excellencies in Himself joined in one, and that immutably. Look upon Him as the Fountain of all excellency, good, and glory that all creatures in the world have. And look upon the Lord every time you come to worship Him as that God whom angels adore, and before whom the devils are forced to tremble. Behold Him in His glory, and this will help you to sanctify His name when you come to Him.

The great reason why people come and worship God in a slight way is because they do not see God in His glory. It is a great mercy for God to give us a sight of Himself, a sight of His glory here in this world while we are worshipping Him. This would keep our eyes and our thoughts from wandering, if we had a sight of the glory of God, and high thoughts of Him.

What is the reason why we wander so as we do? Merely because we do not see God. Suppose that you were in your own house, looking after every feather that was flying up and down. If you were to hear that the king, or any great person, was coming into the room, it would compose your spirits because you have high thoughts of such men as are above you. So let us look upon God in His excellency and glory and have high thoughts of Him. And this is that whereby we are to sanctify God's name when we come before Him in holy duties. First we need a sanctified heart, and then high thoughts of God.

A third thing is high ends, raised ends in worshipping God. Proverbs 15:24, "The way of life is above to the wise." It is on high in this respect: when he worships God, his heart is lifted on high. There is a holy raising of the heart which is well-pleasing to God. Our hearts should be on high in regard of the high ends that we aim at in holy duties. "Lift up thy prayer," said Hezekiah to the prophet in another case. So I say, lift up your soul when you come to worship God in regard of the high ends you aim at.

When we are worshipping God, we should have our hearts set above all creatures and above ourselves. Let not our hearts, then, be groveling upon the ground, mingled with base and drossy things when we come to worship the Lord. Indeed, it is fitting that we should have our hearts low in regard to humility, but not low in regard of any baseness of spirit to mix it with any base and low ends. Now there are low and base ends in worshipping God.

First, we must take heed that we do not subject the worship of God unto our lusts. That is a cursed thing. You are far from sanctifying God's name in worshipping Him who subject His worship to your base lusts. This is an abominable and cursed thing indeed.

QUESTION. You will say, "Who does this? Who is the man, or where is he that will do this, subject the worship of God to his base lusts?"

ANSWER. Whoever makes use of any duty of worship such as prayer, hearing the Word, or whatever it may be, to cloak any kind of wickedness; whoever is conscious of any secret wickedness, and yet shall think to cover it by the performance of duties, and shall reason in this manner, "Who will think me to be guilty of such a vile thing when I pray as I do and am so careful to hear the Word? I hope I shall cover some wickedness this way?"

If there is anyone in this place whose conscience tells them that they subject the worship of God to such a base end as this, the Lord rebuke them this day and speak to their hearts. If I knew any, I would set my eyes upon them and say, as the apostle said to Simon Magus, "I perceive that thou art in the gall of bitterness and in the bond of iniquity," and as he said to him who sought to draw the deputy from the faith, "O thou child of the devil, and full of all subtlety," to damn and undo yourself eternally who seek to cloak any wicked way by any duty of God's worship.

Is it a great evil for a man or woman to make use of any of God's creatures to be serviceable to their lusts, like meat and drink, and so on? What a damnable thing it is, then, to make use of any duty of God's worship, sometimes extraordinary worship such as fasting and prayer, to be a cloak to cover their wickedness! You are so far from sanctifying God's name that you pollute God's name. You do what lies in you to cast dirt in the face of God Himself who do so.

The second base end is to subject the duties of God's worship to the praise of men, to perform duties of God's worship for the esteem of men and because we shall be well thought of. Take heed of this, you young ones, and others who would be esteemed well of by those with whom you live. It is a desirable thing to have a good esteem from those who are godly, but take heed that you do not subject the duties of God's worship to this.

Indeed, it may be an encouragement to you, as David said in Psalm 52:9, "This is good before Thy saints." David encouraged himself to praise God because it was good before God's saints. And, I confess, it may be an encouragement because holy duties are good before God's saints, but take heed that this is not the highest end at which you aim, and that which carries you on in the work, merely to get the praise of men and so that they shall think that you have good gifts and parts, and that, therefore, you are enlarged in that regard.

Take heed of that. Know that in this case you do not worship

God, but you worship men. You make the praise of men to be your God, for whatever you lift up in the high place, that's your God, whatever it may be. Therefore, if you lift up the praise of men and make that your end, you make that your God. So you are a worshipper of men, but not a worshipper of God.

Third, take heed of making self your end. There are some who are not so base and low in their hearts as to make the praise of men their end, but they aim and look at themselves. That is, they look at their own peace and satisfying their own consciences in the performance of duties. Now, though it's true that when we perform duties of God's worship we may expect to receive some good to ourselves, and we may be encouraged to the duties by the expectation of good to ourselves, yet we must look higher. We must look to the honor and praise of God that the name of the blessed God may be honored.

We should think thusly to ourselves, "Now I am going to pray. Oh, that I may pray so as I may lift up God's name. I am going to hear. Oh, that I may hear so as God may be honored by my hearing. It is this which carries me on to hearing the Word and makes me rise readily and to go forth cheerfully. I hope that God may have some honor by my hearing this day, and God knows this is the thing I aim at. I do not come for company, nor to be seen of men. Neither do I come merely to satisfy my own conscience. Others go and hear such truths of God as do good for their souls, and if I should neglect them merely for my own ease, my conscience would not let me be quiet."

However, there are many whose consciences will be quiet enough, though they lose opportunity in the worship of God. But yet there are others whose consciences cannot do so. Their consciences would tell them when they are lying and turning themselves upon their beds, "How do you know but that God has something to speak to your heart this morning that may never be spoken to your heart at any other time?" Therefore, they cannot be quiet unless they attend upon God in the duties of His worship; but still this is not enough merely to satisfy conscience.

Your main end must be that you may know this day some part of the mind of God, that God may speak to your heart, that you may be so fitted to honor the name of God that you may be enabled to live to His honor the following week so much better.

Your thoughts should be in this manner: "Lord, I find a drossy, carnal heart. I am busy in the world in the week time and I find that my heart is sullied and defiled and entangled with the business of the world. But, Lord, Thou hast appointed Thy Sabbath and Word to be a means to sanctify my heart and to cleanse it. O Lord, communicate Thy grace to my soul through Thine ordinances upon this day so that I may be enabled to better live to Thy honor this following week. Lord, I come into Thy presence to this end, that I may know some part of Thy will, and that I might get Thy Spirit to be conveyed through this Word of Thine into my heart." This should be your end whenever you come, and not just self.

I will give you two or three Scriptures to show that God little regards any duties where self is the highest end. The first is Hosea 7:14: "They howled upon their beds, but they cried not to Me." The Lord there acknowledged that they were very much affected in their prayers, but what was it? It was but a howling upon their beds. How so? It was because they only cried for themselves. "They have not cried unto Me," said the Lord, "with their hearts when they cried upon their beds. It was merely for corn and wine and oil, but not unto Me. They aimed at themselves and not at Me."

In Amos 5:22, the Lord professes that He rejected the fat of their peace-offerings. "Though ye offer Me burnt-offerings and your meat-offerings, I will not accept them, neither will I regard the peace-offerings of your fat beasts." They were careful to offer their fattest beasts in their peace-offerings, and will not God regard them? It was in their peace-offerings that they offered their fat beasts, and there they were to eat a great part of it themselves. Indeed, the burnt-offering was wholly offered unto God. God had all that. But those that offered the peace-offering ate a great part of it themselves. Now they were very careful in those offerings that they were to partake of themselves to offer fat beasts. You do not see the Holy Ghost taking any notice of fat beasts in their burnt-offerings.

Now the note from hence is this: in those things where men are interested themselves, they will be very careful to have the best things. But the Lord said, "You were very careful to offer fat beasts in your peace-offerings where you may feed yourselves, but for those offerings wherein I have all, there you are not so careful, and therefore I do not regard them."

The third Scripture is Zechariah 7:5. There they kept many days in seeking God (it is an observable Scripture for these times). "Speak unto all the people of the land, and to the priests saying, 'When ye fasted and mourned in the fifth and seventh month, even those seventy years, did ye at all fast unto Me, even unto Me?'"

Mark the phrase: "you fasted in the fifth and seventh month, and for seventy years together," but, said the Lord, "did you at all fast unto Me?" And then mark how it is repeated twice, "unto Me?" This notes that when we fast, pray, or do anything in the worship of God, we should be sure to aim at God more than ourselves so that God may not say of us another day, "Do you do it to Me, even to Me?"

QUESTION. You may ask me this question, "How may I know that I am acted by self-ends in holy duties? For it is a hard thing for one to know one's own heart, as to when it is acted by principles of self and when we aim at God in holy duties."

ANSWER. Now for that I will give you these notes to see whether you acted from yourselves or not:

First, see if a man loves holy duties, though he finds no present good comes from them, simply because they are such things as God requires. And, therefore, though I get nothing from them, yet this is enough to carry me on, and to carry me on readily and willingly in the worship of God. Those who can delight in God's worship, even at that time, though they find nothing coming into themselves, aim at God in holy duties.

But when we do not find that which we desire coming in, we begin to be weary of worship and say, "Why have we fasted and you do not see it?" This is an argument that you acted by self rather than by God.

Second, to know whether we are acted by self-ends or rather by high ends for God, those men who can rejoice in others who are able to honor God in holy duties more than themselves have good evidence to their own souls that when they worship God they are acting by higher ends than self. But now those who see others more enlarged in the worship of God and envy them and are grieved and troubled, know that self is a great ingredient in those duties that they perform. If your heart were raised to God, though you cannot yourself be enlarged in holy duties, yet your soul would be glad that any others are. Though I have a wretched and vile heart of my own, yet blessed be God that there are any others who can worship God better than I can.

Third, a man who is acted by self in holy duties regards holy duties only a little except in times of extremity, in times of fear, or in sickness, or in dangers. But one who has high ends in holy duties makes duties of God's worship to be the joy of his soul in midst of prosperity—and that is an evident sign that you are not acted by self-ends, but by higher ends.

Can you say in the midst of your abundance, "Lord, Thou givest me all conveniences in this world, and all outward things that I lack, but Lord, this is that which is the joy of my soul. This is that which makes my life comfortable, even communion with Thyself in the duties of Thy worship, that I have free access unto the throne of Your grace to worship Thee, the Lord, and there meet with Thee when I am in the performance of holy duties. O Lord, Thou that knowest all things know that this is the thing that makes my life comfortable. It is not that I have a table furnished with a variety of dishes, and that I can have liberty of time to go into company and spend according as I please, but Lord, those incomes of Thy Spirit that I find in the duties of Thy worship, those are the things that make my life blessed unto me."

Such a man as is able thus to appeal to God when he worships God is surely acted by high ends and not by self-ends. And that's the third thing that is necessary for sanctifying God's name in holy duties: you must have a sanctified heart, high thoughts of God, and high ends.

In the fourth place, there must be much reverence and much fear when you come into the presence of God to worship Him. You do not glorify God as God unless you come into His presence with much fear and reverence for His great name. Fear in worshipping God is so necessary that many times in Scripture we find that the very worship of God is called the fear of God. They are both put for one. I might give you divers Scriptures for that.

And, hence, it was that the name of God was called "the fear of Isaac." Jacob swore by "the fear of his father, Isaac," because

Isaac, being a great worshipper of God, kept his constant times to worship God, and worshipped Him in such a constant way that, except for David and Daniel, we do not find mention of the constancy of any in worshipping God as we do of Isaac; for it is said that he walked into the fields of the evening as he was wont to do to meditate and pray. And therefore God is called "the fear of Isaac."

Psalm 89:7 is a notable Scripture for this drawing nigh to God with fear: "God is greatly to be feared in the assembly of His saints, and to be had in reverence of all them that are about Him." God is to be held in reverence by all those who are about Him, but in the assembly of His saints He is greatly to be feared. He is "daunting terrible," for so the words are, in the assembly of His saints.

When you come nigh to God, you need to have your heart possessed with so much fear. So in Psalm 2:11, the kings and princes of the earth are called upon to serve the Lord with fear. Let them be never so great, yet when they come into God's presence, they must serve Him with fear. And so Psalm 5:7: "In Thy fear will I worship toward Thy holy temple."

Now this fear of God must not be a servile fear, but a filial and reverential fear. For, my brethren, there may be a great deal of slavish fear where God is not honored. There may be fear from some terrible apprehensions of God, which yet is not owned by God to be this grace of fear.

I'll give you two notable Scriptures for that, in Deuteronomy 5:23–24, and compared with verse 29: "It came to pass when ye heard the voice out of the midst of the darkness, for the mountain did burn with fire, that ye came near unto Me, even all the heads of your tribes and your elders. And ye said, 'Behold the Lord our God hath showed us His glory and His greatness, and we have heard His voice out of the midst of the fire. We have seen this day that God doth talk with man, and he liveth, now therefore why should we die? For this great fire will consume us. If we hear the voice of the Lord our God any more, then we shall die.' "

See with what terror they were struck at the apprehension of God's appearance. You would think surely the men feared God much, but mark in verse 29: "Oh, that there were such a heart in them that they would fear Me." Why, did they not fear the Lord? Were they not struck with fear that they thought they should die? They saw His presence so terrible that they were afraid they would die, and yet, "Oh, that there were such a heart in them that they would fear Me!" So it appears from this that one may be struck with much terror in the apprehension of God's presence and yet have no true fear of the name of God.

So some of you, it may be, in time of thunder or danger are filled with terror, but yet it may not be said presently after, "Oh, that there were the fear of God in the heart of this man or woman, this youth or maid. They are terrified sometimes, but yet there is not a filial or reverential fear of God in them."

I find in I Kings 19, where you have the story of God's appearing in that most terrible manner unto the prophet Elijah by fire, by thunder, and in a mighty wind, that the prophet was not as struck with fear of God's presence when He appeared in the mighty wind or earthquake or fire as when He appeared in a small, still voice. Therefore in verse 13 it is said, "And it was so when Elijah heard it," that is, the soft voice after the fire and earthquake, and the mighty wind, "that he wrapped his face in his mantle and went out and stood in the entrance of the cave, and behold there came a voice unto him and said, 'What doest thou here, Elijah?' " Then his heart was struck with fear where was most of God's presence (though it was in a soft voice) more than when the fire and earthquake appeared.

It is a good sign of a gracious fear when the soul can be struck with more fear from the Word, and from the sight of God in enjoying communion with Him in His worship, than when God appears in the most terrible way of His works, or when there is terror in a man's conscience through fear of hell; when God appears as though He would send him down presently to hell, though God expects to be feared then. But when the soul is enjoying communion with God in holy duties, and the more communion he has with God, the more he is struck with reverence and the fear of God, this is a sanctifying fear. And then, the heart sanctifies the name of God, indeed, when it is so possessed with fear in the duties of worship.

Now this fear of God should indeed be in the soul, and expressed outwardly when you are in the assembly, by such reverent carriage in prayer that if a heathen were to come in, he would see God's name sanctified and might say, "How great is this God that these people worship!"

And likewise, this fear must be an abiding fear, not only at that instant when you are worshipping God, or speaking of any of God's titles and names, but a fear that must abide upon your hearts after duty is over. That is, after you have come out of your closets, one may perceive the fear of God upon you, and so walking all the day long in the fear of God as it becomes those who have been solemnly setting themselves to worship Him. Now this fear and reverence is contrary to the slightness, vanity, the boldness and presumptuousness there is in the hearts of men and women when they are worshipping God.

Fifth, the duties of God's worship must be full of strength, for they are not suitable to God otherwise, because God is a God infinite in power and glory Himself. Therefore God cannot endure vain worshipping. Isaiah 1:13: "I hate vain oblations."

Vanity of spirit in worshipping God is very hateful to God. It defiles the name of God. God is dishonored by the vanity of men's spirits. Now this strength is threefold:

First, the strength of intention. We must intend our work as if it were for our lives. If ever we are seriously intentive or attentive about anything, it must be when we are worshipping the name of God. When you are coming to pray, be intent about it. You see some who, when they are going about in the street, intent on their business, if their friends meet them, they give them no mind. One may perceive that they are mightily intent about their business.

My brethren, look upon every duty of worship as a great thing that you must be intent in your thoughts about, and not give way to wandering thoughts. I read of one martyr who, when he was to die and the fire was kindling, the officer said, "What, will you not speak when you see the fire kindling?" Said the martyr, "I am speaking to God." That is, he was praying and he did not mind at all what they were doing.

Oh, what little things take our thoughts away from holy duties! When every toy, every feather, every light matter calls them off, is this to sanctify God's name? Would we not account it a dishonorable thing if we were talking to someone about serious business, and, while we were talking, he would turn and talk to everyone who passed by? If a superior is talking with you, he expects that you should mind what he says; but if God is speaking to you and you are speaking to God, every vain thought that comes by, you are turning aside too, as if it were a greater thing to talk to vain thoughts and temptations than to the great and glorious God—is this to worship God?

Therefore, that is the very time that the devil chooses to bring temptations, when we are in holy duties; for the devil knows then that he does two works at once. He disturbs us in our duties and calls off our hearts to that which is wicked, and aggravates our sin exceedingly. It may be that you will not dare to commit the sin the temptations turns your thoughts upon, yea, but the devil has spoiled the duty by it. The Lord expects that there should be strength of intention when you are upon the duty, and there is no time to parley with temptations now, whatever thoughts come in. The truth is, though they are good thoughts that come into your mind at the time you are praying, yet if they are not pertinent to the duty you must cast them away as the temptation of the devil.

QUESTION. You will say, "Can anything that is good come from the devil?"

ANSWER. Certainly. That which is materially good and comes unseasonably may be from the devil. The devil may take advantage by what is in itself materially good, and bring that in an unseasonable time, and so he may turn it to evil. For example, when you are hearing the Word, it may be that the devil thinks he cannot prevail to cause you to have your heart running about uncleanness. "Yea, but," says the devil, "if I can inject good thoughts, I will put into their minds some place of Scripture that is in no way pertinent to this so as to divert them."

The devil gets much by this; therefore look to it and know that God expects the strength of your spirit in duty, that is, strong intentions. You are worshipping God, and therefore you need to be intent about what you are doing. Indeed, sometimes before you are aware evil thoughts will come into your minds.

Perhaps a man is keeping a door and there is a crowd of people who would come in. Perhaps the man opens the door for some gentleman he hears at the door, but when he opens it for one to come in, forty others will crowd in. And so it is many times with the soul. When it opens the door for some good thought, a great many evil thoughts will crowd in. Those people might come in if they would stay their time, but they should not come in now. Worldly businesses are not in themselves lawful, if they will stay the time they may come in, but they must be barred now at this time. There is required a strength of intention.

Second, strength of affection is required also. That is, the affections must work mightily after God, striving with God in prayer. If ever you had a heart inflamed with anything, it should be when you are praying or attending upon the Word as the heathens who worshipped the sun. Sometimes I have told you that they would not have a snail, but a flying horse. They would offer that which was swift. So when we come to the living God, we must have living affections, our affections boiling, and that will be the way to cure vain thoughts.

As the flies will not come to honey if it is boiling hot but when it is cold, so if the heart is boiling hot and the affections working, it will keep out vain thoughts and temptations. It is a sign of the breath of life when it is warm; but artificial breath, you know, is cold. For example, the breath that comes out of the body is warm, but the breath that comes out of a pair of bellows is cold. So the breath of many people in prayer is discovered to be but an artificial breath because it is so cold. But if there were spiritual life, then it would be warm. There must be strength of affection.

Third, there must likewise be the strength of all the faculties. We should stir up whatever we are, have, or can do to work in prayer. Then the bent of mind, conscience, will, and affection, yea, and the body should be put to also. And those who worship God to purpose spend their bodies in nothing so much as in worshipping God. It will be a sad thing another day when this shall be charged upon you, "You have spent the strength of your body upon lusts; but when did you spend any strength of the body about any holy duty?"

What a riddle this is to most people, to tell them of spending the strength of their bodies in prayer, or hearing the Word, or sanctifying a Sabbath. They think the Sabbath is a time of rest. I confess it is a time of rest from outward labor, but it is a time of spending strength in a spiritual way; and those who worship God rightly on the Sabbath will find themselves spending a great deal of strength—and blessed is the strength that is spent in the worship of God rather than in the ways of sin, as most spend their strength. If God gives you a heart to spend your strength in His worship, you may think thusly, "Lord, Thou might have left me to spend my strength in sin. How much better is it spent in worshipping Thy name?"

There is one notable Scripture in Jeremiah 8:2 that shows how much strength the idolaters put forth in worshipping their idol. They would not do it in a vain and slight way, but their hearts were much in that false worship. The text says, "And they shall spread them before the sun, and the moon, and all the host of heaven." Now mark it, "whom they have loved, and whom they have served, and after whom they have walked, and whom they have sought and whom they have worshipped."

All these are put together in reference to idols. Oh, that it could be said of us in reference to God when we come to worship Him, "whom we have loved, and whom we have served, and after whom we have walked, and whom we have sought, and whom we have worshipped." There are all these expressions to show the strength of their spirits in following after their idols. And that is the fifth thing in our sanctifying God's name.

The sixth is, if you will sanctify God's name in worship there must be a humble frame of spirit. Worship Him with much humility of soul. Abraham fell upon the ground before the Lord and said, "dust and ashes hath begun to speak unto

Thee." Yea, we read of Jesus Christ groveling upon the earth, and of the angels covering their faces in the presence of God. And so we should be humble when we come before the Lord.

There is nothing that abases the soul of man more than the sight of God; and the great reason for the pride of all men's hearts is because they never knew God. If you did but see God, your heart must be abased; and when does the soul see God if not when it comes to worship Him? Job 42:5–6: "I have heard of Thee by the hearing of the ear, but now my eye seeth Thee, wherefore I abhor myself and repent in dust and ashes." Now this humility must be in the sense of our own meanness and baseness. Psalm 34:6, "This poor man cried to God."

They are poor souls who come into God's presence who sanctify God's name most, even those souls who apprehend and are sensible of their own baseness and meanness before God. This poor man cried to God. We used to say, "Give that poor man something." It affects the heart of God when He sees much poverty of spirit. When we come before Him we must be sensible of our infinite dependence upon God. Come as the woman of Canaan did: "O Lord, even dogs receive crumbs, and though I am a dog, yet let me receive crumbs." Here is humility of spirit. Now this humility of spirit appears in these things:

• Admiring God's goodness that we live at this time, and that we have liberty to come before Him. We might have been past praying and worshipping God. Think thusly: "What a mercy it is that we are not banished out of God's presence, that the Lord has not spurned us out of His sight as filth and cast us out as everlastingly abhorring. While others have been praying, we might have been yelling under the wrath of the eternal God."

Come with this apprehension of yourself, and adore God's goodness that you are alive to pray and alive to hear God's Word, and that it is not only a duty, but a rich privilege and mercy that

God will admit you into His presence. Again, it is the goodness of God that He will condescend to look upon the things that are done in heaven. Now if the Lord humbles Himself to behold the things that are done in heaven, how much does the Lord humble Himself to behold me, a poor, vile captive as I am in myself? And yet, that God should not only behold me before Him, but invite me to come into His presence, what mercy and goodness is this!

• Our hearts must be taken off from the thoughts and apprehensions of all excellencies in ourselves. We must not come in the pride of our hearts because we have more abilities than others. What do all your parts do to commend you to God? You have ability in expressing yourself in prayer; why does that commend you to God? Whatever is natural in any of our duties is nothing to God, only that which is from His own Spirit; and therefore you should come in your own thoughts as vile, as if you had no parts or abilities at all. Lay aside all such apprehensions of yourself, for, the truth is, some poor, broken-hearted sinner who can only sigh out a few groans to God, and is not able to speak two or three sentences together in a right language, but only breathes out his soul to God, may be a thousand thousand times more acceptable to God than you who are able to make great orations when you come before Him.

• You must come without any righteousness of your own. You must never come into God's presence but as a poor worm; and if there is any difference between you and others in outward respects, it is nothing to you. When you are in the presence of God, you are as a base, vile worm, though you are a prince or an emperor.

• Your heart must be taken off from what you do. If you have any abilities of grace, still your heart must be taken off there. There may be pride not only from one's parts, but it may be that God has given you enlargements in prayer, and the devil will come in and seek to puff up your heart because of this. But your heart must be taken off there, and you must deny yourself in all. When you have done the best service of all, still you must conclude that you are an unprofitable servant. When you have prayed your best, yet rise with shame and take heed of having your heart puffed up even through the assistance of the graces of the Spirit of God in holy duties.

• Last, you must come with a humble resignation of yourself to God, to be content to wait upon God as long as He pleases, to wait upon God in regard of the time, and of the measure, and of the manner of the communication of Himself, in regard of the means by which He will be pleased to communicate Himself. Wait upon Him. Let me have mercy even though it is at the last hour. This is a humble heart in prayer; and when we come with such a poverty of spirit as this is, we may expect that the Lord will accept us. "Give this poor man something," God will say. "This poor man cried and the Lord heard him."

In the seventh place, we must bring that which is God's own in sanctifying God's name. I spoke to this before in the point of preparation, that in God's worship we must give Him His own. I will only mention it here in the sanctifying of God's name in two regards: first, to give God His own, as for the matter of it; and, second, to give God His own, that is, what comes from the work of His own Spirit, or else we do not sanctify God's name.

I will give one text further about the matter of it. In Exodus 39, if you read the chapter, you shall find that there is said ten times that "they did as God had commanded Moses." And then in the close of the chapter, when they had done as God had commanded in His worship, the text says, "Moses blessed them." That people is a blessed people who observe the worship of God as God has commanded them. But the main thing is, all

that we do must be acted by the Spirit of God. It is not enough
to have true silver or gold, but it must have the right stamp or
else it cannot go for current coin.

And so it is not enough that the things that we offer to God
in His worship are God's own, what we have warrant for out
of God's Word, but they must have the stamp of the Spirit of
God. In the worship of God there are two questions He will ask.
First, "Who required this at your hands?" If you can answer,
"O Lord, Thou hast required it," it is well. But then God has
another question, "Whose image and superscription is this?"
If you cannot give an answer to that, it will be rejected, too.
You must be acted upon by divine principles in all that you
do. There must be the stamp of the Spirit upon that which is
tendered to God or else it is nothing. To open this point fully
would require some time.

Therefore, I will show you how we may know when our
duties act by our natural parts rather than by the Spirit of God.
Then I will show how we may know whether our duties act by
natural conscience rather than by the Spirit of God.

If you act by natural parts, they will not change your heart.
Men who perform duties by the strength of natural parts may
have duties that are as large as others and speak to the edification
of others, but those duties never change their hearts. Now if
you act by the Spirit of God, you will be changed into the very
image of His Spirit.

If men act by natural parts, those will not carry them
through difficulties and discouragements. But if you act by
the Spirit of God, though you meet with such difficulties and
discouragements, you will be carried through them all.

You may know it by this, wherein you account the excellency
of a duty to consist, either in yourself or in others. You perform
a duty; now (it may be) your parts act lively and to your

credit, and yet your conscience tells you that your heart was strengthened. Can you rise up with joy because you have your ends? At another time, perhaps, your heart is more troubled and broken. But you do not express yourself so much, and then you are discouraged. And when you see another perform a duty, if you see any failing in their expression, you pitch upon that and look upon it as a poor thing. You are not able to see an excellency in holy duties unless there is an excellency of natural parts. But those who have the Spirit of God can find the Spirit of God acting in others, though they do not have such natural parts.

Those who act by their natural parts, in secret are far less enlarged than they are before others. Their parts act much before others, but what is there between God and their souls?

They who are so acted will not be very constant. You shall have young ones who begin to look towards religion. Their parts are a little fresh and they are mightily enlarged in holy duties, and the thing is good for them to make use of their parts. But how ordinary it is that after a few years they are more dead and dull than they were before, and have less mind to the duties of God's worship than they had before! Were this the Spirit of God, you would find as much favor and relish in them afterwards as there was at that time.

Natural conscience sometimes puts men upon acting of duties, and this is better than mere natural parts.

If it is only natural conscience, it puts men upon duties, but gives no strength to do them. But when the Spirit of God puts you upon a duty, it gives you some strength to perform it, some strength whereby you get some communion with God.

If it is natural conscience, it puts upon the duty, but does not make the heart glad about the duty and to love the duty. But if it is the Spirit of God, it makes you to delight in it and to love it.

If it is natural conscience, you do not by it increase your communion with God. You do your duties in a rote manner; but now when the Spirit of God puts you upon holy duties, it is not a task done, but you find more and more increase in communion with God. Your heart is more raised to God and closes more with God, and so still more and more in the course of your life.

I had a little converse with God at first when God began to acquaint my soul with His ways, but through His mercy I now find more communion with Him; and so you can bless yourself in God in that converse that you have in communion with Him. You would not lose that communion you have with God in holy duties for all the world. Others have their companions with whom they have communion, and much good it may do them; but the Lord has shown me another manner of communion that my soul can have with Himself in which it has sweet satisfaction. And thus you have had seven particulars for sanctifying the name of God in holy duties.

Again, as natural conscience gives no strength to do the duty, so it does not make the duty to be strong to the soul. That is, there's no strength gotten by the duty. One is not by one prepared for another, "but the way of the Lord is strength to the upright" (Proverbs 10:29); that is, when a gracious heart is in the way of God's worship, it finds the very duty of the worship of God to be strength to it, and so fits it for another duty.

Also, a natural conscience limits itself and is bounded; that is, as much as will serve the turn for its own peace and quiet, so much it will do and no more. But when one is acted by the Spirit of God, no one is enlarged without any limits at all, not bounded to one's own peace; for the more peace a gracious heart has in duty, the more it is enlarged in duty. Now a natural conscience puts you to duty and will act on you when you lack peace, when you are in trouble and fear. But when you are not in trouble and fear, it does not put the heart on to the performance of duty. But the Spirit of God puts the soul on to duty when there is most peace and comfort.

A little will serve the turn to satisfy a natural conscience so that, if they perform the duty, it is enough. But one who is acted on by the Spirit of God in duty must meet with much of God or else he is not satisfied. He goes mourning in the daytime if he has not met with God in the morning in the performance of duty. Thus you see there is much difference between the actings of natural parts and conscience in duty and the actings of the Spirit of God.

The eighth thing is this: when you come to perform holy duties, if you would sanctify God's name, you must consecrate yourselves to God. There must be a resignation of soul and body, estate, liberty, name, and all you are, have, or can do unto God. This is to sanctify God's name, when you consecrate yourselves to God. Professing this in the performance of duty, when you are to pray, would be a very good thing, to actually profess yourselves to be God's, to profess that you give up all that you are, have, or can do to God: "Lord, I am Thy servant. Take all faculties of soul and members of body and improve all. Lay out all to Thine own praise to the uttermost to bring glory to Thy great name." If every time you came to God in prayer you did this, this would be to sanctify yourselves to God.

I spoke before of a sanctified heart, but this is in professing yourselves to God. Do it secretly, at least, in your own thoughts. If you do not express it every time in words, yet do it in your own thoughts. Devote yourselves to God every day. It would be of admirable use if every day, when men and women worship God, either in their closets or families, they professedly devoted and consecrated themselves to God, and, likewise, every time they came to hear the Word or to receive sacraments, God would account His name to be sanctified in such a work as this.

Ninth, that which must make up all, and without which all the other is nothing, is that you must offer up all your worship in the name of Jesus Christ. Let a man or woman worship God never so well, yet when they have done all, if they do not tender it up in the name of Jesus Christ, God will not account His name to be sanctified. You must, by faith, look upon Jesus Christ as the glorious Mediator who has come into the world by whom you have access unto the Father. Act your faith upon Christ, and give your duties up into His hand as by the hand of a Mediator, to be tendered up to the Father by Him.

You have labored what you can to perform duty as well as you are able, yet you must not think to tender it up by your own hand unto God; rather you must tender it up to the Father by the hand of Jesus Christ the Mediator, and so you shall sanctify the name of God in holy duties. We read in Leviticus 16:3 that when Aaron was to tender up the incense, he was "to put the incense on the fire before the Lord, that the cloud of the incense may cover the mercy seat that is upon the testimony, that he die not."

Mark it. It is as much as his life is worth whether he does it or not. Now incense, in the New Testament, is called prayer, and so in the Old Testament, too. It was a kind of emblem of prayer. The offering up of our prayers is the offering up of incense to God, and the mercy seat was a type of Christ. Now as the incense should cover the mercy seat, so our prayers must go up to Jesus Christ, must be upon Him, and so must be accepted by the Father. And as we read in Judges 13:20, when Manoah offered a sacrifice, the text says, "the Angel of the Lord ascended in the flame." This Angel of God here was Jesus Christ, as we might easily make out from this Scripture, and He ascends up in the flame from the altar.

Now though we do not offer such kinds of sacrifices with fire and incense as they did in the time of the Law, yet, when we are offering up our incense, there must be a flame of fervency and zeal. But that is not enough. Together with the flame of the altar, the Angel of God, Jesus Christ, the great Angel of the New Covenant (for angel signifies nothing but messenger), the great Messenger who has come into the world about that great errand of His, to reconcile the world to Himself, He must ascend up in the flame—and so God will account His name to be sanctified. The name of God is not sanctified but through Jesus Christ.

Acting our faith upon Jesus Christ as Mediator is a special ingredient to sanctifying God's name in holy duties. As you know, the Scripture says that the altar sanctifies the gift offered upon the altar. Jesus Christ is the Altar upon whom all our spiritual sacrifices are to be offered; and this Altar sanctifies the gift that is offered upon it. Let never so great a gift be offered upon any other altar, it was not accounted holy or accepted.

So let men, by the natural strength or power that they have, offer up the most glorious and attractive service to God, it is not acceptable unless it is offered up upon the Altar, Jesus Christ. We have an altar now (not the communion table), but Jesus Christ Himself is our Altar upon whom we are to offer all our sacrifices, and this Altar must sanctify the gift. We can never have our gift sanctified, no, nor God's name sanctified in this gift, unless it is offered upon this Altar, and our faith acted upon Jesus Christ.

People think little of this, but much of other things. When we worship God, we should worship Him with fear and reverence, with humility and with strength of intention. Such kinds of things everyone who has any enlightening of

conscience will think of at one time or another, but people
least think of this, which is the greatest ingredient of all that
is required in sanctifying God's name in holy duties—that is,
to come and tender up all to the Father in the name of Jesus
Christ. How many men and women who have been professors
of religion for twenty or thirty years are not yet acquainted with
this great mystery of godliness, to tender up all to God in the
name of His Son?

This is that which upon divers occasions I have spoken
unto, and am willing upon every occasion I have to speak of,
because it is a principle part of the great mystery of the gospel,
without which all our duties are rejected by God and cast away.
Now then, put all these nine things together and see by them
what we ought to do so that we may sanctify the name of God
in holy duties.

(Preached December 21, 1645)

Suiting Our Duties to the God We Are Worshipping

"I will be sanctified in them that come nigh Me."

LEVITICUS 10:3

There is something further to be spoken that may help you to sanctify God's name in holy duties, and that is the various workings of the heart suitable to the various attributes of God; for that is to sanctify God's name: to have the duty be such as is in some way suitable to such a God as we are worshipping. Now then, let us consider what the Scripture says of God, and then let us see what suitable dispositions we should have in us unto those things that the Scripture says of God.

First, you know the Scripture says that God is a Spirit (John 4:24). Then presently Christ says that he who worships God must worship Him in spirit. That is, there must be a suitableness in our worship to what God is. Is God a Spirit? Then all who worship Him must worship Him in spirit and truth. In other words, when I go to worship God, I must consider Him as He is, an infinite and glorious Spirit. Then, surely bodily worship is not sufficient for me. Though I kneel down in prayer, or

111

come and present my body to hear the Word or to receive the sacrament, this is not to worship God as a Spirit.

If our God were as the heathen gods, that is, corporeal, then it would be another matter. Then bodily worship would serve the turn. But God, being a Spirit, must have spiritual worship. Therefore David says, "my soul and all that is within me magnify His name" (Psalm 103:1).

The apostle, in 1 Timothy 4:8, says that bodily exercise profits little. It is no great matter for the body. God looks but very little at bodily exercise, but it is godliness that is profitable. It is the work of the Spirit. When we come to pray, we must pray in the Spirit, that is, we must pray with our souls. We must pour forth our souls before God. And when we come to hear, our hearts must not go after covetousness. We must set our hearts to what we hear. We must hear with our hearts as well as with our ears.

Our souls must be at work in the hearing of the Word. When you hear, it is not enough for you to come and sit in a pew and have the sound of a man's voice in your ears, but your soul must be at work. And so when you come and receive the Sacrament, your souls must feed upon Jesus Christ. Bodily worship without soul worship is nothing, but soul worship may be accepted without bodily worship. Therefore it is the soul that God principally looks at in holy duties.

If you are not able to worship God in your bodies, you may worship Him in your souls; and God regards that bodily exercise in holy duties is worth little. I confess that sometimes bodily exercise may further the soul as a reverend carriage of the body and the like, but it is nothing in comparison. The great work is the work of the soul, for God is a Spirit and must be worshipped in spirit. And God is said to be a Spirit not only in that He is not of so thick a corporeal substance, but it notes the simplicity of God. He is without any composition. Whatever is in God is God Himself. He is absolutely one. There are not divers things in God.

Now then, those who come to worship Him must worship Him in spirit and in truth. That is, there must not be a compounded heart, but you must bring simple hearts before God without any composition of dross in yourselves or any kind of falseness. But in the simplicity of your hearts, you must come to worship God. And thus you shall worship Him with such worship as is some way suitable to Him as He is a Spirit.

Further, consider God as being an eternal God. What suitable dispositions does this require of me when I am to look upon God as an eternal Being? It requires this only, that therefore your heart must be taken off from all temporal good things and set upon that eternal good. You may indeed desire these outward things only in order to your eternal good.

You are worshipping an eternal God. Hence, then, whatever sin you confess, although committed twenty or forty years ago, you must look upon it as if it were now presently committed and be humbled as much before the Lord as if it were now committed at the present.

QUESTION. You will say, "Why so? Because God is an eternal God?"

ANSWER. Yes, for if I understand God's eternity, therefore, if I come to confess the sins that I committed in my youth, they are before God as if they were just now being done with regard to time. Therefore, I must (as much as I can) look so upon them and be humbled for them as if they were sins lately committed.

Many people are troubled for their sins the very day after they commit them, but a little time wears off their trouble. But if you considered that you had to deal with an eternal God, then you would look upon your sins, though a long time since committed, as if they were but now undone.

Likewise, there will be this required from the consideration of God's eternity. You must come with such a disposition of heart as not to think much, though what you desired is deferred and not granted in your time when you would have it. For if there is no time that alters with God, but a thousand years are with God as one day, then that which we account long before it is done is nothing with God. Therefore we must have our hearts so work towards God as towards an eternal God, as one with whom there is no alteration of time at all, with whom there is no succession of time.

If we come to a man and seek anything of him, if he does not answer us presently we think that he will forget it and other things come into his mind. But when we come to worship God, we must look upon Him as an eternal Being and that time alters nothing with Him. Thus, understanding God in a right way will help us a great deal in His worship and to sanctify His name. We cannot sanctify God's name without having serious thoughts about His name, and getting our hearts to work accordingly.

Third, look upon God when you come to worship Him in His incomprehensible Being, that is, as a God who fills all places. His being is as real in the room that we are praying in, the place that we are meeting in, as it is in heaven. Now then, when we come to worship Him, we must consider that this infinite, glorious Being stands before us, looks upon us, and is at our elbow; and, therefore, especially when you worship in secret consider this. It is good to consider it when you are with others, but especially (I say) consider it when you are in secret; and know that when you are most private you have one who looks on you and takes notice of you, which is more than if you had ten hundred thousand witnesses standing by you and looking upon you. For it is the Lord who stands by you and sees your behavior, sees what you do in your worship of Him. Take heed, therefore, that there is nothing done by you that is unbecoming the presence of such a God as the Lord is.

Suppose that some of you were praying, and there was a godly, able minister standing near you. It would be some means to stir up your hearts to mind what you did. But the Lord is not only in the next room, but in the same room and standing by you. Let there be nothing done, therefore, unbecoming the presence of that infinite, holy God who stands by you. Hold this truth forth: "The Lord is present with me. I acknowledge it and I own it, and therefore I carry myself thusly, and all because I would witness to angels and men that I acknowledge that the Lord is present with me in this duty."

Fourth, consider that God is an unchangeable God, that He is immutable. That is another attribute of God, He is unchangeable. Therefore, our hearts must be taken off from these mutable things and set upon God as that unchangeable Good. We must therefore be humbled for our fickleness and unconstantness. There is no shadow of change in God and there is no shadow of constancy in us. Therefore, when we come into the presence of a God who is unchangeable, we should look upon God as being the same now as ever He was heretofore. He has as much displeasure against sin now as He has ever had, and that God who has done such great things for His church in former times is the same God to do good to His people as He ever was.

Make use of this. When you read the Word of God, you find how God has made Himself appear glorious for His people. Now every time I am to worship God, I should think that I am to deal with God who is the same as He ever was, as merciful and gracious, as just and powerful as He ever was, and so my heart is to work towards Him.

Fifth, when I am to worship God, I am to look upon Him as the living God, as that God who has life in Himself and gives life to His creatures.

Then what suitable behavior becomes me? I must come before His presence with fear. It is a fearful thing to fall into His hands who is the living God, who has my life under His feet. He has the absolute disposal over my present and eternal condition. He gave me my life, He has preserved my life, and so may take it away when He pleases and bring eternal death unto me. These things may marvelously help your meditation when you come before Him. You who are barren in your meditations, go over the attributes of God and consider what you may be able to draw from them.

God is the living God. What behavior then is appropriate for me to show towards this living God? Oh, let me be afraid lest my soul departs from the living God. Let me bring a living service to Him. I must not bring a dead heart. Let me take heed how I come before the living God with a dead heart, and with dead service, to sacrifice that which is dead before it comes. It's like carrion that lies dead in the ditch.

Oh, let us be humbled for our dead hearts and dead sacrifices. It is a living God who I am worshipping, and therefore I must pray, "Lord turn away mine eyes from beholding vanity, and quicken my heart in Thy law" (Psalm 119:37). Remember when you come to worship that you come with a quickened heart, for you have to deal with a living God. A man or woman who is of an active spirit cannot endure a dull and heavy servant in the family; but the Lord is a pure act, and nothing else but act. And therefore He expects that all His people should have quick, active, and lively spirits.

Sixth, when you come to worship God, you are to look upon Him as Almighty, and so are to fear His great power when you come before Him. Then you will not be discouraged by any difficulties.

"I come to seek for some great thing, and I come to seek a great God who has all power in heaven and earth, and infinitely more power than there is in all creatures in heaven and earth. I am praying to a God who can create peace, who can create help. My condition cannot be so desperate but this Almighty God is able to help me. Let me make Him the object of my faith since He is so infinitely almighty. What a full object of faith is this God that has all power in Him! Let me, therefore, come to Him as a strong tower." "Run to the name of God as a strong tower" (Proverbs 18:10), who can help in all straits whatsoever.

There would be much drawing forth of our faith if we could present the Lord before us as an infinite, almighty God. When we see outward helps and means near at hand, then we can believe that we may have some succor from Him; but when all outward helps and means fail, then we are discouraged. We do not sanctify God's name, but rather we take this name of God in vain, when our hearts are discouraged with any difficulties. The Lord expects that all His children who come to worship Him should worship Him as the Almighty God, and so have their hearts working towards Him. There would be mighty workings of the spirit towards God if we saw Him by the eye of faith as well as reason.

Seventh, look upon God as an omniscient God, as a God who infinitely understands all things. Now what does this call for?

First, if God is a God of infinite understanding, then let me not bring a blind sacrifice to God; let me not bring an ignorant heart to God. This is the excellency of an understanding creature, to know the rule and end of its own actions. You come to worship an infinite God of infinite understanding. Then know the rule of what you do and know the end of what you do, and come with understanding into His presence.

Second, if He is so understanding, come with a free, open heart to open whatever is in your heart to God. Take heed of keeping any secret resolutions in your own heart. God knows you and can tell how to find you out. God knows all that is in your heart already; all the secret baseness that is in your heart the Lord understands. The Lord's eye is a piercing eye. He sees through and through your heart. It's a vain thing for you to come and conceal anything before Him.

QUESTION. You will say, "If God understands a man's heart, what need is there for him to come and confess?"
ANSWER. Yes, He requires it as a duty that you should come and open all before Him. In spite of your heart, you cannot cover anything from the Lord's eyes, but the Lord will see whether you are willing that He should understand all. God does not require us to come and confess our sins so that He might know something He did not know before, but so that there might be a testimony that you are willing that He should know all that is in your heart. Therefore, when you come to worship Him, ransack every corner of your heart and confess all before the Lord and give glory to His name, as to that God who is an all-seeing God, who knows all the windings and turnings of your heart. Meditate on these things that are presented to you and it will be a mighty means to help you to sanctify His name.

Eighth, God is a God of infinite wisdom. Therefore, when we come to worship God, let us be ashamed of our folly. When you come to have to deal with God, look upon Him as a God of infinite wisdom, and, I say, be ashamed of your folly then.

Exercise the grace of wisdom too when you come to worship God, that is, by propounding right ends (of which we spoke before). One part of wisdom is to have right ends and right means toward those ends; the meditation of the wisdom of God when we come to worship Him will further us to sanctify His name.

And this is to sanctify God's wisdom when you come into God's presence in your greatest straits: deny your own wisdom. Come with a resolution to be guided by the wisdom of God in this manner, "Lord, I do not know how to order my steps. There is much folly and vanity in my heart; but Thou art a God of infinite wisdom. I come to Thee for direction, and I profess here that I am willing to give up my whole soul to be guided by Thy wisdom."

If every time we came to worship God we came thusly, "O Lord, whatever our thoughts have been heretofore, yet if Thou wilt only reveal Thy mind to us, we will hearken to Thee. Lord, we believe that Thy wisdom is Thyself, and therefore we profess to give ourselves up to Thy wisdom." This is to sanctify the name of God.

Ninth, consider the holiness of God. God is a God who is infinitely pure from all sin; and, therefore, when we come to worship God, we must be ashamed of our unholiness. In Isaiah 6, when the prophet heard the seraphim cry, "Holy, holy, holy is the Lord of hosts," he fell down and said, "Woe is me, for I am undone, because I am a man of unclean lips." Is God a holy God? Then let me take heed when I come before Him that I do not bring with me a love for any sin, for the Lord hates it. And let me take heed that I do not cast dirt in the very face of God's holiness, but give up my soul to be ruled wholly by Him.

Labor that there may be a suitableness between the holiness of your heart and the infinite God. Now this is to sanctify God's name, when the consideration of this attribute of God has such an effect on my heart that I labor upon this to come with a suitable heart before God.

Tenth, when you come before God, consider that you come to a merciful God. This should make me to joyfully come into His presence as a God who is willing to do good to His poor creatures who are in misery.

This should make me come with a heart sensible of the need of this mercy. "O Lord, I have had my heart let out to other things heretofore; but now, Lord, Thy mercy is that which my soul longs for as that wherein my chief and only good consists."

This should make me come with expectations of great things from God. Do not come unto God as an empty vine, but as unto a full vine. The more your faith is raised to expect great things from God, the more acceptable you are to God. Certainly the higher anyone's faith is raised when they come into His presence to expect the greatest things, the more acceptable.

It is otherwise with God than men. If you come to men to beg only for a little thing, you may be welcome; but if you come to ask a great matter, they will look askew upon you. But, the truth is, the greater the things are that we come to God for, the more welcome we are in God's presence. And those who are acquainted with God know it, and therefore they come more fully. When they come to ask Jesus Christ Himself and His Spirit, that is worth more than ten thousand worlds. They come with more freedom of spirit than when they come to ask for their health and the like.

It will be likewise another means of sanctifying this attribute of God if, when you come to Him, you come with a merciful heart toward your brethren. Take heed whenever you come to worship God that you do not come with a rugged and cruel heart towards any of your brethren. Therefore you find that

Christ lays this upon you in teaching how to pray. You must say, "Forgive us our trespasses as we forgive our brethren that trespass against us." And you find it repeated again that, if you forgive, then your heavenly Father will forgive, and not otherwise. It is as if Christ should say, "When you come to beg mercy, be sure you bring merciful hearts."

This is a good way to sanctify the name of God in this attribute, for the soul to be solicitous with itself. What is that which will hinder me from the mercy of God and let me avoid it? It is otherwise taking the name of God in vain for me to come to profess what need I have of God's mercy, and yet for all that never regard to avoid those things that may hinder the work of His grace upon me.

Eleventh, consider the justice of God; that is another attribute. Consider that you have to deal with an infinite, righteous, and just God. Do not think that if you are a believer that you have nothing to do with the justice of God, for certainly you are to sanctify the justice of God.

QUESTION. Now you will say, "How should a believer sanctify the justice of God?"

ANSWER. First, he should be apprehensive and sensible how by sin he has put himself under justice, and deserved the stroke of justice to be upon him to eternity. He should consider what he is in himself. It is true that Jesus Christ has come between a believing soul and the justice of the Father, and has taken the stroke of justice upon Himself; yes, but though He has done it, it does not hinder but that you should be apprehensive of what you have deserved.

Second, here is a special thing in sanctifying the justice of God. When we come before Him, we should consider that we have to deal with an infinite, just God, and therefore not dare to come but through a Mediator. Here you have the reason why we must tender up all in the name of Christ, because when we are to come before God, we are to sanctify the name of His justice. It is not enough for you to think thusly, "I have sinned and God is merciful. I will go and pray to Him that He might be merciful." No, God requires the sanctifying of His justice; and there is nothing that sanctifies His justice as much as this, that a poor creature sees the infinite distance that sin has made between the infinite God and itself. The sinner sees that through sin he has made himself liable to justice, and when he sees that there is an absolute necessity that infinite justice must have satisfaction, the sinner thinks, "If it comes to me that I must satisfy the justice of God, I am never able to do it. But there is a Mediator, and therefore I'll fly to Him, and by faith tender up to the Father all the merits of His Son as a full satisfaction to His infinite justice."

When you come thusly before the Lord, you sanctify His name indeed. Many think that when they come to pray they should look upon God's grace and mercy, but not upon His justice. But you must look upon both.

12. Another attribute is God's faithfulness. Consider that you have to deal with a God of infinite truth and faithfulness, and therefore look upon Him as an object of your faith to rest upon. Likewise, you must bring a faithful heart suitable in some way to this faithfulness of God, that is, a heart faithful with Him, to keep within the covenant that you have entered into, and to perform all the vows that you make with God.

Remember that you have to deal with a faithful God. As the Lord delights to manifest His righteousness to poor creatures that seek His face, so this God expects that you should be faithful in all the covenants that you make with Him—and this is to sanctify God's name.

Now, then, put all these attributes of God together, and there you have His glory, the infiniteness of His glory. The shine and luster of all the attributes together is God's glory. I have, then, to deal with a glorious God, and let me labor to perform such services as may have a spiritual glory upon them, that some of the divine luster that is in God may be upon my services. Let me look for glorious things, seeing I have to deal with such a glorious God.

I appeal to any gracious heart. What can you omit of these, or what would you omit? Do you say, "Here's a great deal!"? Can there be too much to make you happy? These things are not only your duty but your happiness. Glory and excellency consists in them.

If anyone were to bring you a great many jewels and pearls, would you say, "Here's a great deal!"? Oh, no, you would say, "The more the merrier!" So I say, this one meditation would take off the thoughts of "a great deal," for in all these my happiness consists, and the more I have of these, the more I shall enjoy God, the more happy I shall be both here and forever.

Now I had thought to have given you some reasons why the name of God must be sanctified, only I beseech you by all that has been said to go away with this thought. What little cause is there that any of us should rest upon any of our duties? If it is required of us to sanctify the name of God in duty, I say we have little cause for any of us to rest on any duties that we perform.

There are many poor creatures that have no other saviors to rest upon but their prayers, coming to church, and taking the communion. Now if in all these the Lord expects that you should thus sanctify His name, you have little cause to rest upon anything that you have done. You have cause, rather, to go alone and mourn for taking the name of God in vain in the duties of His worship. Do not rest in any of your performances. Labor to perform duties as well as you can, but when you have done all, know that you are unprofitable servants after all, and renounce all as in the point of justification. Rest upon something else, otherwise you are undone forever.

Why God Will Be Sanctified in the Duties of His Worship

"I will be sanctified in them that come nigh Me."

LEVITICUS 10:3

We now come to conclude this great argument of sanctifying God's name in holy duties. God expects that we should all sanctify His name in our drawing nigh to Him. Now we will consider divers reasons why God will be sanctified in all the duties of His worship.

REASON 1. It is the very nature of God to will Himself to be the last end, and all other things to work suitably to lift Himself up as the last end. I say, it is essential to Him as anything for Him to will Himself as the highest end, and that all things should work so as to be suitable unto that glory of His, and for the furtherance of it. God would cease to be God if He should not will Himself as the highest end, and so will that all things that have any being should in some way or an other work for Him.

This is the very nature of God. It is that in which I conceive the very nature of God's holiness to consist, willing Himself as the last end, and so to work all things as suitable unto His own infinite excellency. Now as this is God's holiness, so is the holiness that God requires in His creatures (that are capable of holiness) is that they will Him as the last end, and all things suitable to that infinite excellency of His.

Now if this is the nature of God, and if this is His holiness, then certainly it must be a necessary duty in all those who would have communion with God, and would honor God, to will as God Himself wills; that is, that all things should work suitable to the infinite excellency of God so that God may attain the glory of His infinite excellency. This makes it to be a necessary duty that when we come to worship Him we should sanctify His name.

So the first reason is taken from the very nature of God. It is the very being of God that all things should work to Himself, and in such a suitable way as to lift up His excellency and glory.

REASON 2. We must sanctify God in the duties of His worship because it is the special glory that God has in the world to be actively honored. As far as His passive glory, that is, to be glorified in a passive way, He has that in hell. But the special glory that God would have is that He might be glorified actively. Now there is no such way of glorifying the name of God actively as by worshipping Him in a holy manner; and, therefore, God insists that when we come to worship Him we sanctify His name. "For," says God, "if I am not sanctified in My worship, what active glory do I have in the world?" It is the special, active glory that God has in the world to sanctify His name in the duties of His worship.

REASON 3. We have intimated before that the duties of God's worship are the most precious things, the special conveyances of the choicest mercies that He intends to bestow upon His saints; and therefore, though He loses His glory in anything else, He will not lose it in that wherein He especially conveys His mercy and goodness to people. But we spoke of that in showing how we draw nigh to God in holy duties, and it may well come in here again as an argument why we should sanctify God's name.

REASON 4. There is no way for us to be fitted to receive mercy from God through those duties of worship but by our sanctifying God's name. When you come at any time to worship God, what would you have? There is some communion that you would enjoy with God. Now there is no way to make you a fit subject of mercy, or capable of the enjoyment of communion with God, but by such a behavior of soul as that which has been spoken of, to sanctify the name of God. You would be loath to lose those duties of worship that you perform. And, therefore, it is required of you to sanctify His name lest you lose all; for this is what makes you the only capable subject of what good there is to be had.

REASON 5. Now, I say, unless His name is sanctified in our worshipping Him, we will certainly fall off. And, the truth is, this is the very ground of all apostasy in hypocrites. Some who have been very forward in worshipping God when they were young ones, who have later fallen off, were accustomed to worshipping God constantly in their families and in secret in their chambers. And they accounted it the very joy of their lives at that time to be worshipping God. But it is not so with them now as it was before. Yes, they are fallen off from their very profession of religion and have turned loose; and now to be in vain company, to drink or play, is better to them than any service of the worship of God. They prize more to be in company with their sports than to hear a sermon or to be in communion with the people of God in prayer. Heretofore they would not have changed one short time of private communion with God for the enjoyment of a great deal of pleasures and contentment in the world, but now it is otherwise with them.

How does it come to pass that these have apostatized thus from God? Surely here is the ground of it: they did not sanctify God's name in holy duties. At most it was but a work of conscience that put them upon those duties, and they merely had some flashes. There was no real sanctification of their hearts whereby they sanctified the name of God in holy duties, and it is upon this that they have left off. I dare say that there was never any soul who knew what it was to sanctify God's name in worship who was ever weary of worshipping God.

QUESTION. It may be that some of you say, "We have heard that there is much required in sanctifying God's name in duties, and that it is the only way to weary the soul and make it fall off."

ANSWER. Oh, no, there is not any one thing that has been opened for the sanctifying of God's name in duties that any gracious heart can tell how to miss; and the more we sanctify His name, the more we shall be in love with worship. For it is from hence that those who sanctify God's name in worship will hold out, because they will find the sweetness of worship. They will meet with God in holy duties and so come to be encouraged in worship. But as for others who worship God in a formal way, their worship will prove to be tedious to them; for they perform the duties, but do not find God in the duties in that spiritual way as the saints do. If they think they meet with God, it is but an imagination rather than any real meeting with Him. They do not find the influence of God in their souls in holy duties as those do who sanctify God's name in holy duties. Here you see the reason why we are to sanctify God's name in holy duties.

APPLICATION

1. If all that you have heard is required of us for sanctifying God's name, we see how little cause we have to rest upon any duty of worship that we perform. Certainly the duties of worship that we perform are no such things as are fit to be rested upon for life and salvation; and yet, for the most part, there is scarcely anything that people have to rest upon or to tender up to God for acceptance to eternal life but their prayers, their coming to hear and receiving communion, and such duties that they perform. This is all they have to tender up for life and salvation. Perhaps they may speak sometimes of Christ, but the truth is, what their hearts rest upon for acceptance to eternal life is this. And is it but this? It is a weak prop, a rotten reed that you have to rest upon, let the duties be performed never so well.

Suppose we did sanctify God's name to the uttermost, to the highest degree that is possible for any creature to do in this world. Yet such duties are not to be rested upon. Abraham, Isaac, Jacob, and the apostles, the most holy men who ever performed duties in the most holy manner, yet woe to them if they have nothing to rest upon but their duties. Consider, therefore, that what you must rest upon for acceptance to eternal life must be that which has so much worth in it that it will satisfy for all the sins you formerly committed, yes, and for all the sins that you ever will commit.

Now I appeal to anyone's conscience. Is that which you perform—such as prayer, receiving the sacraments, or hearing the Word—such a work that your conscience can think it has so much worth in it that it will satisfy God for all the sins you have ever committed or shall commit? I am persuaded that if people who have rested upon duties heretofore would but seriously have this thought in their minds—that they must rest upon nothing for their acceptance for life and salvation but that which has so much worth in it that it will satisfy God for all the sins they have ever committed or shall commit—this would take them off from resting in duties. Yes, and it must be such as must be the object of the infinite holiness of God to take contentment in. Surely the duties that we perform are no such duties to rest upon.

We read in Exodus 22:31, concerning such things as were torn and rent, that they should cast them to the dogs: "Ye shall be holy men unto Me, neither shall ye eat any flesh that is torn of beasts in the field, ye shall cast it to the dogs, because ye are holy men unto Me." Must the people of Israel manifest their holiness in this, that they must eat nothing torn by beasts but cast it unto dogs? Or was the holiness of the people of Israel such as God required of them that they must eat nothing that was torn by beasts? What, then, is the holiness of the infinite God? Our services that we perform are of themselves such as are torn by our beastly lusts many times. How many are there who bring sacrifices to God that are as carrion that swine have been tearing beforehand; and yet these are the sacrifices that they bring to God. And not only do men think that God should accept them, but they rest upon them for their acceptance to eternal life. How infinitely are these people mistaken! How little do they know of God or the way of acceptance to eternal life! That is the first use.

2. If all this is required to sanctify God's name in duties, that we cannot perform the duties of worship without this behavior of soul, we see that the work of religion is a hard and difficult work for flesh and blood. A main work of religion is the work of worshipping God, for indeed, those who are not religious and godly never worship God to any purpose. Then do we come to

worship God when we begin to be religious and godly. Now it must be a busy work to be a religious and godly man because there is so much required in sanctifying God's name in holy duties.

Many people think it is a very easy matter to worship God. And the worship they tender up to God is an easy matter; there is little in it. If it were nothing else to worship God but merely to go and say a few prayers, to come and hear a sermon, and take a piece of bread and wine, then it would be the easiest matter in the world to come and worship God. But there is more required in the duties of God's worship than you have been acquainted with. There is a power of godliness in it.

That text of Scripture is a very famous one that shows the difficulty there is in the worship of God, and how men are mistaken in thinking it such an easy and slight matter to worship Him. In Joshua 24:16–19, Joshua calls upon the people to worship God. And they said that they would worship Him (so you shall find them professing in verse 16); but mark what the text says in verse 19: "And Joshua said unto the people, 'Ye cannot serve the Lord, for He is a holy God, He is a jealous God, and He will not forgive your transgressions and your sins.'"

It is as if he should say, "You think it is nothing to serve the Lord, and that it is an easy matter to serve Him. You think to put off God with anything. Alas, you cannot serve the Lord, for He is a holy God and a jealous God. You must have other manner of hearts than yet you have, and you must understand His worship in another manner than yet you do. The Lord will be sanctified in those who draw nigh Him, and therefore you cannot serve the Lord."

Know that the work of religion is a very hard and difficult work, for it requires all this. And therefore the soul needs to be very diligent and laborious that would come to worship God in a right manner.

3. Here is a use of humiliation to us all, even to the best of us. Oh, have the best of us all sanctified the name of God! How far have we all come short of the sanctifying of God's name in holy duties! And when we look abroad in the world and see what poor service God generally has from the men and women of the earth, it should make our hearts bleed within us.

Where is that man or woman who, according to the text in Isaiah, stirs himself up to take hold on God? I verily believe that in the opening of this point of sanctifying the name of God in holy duties I have been in the bosoms of many as may have cause to lay their hands upon their hearts and say, "Certainly I have come short of what is required here, and have not been acquainted with this way, this mystery of godliness in sanctifying God's name in holy duties as I ought to be." Oh, be humbled for this, for all the uncleanness in your hearts in the performance of duties!

In Exodus 27:4–5 you read that at the altar where the sacrifices were to be offered the Lord required that there should be a grate made. "Thou shalt make for it (meaning the altar) a grate of network of brass, and upon the net shalt thou make four brazen rings in the four corners thereof; and thou shalt put it under the compass of the altar beneath, that the net may be even to the midst of the altar."

There was a grate for the ashes of the altar to go through, as you have grates in your fires to make them burn clear and for the ashes to fall down. So the Lord would have such a grate for the ashes of the altar to fall down. We have need of such a grate. Oh, the ashes and dirt and filth that there is in our services when we come to offer and tender them up to God! I say that we have cause to be humbled for holy offerings.

There may be many godly people who, through God's mercy, are able to keep you from gross sins. They do not find it any great matter to keep from bad company, swearing, drinking, uncleanness, lying, wronging others, or such kinds of sins as these are. They do not see such need for humiliation in this regard, unless it is for the fact that their natures are as corrupt as any, though they do not break forth into those actual gross sins. But the main work of the humiliation of those who are godly is to be humbled for their thoughts, for misspending time, and for not sanctifying God's name in holy duties. Those are the main things that are the subject of humiliation for the saints, beside the body of sin and death that they would carry about with them. And it would be a good sign that your heart has some tenderness in it when you make these to be the matter of your humiliation.

Carnal people are little troubled for these. If they fall into such sins that their consciences fly in their faces, then they are troubled and humbled; but for such things as these are they are seldom humbled. To be humbled for your holy offerings is a good sign of a gracious heart.

We read that the cherubim have six wings and that with two of their wings they cover their faces. So, my brethren, we need wings, as it were, to cover our best duties. They have wings, and with two they cover their legs and with two they cover their faces. We need not only a covering for our lower parts and meaner duties, but a covering for our holy duties, to cover our faces, our best duties of all. The most heavenly duties we perform need to be purged by the blood of Christ.

In Leviticus 16:14–16 we read of their holy things, that there was need of purging them by blood—and so it should be in our holy duties. Let us be humbled for the best performance we ever performed in our lives. The best needs to be humbled. But then, as for others who have made little or no conscience of sanctifying God's name, how much do they need to be humbled?

You have more to repent of than you thought of, for the truth is that those who have not made conscience of sanctifying God's name in holy duties never in all their lives did any service for the honor of God. You have lived perhaps thirty or forty, it may be sixty years or more, and have never yet honored God in any one thing that you have ever done in all your life.

OBJECTION. You will say, "God forbid! Have I not prayed and heard the Word much, and received the communion often; and yet have I never honored God?"

ANSWER. If you have not been acquainted with this mystery of godliness in sanctifying His name in these things, this is said from God to you this morning: You have never done any one action to the honor of God. You must begin immediately, for your time is not long. Will you go out of this world with the name of God never to be honored by you?

Yea, also, you have lost all your duties; all the time has been lost that you have been in the performance of duties. Now it is an ill thing to idle away time in the things of the world. When a man has an opportunity to advance in the world, if so be that he loses his time and neglects it, we account it a very sad thing to him. But to lose our trading time for heaven (for the times of worshipping God are our trading times for heaven), that's sad, indeed. And yet you who do not make conscience of sanctifying the name of God in holy duties, all the time you have spent is lost.

And you who have been false in the performance of duties and have been hypocrites, not only all your pains and labors are quite lost (for if that were so it might be well with you), but you have aggravated your sins by your holy duties. Those duties that others have enjoyed communion with God in, and furthered their eternal life by, you have aggravated your sins by—yet it was your duty to do them. But I say that by not sanctifying God's name, you have aggravated your sins so much the more.

Those who are godly work out their salvation even in their natural actions. They sanctify God's name in eating and drinking and following their business. They perform those actions in such a holy manner that they honor God in them and further their eternal peace; but as they, in their civil and natural actions, work out their salvation, so you, in the most religious actions, work out your damnation. Certainly wicked men who are not acquainted with this work of godliness to sanctify God's name in holy duties work out their damnation even in the performance of them.

You will say, "Then they had better not do them."

Yes, they are bound to do them, but they are bound to do them in a right manner. Sometimes I have given you this instance, and it is a full and a clear one to show that men are bound to perform holy duties and not to leave them undone, and yet they may further their own damnation while they are doing them. For example, suppose a prince appoints a man to come into his presence on a certain day to petition for his life, which he has forfeited by the law. If this man does not come he may be a dead man. But now if this man is drunk on that day and comes into the king's presence, he may be a dead man too for presuming to come drunk before him. So wicked and ungodly men, whether they worship or not, are in danger of perishing, but more of this when we come to show that God will be sanctified.

4. Here is a use of exhortation, seeing we have this truth thus presented to us and opened before us. Oh, that we had hearts to apply ourselves now to it with all our might, to seek to sanctify the name of God when we draw nigh to Him! The Lord has shown you what it is that He requires of you, to make

conscience of it for time to come. You do not know what blessed communion you may have with God if you make conscience of this. The truth is, if you have not been acquainted with this, you have not been acquainted with the way of a Christian in his enjoyment of communion with God. You do not know what the comfort of a Christian life means.

Try this for the time to come, and you will find more comfort in the ways of godliness, and more thriving in them in one quarter of a year, than you have done in seven years. One Christian who keeps close to God in holy duties, and sanctifies the name of God in them, finds more comfort with God and grows on in godliness more in one quarter of a year than another person does in seven years who goes on in an ordinary, dull, and formal way in the performance of the duties of worship. There are some in our time who cry out regarding duties, "Why do we need to trouble ourselves so much?" Those who do not know how to sanctify God's name think lightly of them; but now apply yourselves as fully as you are able to this that I am speaking of and you will find yourselves to be, as it were, in another world.

You will be able to say, "Well, I have not yet understood what it was to enjoy communion with God in prayer, in the Word, and in sacraments before." This will make your faces shine in your conversations if you will do it.

And to the end that you may do it, there are these three things that I would propound to you:

First, learn to know God more with whom you have to do, and present those things that you have heard before you in your meditation. When you come to God in prayer or in any other duty, and when you are worshipping God, remember that you have to do with God and no one else. Every time you come to perform holy duties, you are as a man or woman separated from all things. Valerius Maximus tells a story of a young nobleman who attended upon Alexander while he was sacrificing. This nobleman held his censer for incense, and, while holding it, a coal fell upon his flesh and burned it so that the smell of it was in the nostrils of all who were about him. Because he would not disturb Alexander in his service, he resolutely did not stir to put off the fire from himself, but still held his censer.

If heathens made such ado in their sacrificing to their idol gods, that they would mind it so as that no disturbance must be made whatever they endured, what care should we have, then, of ourselves when we come to worship the high God? And so Josephus reports of the priests who were sacrificing in the temple when Pompey broke in on them with armed men. Though they might have fled and saved their lives, they would not leave their sacrifice but were slain by the soldiers. They considered it a matter of great consequence. Oh, that we could mind the duties of God's worship as matters of great moment that we might learn to sanctify the name of God in the performance of them more than we have ever done.

Second, when you come to worship, take heed that you do not come in your own strength, for there is more required in sanctifying the name of God than your strength is able to carry you on in. And therefore, act your faith upon Jesus Christ every time you come to worship God, not only as I said before, to tender up your services in His name, but act your faith upon Christ to give you strength to do what you have to do. And what strength you have received from Christ, be sure to stir it up. Many godly men and women have more strength than they know of, and, if they would but stir up that strength they have received, they might sanctify the name of God a great deal more than they do. Therefore, remember that text mentioned before: "None stirs up himself to take hold on God." Quicken your heart and rouse up your spirit when you are to worship God.

Third, whenever you are worshipping God, do not satisfy yourself merely in the duty done, but consider, "Do I sanctify God's name in the duty?" Every time you worship Him, examine your heart as to whether you do it or not. And if you find that you have not attained in some comfortable measure to this that has been presented to you, let the shame and sorrow for that abide upon your spirit until the next time you come to worship God.

At such a time I have been worshipping God, and God knows I have been stirring up my heart in some measure; but I find my heart dead, wandering, sluggish, and dull. I say, when you find you cannot do it according to what is required in any comfortable measure, let the shame and sorrow of heart for it abide upon you until the next time you come to worship God, and that will mightily help you.

You are now praying and cannot get your heart up to what is required. The next time you come to prayer, come in the shame and sorrow of your heart for the lack of sanctifying God's name the last time, and so for hearing the Word or receiving the sacraments; and this will further you mightily for sanctifying the name of God in holy duties.

But that all may be sealed up to you, and, so that I may close the point, know that God will be sanctified in those who draw nigh to Him. There are these two things in the point: if we do not sanctify God's name, God will sanctify His name in a way of justice. If we do sanctify His name, then He will sanctify His name in a way of mercy towards us.

God will manifest that He is displeased with such duties that you perform. He will manifest it in one way or another that He is a holy God, and He does not accept such holy things as you tender up to Him. For, the truth is, if God should accept such unholy things from men, God may be said to be like them. If a man entertains any as his familiar friend who is naughty and wicked, it is his disgrace and dishonor.

A man may sometimes employ in some business those who are naughty and wicked and it may be no disgrace to him, but if he entertains one in his house who is wicked, it is a dishonor to him. So God may employ the most wicked men in the world in some outward services, but if He should accept them in His worship it would be a dishonor to God. And therefore God, that He might sanctify His own name, will manifest His displeasure at one time or another against such duties of worship. You who perform worship in a formal manner and with unclean hearts, I say, it stands against the honor of God. If He will manifest Himself to be a holy God, He must manifest some displeasure against that way of your worshipping Him. This one meditation, one would think, would mightily sink the heart of any man who has an enlightened conscience to think thus: "It stands upon the holiness of God, and He cannot appear to be a holy God unless He, in some way or other, appears to be against me in such duties as I tender up to Him."

QUESTION. Now you will say, "How does God appear that He does not accept them?"

ANSWER. He will appear in these three things:

First, by cursing those who worship Him thus in a formal way. It shall be at first secret, but afterwards it will appear more apparently; and we see it by experience that such as have been professors of religion and worship God in hypocrisy and formality have been cursed in their parts and common gifts.

The judgment of God upon Nadab and Abihu, who did not sanctify God's name, was secret at first. It struck them dead and, though by fire, yet if you read the story you shall find that their clothes were not burned, yet they were burned in their bodies.

So the Lord sometimes blasts men inwardly in their spirits, in their souls, in their parts, in their common gifts. He blasts them, I say, inwardly, though it does not appear outwardly. Yet at length it will appear before men that they are blasted; and in these times of the gospel, the Lord comes with spiritual judgments rather than with outward, temporal judgments.

In the time of the Law, those who did not sanctify the name of God in holy duties, the Lord appeared by some external and visible way upon their bodies. But now in the time of the gospel, God comes with more spiritual judgments upon men's souls, and those are the most terrible judgments. We have a notable Scripture for this in Isaiah 29:13. How God blasts those who do not sanctify His name in holy duties! "Wherefore the Lord said, 'Forasmuch as this people draw near Me with their mouth, and with their lips do honor Me, but have removed their heart far from Me, and their fear towards Me is taught by the precepts of men (mark what follows), therefore, behold, I will proceed to do a marvelous work among this people, even a marvelous work and wonder: for the wisdom of their wise men shall perish, and the understanding of their prudent men shall be hid.' "

It is as if God should say, "What, do they come and draw near Me with their lips and their hearts are far from Me? And do they worship Me in a formal way? I'll take away the wisdom of the wise and the understanding from the prudent."

That is the reason why so many great scholars are cursed in their very parts, because they would worship God according to the precepts of men in a formal way. And so the Lord blasts all hypocrites and formal worshippers in one way or another.

The judgments of God upon the spirits of men were sometimes in the time of the Law, but in the times of the gospel we find generally the judgments of God to be more spiritual upon the hearts and consciences of men. We find by experience that God reveals that He does not accept such as those are; and therefore, when you see any who have made a profession of religion who had excellent parts at first and many gifts, and now are, as we say, nobody, remember this text, that God will be sanctified in those who come near Him.

Second, the Lord manifests that He will be sanctified in those who draw nigh Him by awakening their consciences, many times, upon their sick beds and death beds. The Lord forces them to give glory to Him and there acknowledge that they did not worship God in uprightness, but in formality. And now they are in horror of conscience and cry out in the anguish of their souls upon the apprehension of the dreadful wrath of God that is upon them. Take heed, for the Lord's sake, of this thing when you are performing the duties of worship. Do not rest in the outward duties of worship. Do not rest in the outward duties, for they will never comfort you upon your sick beds and death beds.

You may, perhaps, put off your consciences a little for the present, but when you come upon your sick beds there will be no comfort for you; and then you will be forced to say, "Well, all this while I have but taken the name of God in vain, and now God has rejected me and all my services." And then speak to those who come to your bedside and bid them to take this warning from you.

Take heed that when you worship God you worship Him to purpose. I have spent time in prayer and hearing, but, for lack of this, I find I have no comfort at all. The Lord rather appears to be terrible to my soul and comes out against me as an enemy.

I say now that God's name is sanctified. Whatever becomes of you, He will force glory from you one way or another, and it may be even here at this time of your life; but however, at the great day when the secrets of all hearts must be disclosed before men and angels, then the Lord will appear to be a holy God by rejecting all such services that you tendered up to Him. And it will then be a great part of the work of the Day of Judgment for God to be sanctified in those who worshipped Him by declaring before men and angels how He rejected this formal and hypocritical worship that they tendered up to Him. Oh, that God would strike this upon your hearts, that it may abide upon you every time you come to worship Him to think thusly, "Let me look to it to sanctify His name now, for I hear that God will sanctify it Himself if I do not."

But then, on the other side, if so be that you make conscience of sanctifying God's name in duties, then He will sanctify His name in a way of mercy. That is, He will manifest how He accepts the least degree of holiness, though there is much mixture. God has a way to take away the mixture by the blood of His Son and then to accept any holiness He sees in you. He will sanctify His name by meeting with you and revealing His glory to you when you are worshipping Him.

There is an excellent Scripture for this in Exodus 29:43: "There I will meet with the children of Israel and the tabernacle shall be sanctified by My glory." You who have a gracious heart and are worshipping God in sincerity, you are as a tabernacle of God, and God has His service and worship from you. You are as the temple of God, "and there I will meet with you," says God, "and I will sanctify My tabernacle by My glory." God will sanctify your heart by His glory if you sanctify His name.

Further, you shall, it may be, not always have such glorious comforts, the full beams of the sun rising upon you, but at one time or another the Lord will break in upon you and manifest His glory to you. If you do not have such full comforts now, yet upon your sick bed you will. Though God does not always manifest Himself fully—for sometimes the disease itself may be a hindrance—yet ordinarily those who in their constant way sanctified God's name in holy duties lie comfortably upon their sick beds, and a glorious entrance is made for them into the everlasting kingdom of our Lord and Savior Jesus Christ.

And then again, all things are sanctified unto them. As on the other side, those who do not sanctify God's name, all things are cursed to them. If you do not make conscience of sanctifying God's name in duties, God does not care to sanctify anything for your good. But now those who make conscience of sanctifying God's name in holy duties, the Lord takes care that all things shall be sanctified for their good, for the furtherance of their eternal good.

And however it is here, yet hereafter, at the great Day of Judgment, it will be a part of the glory of God to manifest before men and angels how He accepted those holy services that you tendered up to Him. Hypocrites shall be cast away and abhorred, and you who had an upright, sincere heart shall be owned before God and before men and angels at that great day; and God shall say, "Well, it is a part of the glory of My holiness to make it appear that I have accepted these holy things that these, My poor servants, have tendered up to Me."

And is this not of marvelous use for comforting a gracious heart? Those duties that you think you have lost, and that nothing will come of them, you shall certainly hear of them another day. God will make it appear that there is nothing that He stands more upon than the glory of His holiness; and it is the glory of His holiness that is your strength in this thing, and that makes it certain to you that there must be a manifestation of your acceptance. Therefore take these truths to your heart about sanctifying the name of God. You have had only the point in general opened to you. Oh, that the Spirit of God would bring things into your remembrance!

SERMON VIII

Sanctifying the Name of God in Hearing the Word

Part 1

"I will be sanctified in them that come nigh Me."

LEVITICUS 10:3

I have preached many sermons upon that point of sanctifying the name of God in the duties of His worship. I spoke to the point in general the last Lord's Day. I do not intend to look back to anything that was said, but will proceed to show how the name of God should be sanctified in the particular duties of His worship. Now the duties of God's worship are especially these three—hearing the Word, receiving the sacraments, and prayer.

Other things come under worship, but these are the three chief duties of worship; and I intend to speak to all these and show how we should sanctify the name of God in drawing nigh unto Him in the Word, the sacraments, and in prayer.

We might choose several texts for all these, but they fall fully within the general; and therefore it shall be sufficient to ground the sanctifying of God's name in these duties of worship upon this text.

That which I am to speak to this morning is sanctifying the name of God in hearing the Word. If you would have the ground of what I am to say concerning this, you may have it in Luke 8:18: "Take heed therefore how you hear." It is not enough to come to hear the Word, although that is good, and there is no question but that God is pleased with the willingness of people to come to hear His Word; but you must not rest barely in hearing, but take heed *how* you hear.

Now this is a point of great consequence, and I hope it may help to make many sermons profitable to you. And the point, I hope, is seasonable and will be very suitable unto you. Those who come to hear early in the morning, and are willing even in hard weather to come out of their beds, give some good testimony that they desire to honor God in their hearing and to get good by their hearing. And it is a pity that labor and pains should be bestowed and no profit, but rather hurt, gotten by it, God forbid. Therefore now I am to speak to a point that may help you so to hear as may recompense all your labor and pains in hearing. I'm preaching to those who come to hear so that they may get good and benefits by it. There is a great deal more encouragement than to such as come in a formal way because they are used to coming. Therefore, this point being a great point, I shall open it somewhat largely and shall cast it unto this method:

First, I shall show you that hearing God's Word is a part of the worship of God, for otherwise I could not ground it upon my text.

Second, I shall show you how we are to sanctify God's name in hearing His Word, either in regard to preparation unto it or our behavior in hearing His Word.

Third, why it is that God will be sanctified in this ordinance of His.

Fourth, how God will sanctify Himself in those who do not sanctify His name in hearing His Word.

Fifth, how God will sanctify His name in ways of mercy to those who are careful to sanctify His name in hearing His Word.

These are the five principal things that concern this argument, but I will deal only with the first one here.

1. Hearing God's Word is a part of God's worship. You heard in the opening of the worship of God in general what it was. I told you that it was a rendering up of the creature's homage to God, a testimony of the respect that the creature owed to God. Now if that is the nature of worship, certainly hearing God's Word is a part of the worship of God, for in hearing God's Word.

In hearing God's Word we profess our dependence upon God for knowing His mind and the way to eternal life. Every time we come to hear the Word, if we know what we are doing, we do this much: we profess that we depend upon the Lord God for the knowing of His mind and the way and rule to eternal life. It is as much as if we should say, "Lord, of ourselves we neither know Thee, nor the way and means how we should come to be saved; and, therefore, that we might test our dependence upon Thee for this thing, we here present ourselves before Thee." Now this is a testimony of the high respect we owe to God.

Hearing God's Word is a part of His worship because in it we come to wait upon our God in the way of an ordinance beyond what the thing in itself is able to do, and therefore it is worship. I wait upon God when I am hearing the Word, if I know what I am doing, to have some spiritual good conveyed to me beyond what there is in the means itself. This makes it to be worship.

When I am busied in natural and civil actions, I must profess that these things can do me no good without God; but

I do not wait upon God in an ordinance for the conveyance of natural good beyond what God has put into the creature. It is His blessing with it that God, in the ordinary course of His providence, conveys such natural or civil good in the use of those creatures. But now when I come to hear the Word, I come here to wait upon God in the way of an ordinance for the conveyance of some spiritual good that this ordinance does not have in itself. Take it materially, but merely as it has an institution in it and is appointed by God for the conveyance of such and such things.

God appoints meat to nourish me and, together with His appointment, He has given a natural power to meat to nourish my body. That, in an ordinary course of providence, is enough for the nourishment of my body. But when I come to hear the Word, I must look upon that not only as a thing appointed to work upon my soul and to save my soul by, not as a thing that has any efficacy put into it in a natural way as the other has. It is not the nature of a thing that carries such a power in it, but it is the institution of God and the ordinance of God in it. Now then, when I come to wait upon God in an ordinance for the spiritual good that is beyond the virtue of any creature to convey to me, certainly I worship God. That is a special part of worship, to wait upon God in this way.

Therefore, in these two respects, hearing God's Word is a part of the worship of God. And I beseech you to remember these two things every time you come to hear. "I come now to give a testimony that I am not able to understand God and the way to eternal life of myself, but I depend upon God for the knowledge of it. And here I come to wait upon God for the conveyance of that good to my soul that is not in the power of any creature to convey." Now I worship when I do these.

But further (you shall find it more plain when we come to

open how we should sanctify God's name in the hearing of His Word), this is divine service, as much as any can be performed. Heretofore, our prelates, and those kinds of men, made all the worship of God to be in their divine service (as they call it), which was of their own inventions, and made light of the preaching or hearing of the Word. But the Word is a great part of that divine service that God requires of us in His worship, and in it you tender up your homage to God.

Therefore, when you come to hear, you must not only think, "I come to get something. I come to understand more than I did, and to hear such a man's parts," and the like, but remember that you come to tender up your homage to God, to sit at God's feet, and there to profess your submission to Him. That is one end of your coming to hear sermons.

QUESTION. You will say, "What should be done in the hearing of God's Word so that God's name may be sanctified?"

ANSWER. In the duties of God's worship there must be preparation, and then an answerable behavior of the soul. So here there must be a preparation of the soul to this work, and then an answerable behavior of the soul in it.

There must be a preparation of the soul so that, when you come to hear, you may receive the Word with all readiness. The soul must be made ready. Acts 17:11: "These were more noble than those of Thessalonica, in that they received the Word with all readiness of mind." The word is "with all alacrity," as well as readiness. Their minds were in a fit preparation to receive the Word, and the text says that they were more noble. The word that is translated "more noble" signifies better bred. I do not take this Scripture to mean that these men were earls or lords who received the Word with readiness, but they were men of a more noble disposition. They were well-bred men, for so the

Greek word signifies.

A man who sometimes preaches to a company of rude people who never had any good breeding will find that they will behave themselves rudely. They slight the Word and, like the swine, regard acorns rather than pearls. And the Word is seldom profitable to a company of rude people who have no breeding at all; but there is more hope in preaching to men who have breeding. Men who are exercised in arts and sciences, who have some understanding and some ingenuity in them, will hearken to reason. Now there is a great deal of spiritual reason in the Word. There is a great deal to convince men who are rational men. Let a man be a rational man and be willing to attend to the Word, and I say that there is a great deal of reason to convince him in it; and it is a sign of good breeding of men of ingenuity to be willing to hear the Word.

Who are those in a parish but the ruder sort, who so disregard the Word as not to hear it? There are many, I confess, who are men of parts. Perhaps the Word does not prevail with their hearts to convert them, yet, if they have any good breeding at all, if the Word is preached in a convincing way so that they see there are pains taken, and preached as the Word of God to them, they will grant their presence at least. But the rude multitude that knows nothing at all would rather be in alehouses drinking and swilling. They never care to hear the Word as in such a place as this.

There are very few of your miserable people who come to hear the Word. What place is there more full of miserable, poor people than this place, and yet what a poor appearance is there of such people at the hearing of the Word? But now those who have any ingenuity in them at all, or any breeding (for so the word is), will "receive the Word with readiness." But this breeding here spoken of was a little higher than natural breeding. They were spiritually noble, and so they had a readiness in their hearts in receiving the Word. Now this readiness of heart in receiving the Word consists in these particulars:

First, when you come to hear the Word, if you would sanctify God's name, you must possess your souls with what it is you are going to hear, that what you are going to hear is the Word of God. It is not a man speaking that you are going to attend, but you are now going to attend upon God, and to hear the Word of the eternal God. Possess your souls with this. You will never sanctify God's name in hearing His Word otherwise. Therefore you find that the apostle, writing to the Thessalonians, gives them the reason why the Word did them as much good as it did. It was because they heard it as the Word of God. 1 Thessalonians 2:13: "For this cause also thank we God without ceasing, because when ye received the Word of God, which ye heard of us, ye received it not as the word of men, but (as it is in truth) the Word of God, which effectually worketh also in you that believe."

Mark, it came effectually to work because they received it as the Word of God. Many times you will say, "Come, let us go hear a man preach." Oh, no, let us go hear Christ preach, for as it concerns the ministers of God that they preach not themselves, but that Christ should preach in them, so it concerns you that you do not come to hear this man or that man, but to come to hear Jesus Christ. "We as the ambassadors of Christ do beseech you," said the apostle.

Second, possess your hearts likewise with this consideration: "I come to hear the Word as an ordinance appointed by God to convey spiritual good to my soul." This is a very useful consideration. It especially concerns men of understanding and parts for helping them to hear, for when men of understanding and parts come to hear, this temptation is ready to come upon

them, that unless they hear some new thing that they did
not understand before, why should they come? "I am able to
understand as much in such a point as can be said; and when I
have come and heard many times, I have only heard that which
I knew before." Upon this they think there is no use in coming
to hear.

Now this is a great mistake. When you come to hear the
Word, you do not always come to hear what you did not know.
It may be that sometimes God may dart something that you
did not think of before or so fully understand. But suppose it
is not so. You are to come to it as an ordinance of God for the
conveyance of spiritual good to your souls.

OBJECTION. You will say, "Cannot we sit at home and read a
sermon?"
ANSWER. But has God appointed that the great ordinance for
the converting and the edifying of souls in the way of eternal
life? True, there is some use of it, but the great ordinance is the
preaching of the Word. Faith comes by hearing, the Scriptures
say, and never by reading. So that even though when you come
to hear you do not hear that which you did not hear before, yet
you come to attend upon this ordinance for the conveyance
of some spiritual good that, it may be, has not been conveyed
before, or in a further degree than has been conveyed before.

And so you should come to hear the Word with your hearts
possessed with the meditation that it is the Word of God and
the great ordinance that God has appointed for the conveyance
of spiritual good. "Now I come in obedience to God, and in
this I testify my respect to God, that I will attend upon this
ordinance of His for the conveyance of spiritual good to me.
And although I may think that this or the other means may do
the deed as well, yet because God has appointed this to be His

ordinance, therefore, in obedience to Him, I will attend upon this means rather than upon the other means."

As you know, Naaman thought the other waters would have been as good as the waters of Jordan to have healed him; but if God appointed the waters of Jordan to heal him rather than the other waters, then he must wash there. There is no question that the other waters had as much natural virtue in them, but because the waters of Jordan were the ordinance that God had appointed to cure his leprosy with, he must come and wash in those waters rather than any other. So because the preaching of the Word is the great ordinance that God has appointed to convey Himself by, therefore He requires that you should show your respect to Him so far as to attend upon Him in that ordinance.

The second thing that is to be done in way of preparation is to plow up the fallow ground of your hearts and not to sow among thorns, as you have in Jeremiah 4:3 and Hosea 10. The Word of God, you know, is compared to seed in that parable of Christ in Matthew 13, and an audience is compared to the ground. I suppose you are all acquainted with that parable of the sower, that it is to set out the ministry of the Word and what fruit it has upon the hearts of men. A congregation is like the field and a minister preaching is like the sower who sows the seed in the field. He does not know which truth will prosper. The seed being sowed in some part of the ground is lost, and in another part it grows. So in one pew the seed of the Word is lost, and in another pew it grows up. But now, if people who are compared to the ground would so hear the Word that God's name may be sanctified in it, their hearts must be plowed. If one should sow seed upon green soil, sow it in the fields upon green grass, what would become of it? The ground must first be plowed for the preparation of the seed.

QUESTION. But you will say, "What is the meaning of the plowing of our hearts for the preparation of the Word?"

ANSWER. The meaning is nothing else but this, the work of humiliation, the humbling of the soul before the Lord when it comes to hear God's Word.

Humble it in these two regards. First, be humbled for your ignorance, that you know as little of God's mind as you do. Second, be humbled for all the sinfulness of your hearts. Be sensible of the miserable condition that you are in. If you can get your hearts broken with the sense of your sin and misery, and so come to hear the Word, it is very likely the Word may be of mighty use, and God's name may be very much sanctified in your hearing the Word.

QUESTION. You will say, "Must we plow up our hearts before we come to hear? It must be the Word that plows us. The Word is the plow, and so the ministers of God are compared to plowmen in the Word: 'He that puts his hand to the plow and looks back is not fit for the Kingdom of heaven.' "

ANSWER. It is true that it cannot be expected that the heart should be thoroughly plowed as it ought except by the Word. Therefore, at the first coming to hear, there is no hope that men will sanctify God's name until the Word gets in to plow them; and so, by getting at one time into their hearts, they come to be prepared for hearing at another time. And yet something may be done before by that natural knowledge that men have. They may come to know themselves to be sinners, and come to understand themselves to be very weak and ignorant, by some knowledge that they may have by the works of God, by conference with others, and by reading and the like. And so they may, in some measure, come to have their hearts humbled. It is good to make use of these to humble the heart; but now you who have heard the Word often and have not yet sanctified God's name, there are truths that you have heard heretofore that, if you had made use of them in private to have plowed up your hearts, they would have prepared your hearts for the next time of hearing the Word. If therefore you would hear the Word with a great deal more profit than formerly, your hearts must be plowed by humiliation.

The heart must be plowed by laboring to get out those thorns that are in the heart, those lusts that grow deep in the heart like thorns grow in the ground. Labor to pluck them out; that is, when you come to hear the Word, get your heart into that frame so as to be willing to profess against every known sin that you have found in your heart. Labor to find out those lusts that are in your heart, and then profess against them, that you are willing to have them to be rooted out of your heart. If men and women would only do this when they come to hear, then God might see in them that they have, before they came, professed against every known sin. This would be an excellent thing indeed.

Again, when you come to hear the Word, come with a resolution to yield whatever God shall reveal to be His mind. "I am now going to hear Thy Word, O Lord, to wait upon Thee, to know what Thou hast to say to me. And Thou, who art the Searcher of all hearts, know that I go with such a resolution to yield up myself to every truth of Thine."

How would the name of God be sanctified if you came thusly to hear the Word, if you came with such a resolution as that in Job 32:34: "That which I know not, teach Thou me, and if I have done iniquity, I will do no more." In Isaiah 2:3 you have a prophecy of how the Gentiles should come to the Word: "And many people shall go and say, 'Come ye, and let us go up to the mountain of the Lord to the house of the God of Jacob, and He will teach us His ways, and we will walk in His paths.' " Here is a blessed disposition when you come to hear the Word.

Some of you come together in streets and lanes and over the fields. When you come together and meet with one another as you walk over the fields, make use of this text. Oh, that this prophesy might be fulfilled in your coming over the fields every Lord's Day morning, and at other times that you would say to one another, or when you call upon one another to go to hear, "Let us go up to the house of the Lord and He will teach us of His ways and we will walk in His paths. We are resolved that whatever the Lord shall teach us to be His ways, we will submit to it." This is a due preparation of the heart for sanctifying God's name in hearing the Word.

When you come to hear the Word, come with longing desires after the Word. Come with an appetite for it as in 1 Peter 2:2: "As newborn babes desire the sincere milk of the Word that ye may grow thereby." Do it as newborn babes. Now you know little babes do not desire milk to play with, but only to nourish them. Children of three or four years old may desire milk to play with, but newborn babes never care for it but when they are hungry. And so it is true, many come to hear the Word to play with it; but you should come to hear the Word as newborn babes, with a hungering desire after the Word so that your souls may be nourished thereby.

That would be excellent if every Lord's Day, and at other times, you came as hungry to the Word as you ever went to your dinner or supper. The Word of God should be more to you than your appointed food, and then you are likely to grow by it and to sanctify God's name in it.

Pray beforehand that God would open your eyes, and open

your heart and accompany His Word. Thus did David, "Open mine eyes O Lord, that I may understand the wonders of Thy Law." And you know what is said of Lydia, "The Lord opened her heart to attend to the Word that was spoken." Now seeing it is an ordinance, you expect more good from it than what it, of its own nature, is able to convey. You have need to pray, "Lord, I go to such an ordinance of Thine, and I know there is no efficacy in itself. It is not able to reach such effects as I expect, that is, to have my eyes opened, but Lord, open my eyes and my heart. Lord, my heart is naturally locked up against Thy Word. There are such wards in my heart that unless Thou art pleased to put in a key that may fit my heart it will never open. Man is not able to know my heart, and therefore he cannot fit a key to answer every word, to resolve every doubt, to silence every objection. But, Lord, Thou canst do it. Lord, therefore fit Thy Word this day to meet with my heart. Lord, I have gone often to Thy Word, and the key has stuck it in and it has not opened. But, Lord, if Thou wouldst but fit it and turn it with Thine own hand, my heart would open."

Oh, come with such a praying heart to the Word, and thereby you shall sanctify the name of God in hearing His Word. This is to come to the Word as to the Word of God. You must not come to the hearing of the Word as to hear a speech or an oration, but come in such a preparation as this is—and so God will be glorified and you will profit.

QUESTION. What should be the behavior of the soul in sanctifying God's name in the Word when it is come?
ANSWER. Now to that there are these particulars:

First, there must be a careful attention unto the Word. You must set your hearts unto it as did Moses in Deuteronomy 32:46. He said unto the people, "Set your hearts unto all the words which I testify among you this day, which you shall command your children to observe to do; for it is not a vain thing for you, because it is your life." Set your hearts to it; for it is not a vain thing, it is your life. When you come to hear the Word, give diligent attention to what you hear.

In Acts 8:6 it is said, "The people with one accord gave heed unto those things which Philip spake." The word translated "they gave heed" is used often in Scripture. Sometimes it is used as "to beware of something," as in "beware of the leaven of the Pharisees." Beware of them. When a man sees an enemy and is aware of him, he is very diligent to observe how to avoid him. So there should be as much diligence to get good by the Word as one would be diligent to avoid any danger whatsoever.

The word signifies other times "to give heed." As a disciple gives heed unto his master, so they gave heed to the Word. So in Proverbs 2:1–2: "My son, if thou wilt receive My words, and hide My commandments with thee, so that thou incline thine ear unto wisdom. . . ." We must diligently attend to what is said, and not allow our eyes and our thoughts to be wandering. My brethren, there are always things that may challenge attention in the Word.

Think of what would make you attend to anything. You would attend if he who spoke were much above you. If it were a great prince or lord who spoke to you, then you would attend. Now it is true that it is but a man (who, it may be, is inferior to most of you) who speaks, yet know that in him it is the Lord of heaven and earth who speaks to you. And so you know that Christ said, "He that heareth you heareth Me." So though you would not attend in respect of the messenger so much, yet as it is the Son of God who is speaking to you, it may challenge your attention.

If you were to hear a voice out of the clouds from heaven speaking to you today, would you not then listen? The truth is, we should listen as much to the voice of God in the ministry of His Word as if the Lord should speak out of the clouds to us. And I will give you a Scripture for that, that the voice of God in His Word should be as highly regarded by you as if God should speak from heaven to you in an audible voice out of the clouds. 2 Peter 1:18–19: "This voice which came from heaven we heard, when we were with Him in the holy mount." But mark what it says in verse 19: "We have also a more sure Word of prophecy whereunto ye do well that ye take heed."

Mark it, we heard a voice from heaven, said Peter. Yes, but "we have a more sure Word of prophecy whereunto ye do well that ye take heed."

OBJECTION. "There was a voice from heaven which spoke?" you will say, "If we had heard that voice, we would have given heed to it!"

ANSWER. The apostle says, "You have a more sure word of prophecy." Now prophecy in Scripture is taken for preaching. "Despise not prophecy." It is as if the Holy Ghost should say, "You must have regard for the Word of prophecy as you would have regard to any voice from heaven."

Suppose an angel should come and speak to you. Would you not attend to him? Then whatever thoughts you had would be set aside, for there is an angel that has come down from heaven to speak. Now mark what is said in Hebrews 1:1: "God, who at sundry times and in divers manners spake in times past to the fathers by the prophets, hath in these last days spoken to us by His Son, whom He hath appointed heir of all things, by whom also He made the worlds." And then in verse 3, He describes His Son: "And being made so much better than the angels, as He hath by inheritance obtained a more excellent name than they."

If a prophet should come and speak, that is not as much as if the Son of God comes, no, nor as if an angel should come; for Jesus Christ has obtained a more excellent name than the angels, and it is Christ who is the ministry of His Word. "He that heareth you heareth Me."

Second, that which will cause attention is the greatness of the matter propounded. It is true, if a man should speak of some slight and vain things, it does not require as much attention. My brethren, the matters in the Word are the great things of God. It is the voice of God, the great mysteries of godliness, those deep things that the angels themselves long to pry into. Yea, the angels themselves have come to have the knowledge of the mysteries of God by the churches. I have no doubt but in the ministry of the Word among the churches the angels attend and come to some knowledge in the mysteries of godliness, for so the Scripture says in Revelation 22:16, "that they have it in the churches."

Here the greatest things of God's will, the greatest counsels of God that were kept hidden from all eternity, are opened to you in the ministry of the Word. We do not come to tell you tales and the conceits of men, but to open the great counsels of God, wherein the depth of the wisdom of God comes to be revealed to the children of men—and therefore this calls for attention.

Third, suppose they are great things. Yet if they do not so much concern us, there is no great reason for attention. Therefore, that which we speak is your life. It is that which concerns your souls and eternal estates. Your souls and everlasting estates lie upon the ministry of the Word. If that is made effectual to you, you are saved; if that is not made effectual to you, you are damned and undone forever.

If we should come to tell you of something whereby you

might get some good bargain, or how to get great riches, I have no doubts but that you would rise even though it was a cold or rainy morning. But know that when you are called to hear the Word, you are called to hear that which may do you good forever, that for which you may bless God to all eternity with the angels and saints in the highest heavens. If they are such things of such great concern, then there needs to be great attention.

You know what Christ said to Martha when she was troubled about His entertainment in Luke 10:41, "Martha, Martha, thou art careful and troubled about many things, but one thing is needful, and Mary hath chosen that good part which shall not be taken away from her." What did Mary choose? It was this: she diligently attended upon Jesus Christ to hear the Word from His own mouth while Martha was busy in the house to provide for His entertainment. But it is a better thing to attend upon the Word than to entertain Christ in your houses.

You who are of loving dispositions, if a good minister or a good Christian should come to your house, someone in whom you see the image of Christ, your hearts spring within you and you will do anything to entertain them. Well, what if Jesus Christ should come? If you knew that such a man who came inside your doors was the Son of God, how would you busy yourselves to entertain Him? But know, it is a more acceptable service to Jesus Christ to attend upon His Word than to provide for Him in your houses.

And there is great reason, too, why we should be diligent in drawing nigh to the Word and to give ear unto it. Because you find that the Lord expresses Himself in the Scripture as to how He gives ear to us when we speak to Him. God is said to incline His ear, sometimes to open His ear, sometimes to cause His ear to hear; and there are divers such expressions to that purpose. Now if God, when we who are poor wretches speak to

Him, shall bow His ear, bend His ear, open His ear, and cause
His ear to hear, much more should we when we come to attend
upon Him?

2. As there must be an attending to the Word of God, so there
must be an opening of the heart to receive what God speaks to
you. It is true that it is the work of God to open the heart, but
God works upon men as upon rational creatures; and He makes
you to be active in opening your hearts so that when you should
have any truth come to be revealed, you should open your
understandings, your consciences, your will and affections. "O
Lord, Thy truth, which Thou art presenting here to my soul at
this time, let it come in." "Let me receive it," as the expression
is in Proverbs 2:1: "My son, if thou wilt receive My words." And
then in verse 10, "when wisdom entereth into thy heart."

The words of wisdom are the words of God. They must
enter into the heart and get in. It may be that they get into
your ear, but that's not enough. They must get into your heart.
In John 8:37, Christ complained that His word had no place in
the people. That's a sad thing when the Word of God shall have
no place in the heart. If a temptation to sin comes, that has a
place in the heart; but when the Word comes, it has no place
in the heart.

It is a very sad thing that we can find no room for the Word.
We should get room for the Word. "Open ye gates, stand open
ye everlasting doors, that the King of Glory may come in"
(Psalm 24:9). Know that when you come to hear the Word, the
Lord is knocking at the door of your hearts. Have you not felt
it sometimes? Open, oh, open the doors; let all be opened to
receive the Word into your hearts. That is the second thing for
the behavior of the soul.

3. The third thing is the careful applying of the Word (Proverbs 2:2). There must be a careful applying of the heart to the Word, and an applying of the Word unto the heart. All action is by an application of the things that acts unto the subject. There must be an application of the Word unto your soul.

Suppose you come to hear the Word and you hear of some sin that, it may be, you know you are guilty of. Take the Word and lay it to your heart and say, "The Lord has met with my soul this day; the Lord has spoken to me to the end that I might be humbled for this sin and the other sin that my conscience tells me I am guilty of."

Does the Lord put you upon a duty that concerns you? Acknowledge this. "The Lord has spoken to me this day and put me upon the reformation of my family and the reformation of my own heart."

Is there a word presented? Apply that, and do not let the trouble of your heart cause you to cast off that word which God has spoken to you. The application of the Word to the heart is of marvelous use, and it concerns not only ministers in general to lay before people the doctrine of the gospel, but to apply it. And know that it concerns you as well as ministers to apply it, not only when they come to that which is called use, but all the way in the opening of the Word. It concerns you all to apply it to your own souls and to consider, "How does this concern me in particular?"

My brethren, there is no such way to honor God or let good to your own souls as the application of the Word unto yourselves. If a man is asleep, a noise will not soon awaken him; but if you come and call him by his name and say, "John," or "Thomas," that will awaken him sooner than a great noise will. So when the Word makes a little noise when it is delivered only in general, men take little notice of it; but when the Word comes particularly to the souls of men and calls them by name, as it were, this awakens them.

Now God, many times, speaks to your hearts. You should apply it. You know the Word is compared to meat, and it must be applied to the body. Then we worship God in a right way when we take notice of God's Word as concerning us in particular. You have that notable Scripture in 1 Corinthians 14:25, where a poor man comes into the church of God and hears prophesying, hears the Word opened, and the text says, "He is convinced of all, he is judged of all." And then in verse 25: "thus are the secrets of his heart manifest, and so falling down on his face he worships God and reports that God is in you of a truth." That is, when the Word comes and meets with his soul in particular, he finds himself to be aimed at by the Word. Then he worships God and says that God is certainly in them.

Here's the reason now that when you come to hear the Word you do not worship God, because you do not apply it to yourselves. You are ready to say, "This was well spoken to such a one, and it concerns such a one." But how does it concern your soul in particular? Sometimes the Lord even forces men and women to apply it whether they want to or not, so that they think the minister speaks to them in particular, and that nobody but them was spoken to in the congregation. This is a mercy when the Lord does it unto you, but it is a greater mercy when the Lord gives you a heart to apply it to yourselves; and although it may trouble you a little for the present, yet be willing to apply it and account it a greater mercy from the Lord that the Lord will be pleased to speak in particular to your souls.

4. We must mix faith with the Word or else it will do us but little good. Apply it and then believe it. In Hebrews 4:2 it is said that "the Word preached did not profit them, not being mixed with

faith in them that heard it." Wherefore there must be a mixture of faith to believe the Word that the Lord brings to you.

QUESTION. You will say, "Must we believe everything that is spoken? Sometimes there are some things spoken that we cannot tell how to believe."

ANSWER. I do not mean that you must believe everything merely because it is spoken, for you must take heed what you hear as well as how you hear, but do this much at least:

First, whatever comes in the name of God to you (unless you know for certain it is not according to the written Word), you owe so much respect to it as to examine it at least, to try whether it is so or not. As it is said of those well-bred men of whom I spoke, they examined whether things were so or not. Do not cast off anything presently that comes in the name of God. Now anything that has the broad seal upon it, you must not disobey.

You will say, "It may be counterfeit." But do not disobey it until you are sure that it is counterfeit. Oh, that men would just give this respect to all the things that they hear, never to cast them off until they have examined and tried whether they are so or not.

Second, grant enough respect to the Word that is spoken to you to think thusly: "What if all that I hear spoken against my sin, that lays open the dangerous condition that my soul is in, proves to be true? What a case would I be in then?"

This has been the beginning of the conversion of many souls, having just such a thought as this: "It may be things are not as terrible as I hear, but what if they prove that they are? Then I am undone forever. Do I dare venture my soul and my eternal estate upon the hope that these things are not as bad as I hear?"

I believe that if you would put yourselves to it, you would think of it as a bold adventure; and the comfort that any of you have grounded upon this, merely hoping that things are not as bad as you hear, would prove to be a cursed comfort that has no bottom. Grant that respect, therefore, to the Word.

Third, consider this. It may be that I do not see clearly that these things are so that are now delivered. I do not see enough to believe them now, but what if I were dying now? What if I were now going to receive the sentence of my eternal doom; would I not then believe these things? Would I not then think what I hear out of the Word to be true?

It is an easy matter for men to reject the Word while they have their health and prosperity. But if you were to die, and, upon your sick and death beds, if you saw the infinite ocean of eternity before you, what would you say then? Would the Word be true or not? Would you give belief unto the suggestions of the devil then? We find by experience that men easily cast off the Word in times of health, yet when they have come to lie upon their sick and death beds, they found the Word to be true. Believe it now as well as then.

Fourth, consider that if you do not believe, what a case are you in then? "Am I worse than the devils themselves? The Scripture tells me that the devils believe and tremble. Why Lord, do I come to hear sermons, and am I less believing than the devils themselves? They believe that Word that I cast off, and they tremble at it, but my soul is not at all stirred. It is as if there were no reality in such things that have been spoken to me."

There are other things that may further help us towards believing the Word of God, but these shall suffice. And certainly, my brethren, until we come to believe the Word, though we might sit under it for many years, it will do us little good, and we shall never sanctify the name of God by hearing it.

Sanctifying the Name of God in Hearing the Word

Part 2

"I will be sanctified in them that come nigh Me."

LEVITICUS 10:3

5. The next thing for the right behavior of the soul in sanctifying God's name is this: we must receive the Word with meekness of spirit. You have that in James 1:21: "Wherefore lay apart all filthiness, and superfluity of naughtiness, and receive with meekness the engrafted Word which is able to save your souls." Receive it with meekness. The former part of this Scripture, I confess, concerns something that was before about the preparation of the soul; and we shall afterwards, perhaps, in the application, come to open the former part of this verse, "Lay apart all filthiness, and superfluity of naughtiness." Let there be a quietness in your spirits in attending upon the Word, no hurrying.

There is a twofold distemper of passion in many people that is a great hindrance to the profit of the Word and sanctifying God's name in it. The first is a distemper of passion in those who have some trouble of conscience in them. They are troubled for their sin, and their spirits are in a discontented, wicked humor because they do not have that comfort which they desire. Therefore, when the Word of God comes to be preached to them, if it does not suit their hearts in every way, and if they do not find immediate comfort by it, their spirits are in a distemper and a perverseness and they cast it off. If at any time there are not comfortable things spoken in the Word, then there is an anger in their spirits because they are not able to apply the Word to themselves. They think, "This does not concern me."

Now there should be meekness of spirit in those who are in trouble of conscience above all. They should quietly attend upon the Word and wait for the time that God will speak peace to their consciences. "If I cannot find the Word suitable to me at this time, I may at another time. Let me attend with meekness, and let me receive with meekness. The Word is above me, and if ever I have good, it must be by the Word at last." It much concerns those who are in trouble of conscience to have meek spirits.

There is another distemper in others that is worse, that is, those who, when they find the Word come near unto them, relating those sins that their consciences tell them they are guilty of, find their hearts rising against God and His Word, and His ministers, too. Because it would pluck away some beloved corruption, because it rebukes them for some habitual practice of evil, some distemper of heart that they have been or are guilty of, it puts a shame upon them, and therefore their hearts rise against it.

It is a dreadful thing to have the heart rise against the Word. We read of that evil prince, Jehoiakim, in the prophecy of Jeremiah, when the roll was read in his hearing (sitting in the wintertime by a great fire), he took a knife and cut it in pieces and threw it into the fire in anger. I have read that the Jews kept a fast every year to mourn for that great sin. And yet this Jehoiakim was the son of Josiah, whose heart melted at the hearing of the Word. He had a humble and a meek heart when the Law was read; and yet see what a different spirit Jehoiakim had either from his father or his grandfather.

It is a great dishonor to the name of God for men to give liberty to their passions to rise against the Word. Take heed of passion either while you are hearing the Word or after, like many of you who are discontented with what is said. When you come in company, what a fury are many men in upon hearing some things in the Word that come close to their hearts. Remember when you are hearing the Word that it is that which is above you, and it is not fitting for one who is an inferior to show himself passionate in the presence of a superior. It is true, the ministers may be in as low a condition as you, perhaps lower, but the Word they speak is above all the princes and monarchs upon the face of the earth. And it is fitting, therefore, we having to deal with God, that we should behave ourselves in a meek disposition.

6. The next thing for the sanctifying of God's name in the hearing of the Word is this: we must hear it with a trembling heart. For that you have the famous Scripture in Isaiah 66 beginning, "Thus saith the Lord, 'The heaven is My throne, and the earth is My footstool; where is the house that ye build unto Me, and where is the place of My rest? For all those things hath My hand made, and all those things have been,' saith the Lord, 'but to this man will I look, even to him that is poor, and of a contrite spirit, and trembleth at My Word.'"

This is a most admirable Scripture. Mark how God lifts Himself up in His glory. He is so great a God that "the heaven is My throne, and the earth is My footstool. Where is the house that ye build unto Me?"

But then a poor soul may say, "How shall I be able to stand before this God who is so glorious?"

God says, "Do not be discouraged, poor soul who trembles at My Word, for I look to you."

Observe that God has a regard to that soul who trembles at His Word rather than to any who should build the most sumptuous buildings in the world for Him; for God says here, "The heaven is My throne, and the earth is My footstool; where is the house that ye build unto Me, and where is the place of My rest?" They have built a glorious temple to Me, but what do I regard that? says God. I regard one who trembles at My Word more than that great house which you have built unto Me. It is a notable Scripture to show what a high respect God has to one who trembles at His Word. He regards them more than this glorious temple that was built unto Him.

If you were to build such a place as this was for the service of God, you would think it a great matter. But it is not as highly regarded as if you could bring a trembling heart to God's Word. That's a special thing wherein the sanctifying of the name of God consists: when we come to see the dreadful authority that there is in the Word of God, when we are able to see more of the glory of God in His Word than in all the works of God besides; for there is more of His glory in the Word than there is in the whole of creation of heaven and earth.

Take the sun, moon, and stars. You who are mariners have seen much of the glory of God abroad, that one would think might strike terror into all your hearts; but know that there is more of the dreadfulness of God's name in His Word than in all His works. Psalm 138:2: "Thou hast magnified Thy Word above all Thy name." The Word is magnified above all the name of God whatever; and it is a very good sign of a spiritually enlightened soul when he can see the name of God more magnified in His

Word than in all His works besides.

I appeal to your consciences in this thing. Have you ever seen the name of God to be more magnified in His Word than in all His works? I may with a very good conscience affirm that there is no godly soul upon the face of the earth, who has the weakest degree of grace, but has seen more of the glory of God revealed in His Word than he has seen in all the works of God besides, and his heart is more taken with it. It requires, therefore, a trembling frame of heart when we hear it.

And then further, when it is considered that the Word is that which binds the soul over either to life or death, men's eternal estates are to be cast by the Word, certainly then it requires a trembling heart to hear that by which the eternal estate of man is to be cast. We do not sanctify God's name when we come to hear the Word unless we come with trembling hearts. And they are the most likely of all men and women to understand the mind of God.

As for such as come with conceited spirits, thinking that they understand as much before they came and that their reach of wit or capacity is beyond the capacity of any who shall open the Word unto them (yet that would not be so much if it but only rested upon the man and did not reflect upon the Word itself), now these who are rich in their own thoughts and understandings are sent away empty. But those who come with trembling hearts to the Word are the men who are likely to understand God's counsels revealed in His Word.

In Ezra 10:2–3: "Shechaniah the son of Jehiel, one of the sons of Elam answered and said unto Ezra, 'We have transgressed against our God and have taken strange wives. . . . Yet now there is hope in Israel: concerning this thing, now therefore let us make a covenant with our God according to the counsel of my Lord and of those that tremble at the commandment of our God.' "

So those who tremble at God's Word are such as are most fit to counsel; they understand most of God's mind. And that's another particular of the behavior of the soul in sanctifying God's name in hearing His Word.

7.   The next thing is a humble subjection to the Word that we hear. Our hearts must bow under the Word that we hear. It is a very remarkable Scripture that we have in 2 Chronicles 36:12. There it is said concerning a great king, Zedekiah, "He did that which was evil in the sight of the Lord his God, and humbled not himself before Jeremiah the Prophet, speaking from the mouth of the Lord." It is a very strange expression we have in the book of God, as strange as any we have, that Zedekiah, a great king, should be charged with this as a great sin, that he did not humble himself.

QUESTION. "Humble himself? Before whom?" you will say.
ANSWER. We are bound to humble ourselves before God, but here it is that he did not humble himself before Jeremiah the prophet. Why before the prophet? "Because he spake from the mouth of the Lord." If it is any messenger who speaks from the mouth of the Lord, God expects that we should humble ourselves. So that if any truth comes to be delivered unto you, the Lord expects that you should fall down and yield obedience to it. Whatever your thoughts, your judgments, your opinions have been heretofore, if anything comes in the Word against it, you must submit your judgments, submit your very consciences, you must submit your wills. Whatever your hearts have been set upon, though it has been never so contentful to your spirits before, yet now submit and yield, though it goes never so cross to your minds, your wills, your ends. All must be submitted and laid down flat before the Word so as to be willing to deny

yourselves of anything in the world.

When a man or woman can say, "Lord, it is true, I confess before I heard Thy Word opened in the evidence and demonstration of the Spirit unto me, I was of such a mind, and my heart went after such and such contentments, and I thought it impossible that my heart should ever be taken from them. But, O Lord, Thou hast been pleased to plainly show me by the opening of Thy Word in the evidence of Thy Spirit what Thy mind is. Now, whatever becomes of my name, of my comforts, of my contentments in this world, Lord, here I cast down all before Thee. I submit to Thy Word"—this is a gracious frame. Now is the name of God extolled and lifted up in the hearing of the Word. The name of God is sanctified in such a work of spirit as this.

I have read of a German divine writing to Oecolampadius, another famous German divine. He has this expression, "Oh, let the Word of God come, and though we had 600 necks, we would submit them all to the Word of God."

So should be the temper of those who hear the Word and desire to sanctify God's name in it: "Let God speak and we will submit. Though we have 600 necks, we will submit all we are or have to this Word of the Lord. It is the Word of God that we are willing should triumph over us."

To have a congregation lie down under the Word of God that is preached to them is a most excellent thing, and God's name is greatly sanctified. We do not, brethren, desire that you should lie down under us. We are not only willing, but we are very desirous that you would examine what we speak to you to see whether it is according to the Word of God or not. But if we speak to you that which is the word from the mouth of the Lord, know then that God expects that you should submit your estates, your souls, your bodies, all that you are and have, to this Word. And that is another particular of the sanctifying of the name of God in hearing the Word, there must be a humble submission to it.

8. Another particular wherein the behavior of the soul for the sanctifying of God's name consists is this: the Word must be received with love and joy. It is not enough for you to be convinced of the authority of it and to think thusly, "I must yield to it. This is the Word of God and if I do not yield to it, I must expect the plagues and judgments of God to follow it." That is not enough, but you must yield to it with love and with joy. Unless you receive the Word with love and with joy, it is not sanctified. You do not sanctify God's name, nor is it sanctified unto you.

You must receive the Word not only as the true Word of the Lord, but as the good Word of the Lord. In 2 Thessalonians 2:10, we find it to be the cause of men's being given over to a spirit of delusion, "Because they received not the Word of God in love." It is spoken of Antichrist that at his coming he shall come with all deceit, and he shall prevail with them who perish. Who are they? "They that receive not the love of the truth that they might be saved."

It is not enough, my brethren, to receive the truth that we might be saved, but we must receive the love of the truth if ever we would be saved. Good is the Word of the Lord to my soul, and we must receive it with joy as well as love. Proverbs 2:10: "When wisdom entereth into thy heart, and knowledge is pleasant unto thy soul: then discretion shall preserve thee, understanding shall keep thee."

That is a great matter when the Word reveals some truth to your understanding, and you can so receive it that it should be pleasant to your soul, that your soul rejoices in it. It is a good Word; it is that which does me good at the heart. When a people can hear the Word, and with the Word coming near to them can say, "This Word does me good at the heart; it is pleasant to my soul," that is excellent. In Acts 2:41, the godly are described, those who receive the Word so as to sanctify God's name in it, by this, "they gladly received the Word and were baptized, and the same day there were added unto them about three thousand souls." There were three thousand who gladly received the Word! What an audience Peter had at this time! Then the Word did them good when they gladly received it.

OBJECTION. But it may be said, "We read in Matthew 13 of the stony ground, the hearers who were not good and did not profit by the Word so as to be saved; yet they received the Word with joy. And it is said of Herod that he heard John the Baptist gladly. It seems then that it is not enough to receive it with gladness."

ANSWER. First, there must be more than that which hypocrites may have. If that is wanting, we cannot sanctify God's name.

But you will say, "We must go further or else God's name is not sanctified."

That I confess. Therefore when I speak of gladness and joy, know that I mean another kind of joy than the stony ground had; and so certainly the pleasantness that is spoken of in Proverbs, which I mentioned before, and the gladness that the three thousand received the Word with is different from the gladness of the stony ground.

If you ask me how it differs, I would answer that differs thusly. The gladness of a hypocrite in receiving God's Word arises either from the novelty of it—because it is a new thing and he gets new notions that he did not have before—or else he is joyful from some other carnal excellencies that he finds going together with the Word, some esteem or honor that he shall get by it, some selfishness that there is there that makes his heart to be glad; for there is a great deal of natural and carnal excellency that goes along with the Word many times. But this gladness that is spoken of in Acts and in Proverbs is the gladness that arises from the apprehensions of the spiritual excellencies that there are in the Word, that it is that Word that reveals God and Christ to my soul, that Word that comes nearest to my soul to the mortifying of my lusts and the sanctifying of my heart. What makes me rejoice in the Word is the holiness and spiritual excellency that I see to be in that Word.

"Thy Word is pure," said David, "and therefore doth Thy servant love it and rejoice in it." This no hypocrite can say. "I see the image of God in His Word. I see the very glass of God's holiness in His Word. I feel that in the Word which may bring my soul to God, wherein my soul enjoys communion with God and Jesus Christ—and it is this that gladdens my soul."

If we receive the Word with joy thusly, we shall come to sanctify the name of God in the hearing of it.

9.   If we would sanctify the name of God in His Word, we must receive the Word into honest hearts. This you have in Luke 8:15, in "the Parable of the Sower." You find there that there are divers grounds that receive the Word, and those divers grounds are meant as divers sorts of hearts. There is first the highway ground, that is, such as hear the Word and never regard what they hear; and as soon as they go out of the congregation, the seed of the Word is quite gone, and it is as if they had not heard at all.

And then there is the stony ground and the thorny ground, that is, those who hear with joy (as was spoken before), but the cares of the world choke the seed of the Word. As soon as those cares are gone, they are upon their worldly business and their thoughts and hearts run that way.

But then there is the good ground, that is, those who receive the seed of the Word into a good and honest heart. A good and an honest heart are both joined together. By a good heart is meant a heart that does not have malice in it, a heart that desires to empty itself of everything that is against the Word and that is not suitable to the spirituality of the Word; a heart, I say, that entertains nothing in it that in any way opposes the Word. A good heart is a heart that (as the apostle says in James 1:21, and that place may very well come in here to be opened) is "cleansed from all filthiness and superfluity of naughtiness." The word that is there translated "filthiness" signifies excrements, that which is unclean, that which comes from the body. Such is the sinfulness of your hearts. You come to hear the Word, if it be, with evil hearts. You mingle that very filthiness which is as vile before God as excrements are.

"And superfluity of naughtiness." By that, I take, is meant as if the Holy Ghost should say, "Do not think it is enough to purge away filthiness, that is, notorious, stinking evils, abominable sins, that you do not come with such filthy, vile hearts. But whatever there is in your heart that is in any way against the work of grace is a superfluity of naughtiness, all kinds of evil thoughts and evil affections that are more than needs. Look into your hearts and affections and see whatever you find there that is more than ought to be, running out into anything that they should not. Labor to purge that out," He says, "Do not satisfy yourselves in any kind of evil whatsoever."

It may be that you are cleansed from the notorious evils of the world; but if there remains any naughtiness, any kind of drossiness in your hearts that is not grace, it is to be purged out, for it is superfluity. So that is a good heart that entertains no kind of evil in it. It may be there is some evil, but it desires to purge it out, not only that which is filthy, nasty, and abominable, but if there is anything that should not be there, a good heart is against it. And that is a good heart that is willing to receive anything that God reveals. As we used to say, "Such a man is a good man, that is, you can propound nothing to him that is fit to be done but he is willing to hearken to you."

A good man has no kind of evil ends in him, no evil designs at all, but he is willing to hearken to everything that is good. So a good heart is ready to entertain whatever is good. If it is a good thing, his heart is suitable to it and runs immediately to it. Having a good heart, it immediately closes with the good Word of the Lord.

QUESTION. "But what do you mean by an honest heart?"
ANSWER. By honesty of heart, certainly more is meant than such a one that we call an honest man, that is, a man who is honest in his dealings with his fellow man. There is many a man who is accounted a very honest man in the world, but does not have an honest heart. I beseech you to observe it. That man who has an honest heart before God is one who receives the seed of the Word so that he goes beyond the highway ground, the stony ground, or the thorny ground. He goes beyond those three sorts of professors. He is one who has an eminency in his profession of religion beyond those three.

Now the world accounts many honest men who do not go beyond any of those three. Yes, the world ordinarily accounts any of those three to be honest men. Take the highway ground. Are there not many honest men in the world who do not regard the Word of God at all, but only come to hear a sermon and, as soon as they are done, as it came in one ear, so it goes out the other? I fear there are some men and women who are accounted honest men and women in the world who can hardly give an account of any one sermon they have heard in all their lives. Hardly, I say, but the Word that they heard is immediately taken away from them, and yet these are accounted honest men in the world. But this is not the honest heart that the Scripture speaks of. And there are many who go further than these, who come to hear the Word with joy, and yet they do not have this honest heart. Yes, they may hear the Word and not have this honest heart. By this honest heart I take, therefore, to be meant this: a heart that deals squarely and truly with God, behaving itself in a becoming manner that is suitable to that authority and excellency that there is in the Word of God.

Now, for examples, first, among men, he is accounted an honest man who deals squarely and truly with men in all actions. Such a man, you will say, is an honest man, as honest a man as ever broke bread. That is, he is one who will deal squarely with men not only in one thing, but turn to him in anything and you shall find a proportion between one act and another.

So this is an honest heart, not one who only will be forward for God in some one action wherein he may enjoy himself as well as God, but one who deals squarely with God. Let God put him upon duty, upon any service, God shall find him still to be the same man. Put him upon any easy service (as many will embrace that), or put him upon a difficult service, it is all one if it is the mind of God. You shall find him square in everything. Though he is put upon that in which he is likely to suffer a great deal, yet he goes on according to his principles. An honest heart is one that has received gracious principles and acts accordingly. All the world cannot take him off from his principles of godliness, which the Lord has put into his heart.

Second, an honest man is one who provides things honest before men, who does all things in a seemly way in all those relations that he has with others. That we account as honesty. So when a man's behavior towards the Word is such as becomes the Word of that God with whom he has to deal, then look what excellency, what glory there is in the Word of God. Such a suitable behavior there is in the heart of a man to it; and this is an honest heart. So there are those two things: when a man is square with God in one thing as well as another, and when there is a suitableness to the behavior of the soul to what excellency there is in the Word, when the heart of man will not abuse the Word at all, but behaves itself honestly, according to the gravity, holiness, and weight that there is in the Word. And now with such a good and honest heart, we are to receive the Word if we will sanctify God's name in it.

10. If we will sanctify God's name in the Word, we must hide the Word in our hearts. We must not only hear the Word, but keep it, preserve it, and then we declare that we account the Word of God to be worth something indeed. For what is it to sanctify God but such a behavior towards Him as may testify the excellency of the name of God. So the behavior of the soul in hearing the Word must be such as must give a testimony to the excellency of the Word and manifest the high esteem I have of it.

Now if I received a thing that is of great value, and I slight it and let anybody take it from me, I do not give a testimony to the excellency of that thing. But if I take it and lock it up, and keep it under lock and key, I thereby give a testimony of the esteem that I have of the excellency of that thing. So now when I come to hear the Word and meet with truths that have gotten into my soul, I must close with them and be resolved within my heart as I am hearing them so as to say, "Well, I will keep this truth through God's grace. This concerns me and I will make much of it, and, although I forget other things, yet I hope I shall remember this, to sanctify God's name in hearing the Word."

In Isaiah 42:23 the Holy Ghost says, "Hear for the time to come." When we come to the Word, we must not only hearken for the present. Many of us, while we are hearing, find our hearts stirred for the present. Oh, that we could but have that affection of the heart always as we have when we are hearing the Word!

How many of you have said when you have been hearing such a sermon, "Oh, then I thought I could have gone through fire and water for God!" I only mark it, you must hear for afterwards. And in Psalm 119:11, the prophet David protested that he hid the Word in his heart, that the Word was sweet to him. He said, "Thy Word have I hid in my heart that I might not sin against Thee."

You who come and hear those truths upon the Lord's Day, if you would hide them thusly in your hearts and keep them all the week, they would help you against many of the temptations you meet with. You go about on the weekdays into company, and there you meet with a temptation and it overcomes you. Then you complain, "Alas, I am weak. I have met with a temptation and it has foiled me." But had you hidden the Word in your heart that you heard on the Lord's Day, it would have kept you from the strength of your temptation so that it would not have overcome you.

Those who are truly godly have care to hide the Word in their hearts. When they hear it they think, "This Word shall help me against such and such sins that I am prone to by nature. And when a temptation comes to that sin, I hope I shall have use of the Word that I heard this day."

Suppose you hear a word against passion. Then you should hide that word in your hearts against the time that temptation comes to passion. And when you hear a word against sensuality and the abuse of the creatures, you should hide that word against the coming of that temptation. When you hear a word that speaks of obedience to parents, and servants of duties to governors, now you should hide that word in your hearts against that time. "I have hid Thy Word in my heart that I might not sin against Thee."

You say that you would fain withstand and not be overcome with temptations? Why, here is the way. Hide the Word within you so that you may not sin against Him. And so in Proverbs 2:1, you have a Scripture to the same purpose, about hiding the commandments within us. Then in 1 John 2:4: "I write unto you young men because you are strong, and the Word of God abideth in you and ye have overcome the wicked one." I have written to you young men. You are young; you have strong natures, and so strength of nature for God. But how does this come to pass? "You are strong and the Word of God abideth in you."

Here is an excellent Scripture for all young men. You have your memories fresh, and if you will exercise your memories about anything, it should be in the Word of God. It is a comely and an excellent thing to see young ones having the Word of God abiding in them. So that if you come to them, not only a week, but a month after they have heard the Word, they are able to give you an account of it. I am verily persuaded that there are many young ones in this place who are able to give you old ones, if you ask them, an account of what it is to sanctify God's name in the duties of worship. Why? Because the Word of God abides in them.

It is the honor of young men to have the Word of God abiding in them, and thereby they overcome the wicked one. On the other hand, many young people who come to hear the Word, it may be, are drawn to it by others, or it may be they love to have a walk in the morning, but the Word of God abides not in them; and therefore, when the wicked one comes with temptations the week after, they are overcome by him. But those who have the Word of God abiding in them overcome the wicked one.

So in John 8:31 you have a very remarkable Scripture for the purpose of keeping the Word after we have heard of it: "Then said Jesus to those which believed on Him, 'If you continue in My Word then you are My disciples indeed.' " I beseech you to observe it. It is said that the Jews believed in Christ, and yet Christ said, "If ye continue in My Word *then* are you My disciples." Why, were they not the disciples of Christ who believed in Him?

By this believing, therefore, we must understand some general notion that they had of Christ. They began to think that Christ might be the true Messiah. They had some kind of imperfect believing, but they were not thoroughly brought off. Now Christ says, "If you continue in My Word, you are My disciples." It is as if He should say, "Do not think it enough that you come to hear Me and are taken by what I say. You must continue in My Word, and then you are My disciples."

Christ will not own that man or woman to be His disciple who does not continue in His Word. Oh, that you would consider this, you who satisfy yourselves in having some flashes of affection when you are hearing the Word. Do not think that you are the disciples of Christ because of them. Titus 1:9: "Holding fast the faithful Word as you have been taught." That is, the thing you should labor for is to hold fast the faithful Word. Hold it fast so that it may not be taken away from you, and so you shall come to sanctify the name of God in the hearing of His Word.

11. The last thing that I shall speak to is this: If you would sanctify

the name of God in hearing His Word, turn it into practice or otherwise the name of God is blasphemed, or at least is taken in vain by you if you do not turn what you hear into practice. So you have it in James 1:22: "He that is not a forgetful hearer, but a doer of the Word, this man shall be blessed in his deed." And verse 22: "Be ye doers of the Word, and not hearers only deceiving your own selves."

The word that is translated here "deceiving your own selves," is a word taken from logicians, and signifies to make a false syllogism. A man who hears the Word and does not do it reasons, as it were, thusly, "Those who come to church surely are religious people; but I come to sermons, and therefore I am religious."

Now this is a false reasoning, and you only deceive yourself. Be not a hearer only, but a doer of the Word so that you may not deceive your own soul. So Romans 2:3: "Thinkest thou this O man that judgest them that do such things and doest the same, that thou shalt escape the judgment of God?" It is as if he should say, "You have the Word, and you are able to judge thereby what you hear; but yet you are still wicked in your lives. This is despising the riches of the goodness of God towards you." And in Philippians 2:16 you have a remarkable text where the Holy Ghost said of the Philippians that He would have them "hold forth the Word of life."

It would be a most excellent thing if it might be said of this congregation that as they come diligently to hear and are willing to take pains to get out of their beds so early in the mornings, so all week they hold forth the Word of God. You who are servants, it may be that your masters are evil and the families are evil from whence you come. Now when you go home, though it may be that they will not let you repeat the sermon, yet you are to hold forth the sermon in your practice and conduct.

How the name of God is glorified when we hold forth His Word! This is to let not only your light shine, but the light of the Word shine before men so that they may behold it and glorify your Father who is in heaven.

So put all these eleven particulars together and then you have made good that expression we find in Acts 13:48, "that the Word of God was glorified." And to the same purpose we have another expression in 2 Thessalonians 3:1: "Finally, brethren, pray for us, that the Word of the Lord may have free course, and be gloried even as it is with you."

This is the commendation of a people, that they glorify the Word of God. I beseech you, brethren, in the name of Jesus Christ this morning that you who are hearers of the Word would glorify the Word, and glorify the name of God in the Word. Oh, that not one of you would be a disgrace or shame to the Word of God. This is the charge that God lays upon you if ever you would expect to receive any good from the Word, or to look upon the face of God with comfort whose Word it is. Do not be a shame to His Word and to the ministers of the Word.

Put all these things together, I say, and learn to make conscience of sanctifying God's name in hearing the Word so that there may be none of you who may give any just occasion to others to say, "Is this what it means to hear sermons?" If you should open the mouths of men to say so of you, the Word of God, as much as lies in you, would be disgraced by you. You should rather think thusly, "It would be better for me that I should die, and that I were under the ground and rotting there, than that the Word of God should ever be disgraced by me. Let me hold forth the glory of the Word. The Word is that which has done good to my soul. The Word is that which I would not for ten thousand worlds but have heard it; and shall I disgrace this Word? Shall I give any occasion that this Word of the Lord should be spoken ill of because of me? Oh, God forbid!"

Therefore, if you do not regard yourselves and your own honor, yet regard the honor of the Word. If ever you have gotten any good by the Word, you should go away with this resolution, "Well, I will labor all the days of my life to honor this Word of God that I have gotten so much good by." If this were but the resolution of every one of your hearts this morning, it would be a blessed morning's work.

SERMON X

Why God Will Have His Name Sanctified

"I will be sanctified in them that come nigh Me."

LEVITICUS 10:3

N

ow follow the reasons why God stands so much upon having His name sanctified in the ordinance of hearing His Word.

REASON 1. Because there is so much of God in His Word, therefore we should sanctify God's name. If it were possible that there could be sin in heaven, that sin would be greater than sin committed here. Therefore, the sin of the angels when they were in God's presence in a more special manner was the greater. The name of God being in anything, the greater will be the evil if we do not sanctify God's name in it. Now there is more of God in His Word than in all His works of creation and providence. Psalm 138:2: "Thou hast magnified Thy Word above all Thy name." There being, therefore, so much of God in His Word, we must sanctify the name of God in it.

REASON 2. God has appointed His Word to be the great ordinance to convey the special mercies that He intends for the good of His people. That we spoke to before in the general in showing how the duties of God's worship are as a channel for the conveyance of special good to the saints. But none is more so than the Word; that's the ordinance to convey the first grace to those who belong to God's election. The sacrament is for strengthening, and therefore there is more in the Word than in the sacrament; and yet everyone thinks in conscience that he is bound to come carefully to the sacrament and to sanctify God's name there.

It is an easy matter to convince men and women that they are bound to sanctify the name of God when they come to receive the holy communion more than for the hearing of the Word. They do not think so much of that; but certainly the Word is appointed to be an ordinance of conveying more blessing than the sacrament because it is appointed to convey the first grace, and to convey strength of grace as well as the sacrament. Now being appointed to convey such great things to the soul of the elect, both the first grace and strengthening of grace, comfort, and assistance thereof, the Lord expects to have His name sanctified in it.

3. The name of God must be sanctified in the Word because the Word is very quick and lively. It works men or women to life or death, to salvation or damnation. Hebrews 4:12: "The Word of God is quick and powerful, and sharper than any two-edged sword, piercing even to the dividing asunder of soul and spirit." It is very quick of operation, the text says. That is, when God has to deal with men by His Word, He will not stand dallying and trifling with them; but He is very quick with them, either to bring their souls to life or to cast them away. "The time of men's ignorance God winks at, but now He calls all men to repent" (Acts 17:30).

Let them look to it now, God did forbear in the time of ignorance, but He will not forbear so when the Word comes.

"Now is the axe laid to the root of the tree." And when was that? When John the Baptist came to preach repentance because the kingdom of heaven was at hand. Though the tree was barren before and did not bring forth good fruit, yet it might stand still and not be cut down; but when the powerful ministration of the Word comes, then the axe is laid to the root of the tree. Either come in now and be saved, or resist the Word and perish. And therefore that is very observable when Christ sends out His disciples to preach in Mark 16:15–16. He says, "Go ye into all the world and preach the gospel to every creature, and he that believeth and is baptized shall be saved; but he that believeth not shall be damned."

It is as if He should say, "There shall be quick work made with them. Go and preach, and those who belong to My election shall be brought in to believe and be saved, and the others shall be damned."

It is as if God should say, "If they will come in and embrace the gospel, they shall be saved. If they will not, they shall be damned, and there is the end of them."

So I say that we have need to look to it that we sanctify the name of God in His Word upon these three grounds, because there is so much of God in His Word, because He has appointed it to convey the greatest mercies unto His saints, and because God is very quick in His Word one way or another.

APPLICATION

USE OF REPREHENSION. This is to all those who do not sanctify God's name in hearing the Word. And herein we shall show their fearful condition, and how God will sanctify His name upon them in ways of judgment. And then when we come

to the use of exaltation, to exhort you to sanctify the name of
God, there we shall show you likewise how God will sanctify His
name in ways of mercy upon those that sanctify Him in ways of
obedience in hearing His Word.

1. Certainly if to sanctify the name of God is that which we
have spoken of, God's name is very little sanctified by people
who come to hear His Word. We have no cause to wonder that
so little is gotten by the Word because there are so few who
make conscience to sanctify God's name in hearing it. There are
some who are so far from sanctifying God's name in it that they
altogether neglect it and make it a matter of nothing whether
they come to hear it or not. Christ said in John 8:47, "He that is
of God heareth My Word; ye therefore hear them not because
ye are not of God." Certainly he who has the knowledge of God
and any interest in God, he who belongs to Him, nothing is
more sweet to him than hearing His Word. But because you are
not of God, Christ says, therefore you do not hear His Word.

Those men and women who have no interest in God, but
live without God in this world, do not regard to hear His Word.
Oh, how many we have who belong to this place who do so! How
many live without God in the world and declare to all the world
that they are not of God! They have no part nor portion in God
in that they do not hear His Word. There are some who come
to hear it, but they come to hear it as a matter of indifference,
in a mere formal and customary way, for company's sake or to
satisfy others. These are poor and low ends. You should come
to hear the Word expecting that God will speak to your soul for
the furtherance of your external good; but your consciences
may tell you what vain and wandering hearts you have when
you come to hear it.

"The eyes of the fool," Solomon said, "are in all the corners
of the earth," wandering up and down, little minding that you
have come to hear God Himself speak to you in the ministry of

man. And if so be that it is minded, yet ordinarily the hearts of men put off the Word; and if it comes near to anything they do, then they shift it from themselves to others. We have a notable Scripture in Hebrews 12:25 for such men as shift off God's Word when it comes near to them: "See that ye refuse not Him that speaketh, for if they escaped not who refused Him that spake on earth, much more shall not we escape, if we turn away from Him which speaketh from heaven."

See that you do not refuse him who speaks the Word; see that you do not put him off. And that this is the significance of it, if you compare it with Luke 12:18, you shall find that there the same word is used where, speaking of those who were invited to the supper, it is said, "They all with one consent began to make excuse." They began to shift it off, that is the same word. Oh, take heed of this, that when you are hearing the Word and Christ comes and speaks to your hearts, and you begin to think that it may concern you, and your consciences begin to stir, take heed that you do not shift Him off. Take heed that you do not put away the Word from you by any kind of pretense whatsoever.

It may be that you will say, "If I were certain it was the Word of God and that God spoke to me, God forbid but that I should submit to it."

But though it may be that the hearts of men are not so notoriously rebellious as to resolve to sin against the Word, which they will acknowledge to be the Word of God, yet this is the deceit of the heart. When the heart has no mind to obey, it will shift off the Word and have pretenses and put-offs. Oh, take heed that you do not shift off Him who speaks from heaven by making any kind of excuse whatsoever. But when you hear, if the Word of God comes to your conscience, do not listen to the vain reasonings that are against it.

There are others who cannot tell how to shift off the Word, but it will come upon them when they are hearing it. It may be that they are a little stirred, but it is immediately gone so that they are far from holding the Word, far from keeping it in their hearts. Oh, how many of you have been stirred when you have been hearing the Word! And how happy it would have been for you if you had hidden those words in your heart that the Lord has spoken to you in the ministry of it. If you had but the invitations of the Spirit now that you have sometimes had, how happy would it be for you? But it is with many in hearing the Word as it is with you mariners when you go abroad. Your friends come with you, take their leave of you, and then you see them stand upon the shore for a while. But when you sail a little further, your friends are out of sight and then you only see the shore. You sail on a little further and then you only see the houses. You sail a little further and then you only see the steeples and the high places. You sail yet a little further and then you see nothing but the ocean.

So it is in hearing the Word. It may be when you go home there are some things that are fresh in your minds, but on Monday mornings you have lost some. But then there are some others who yet present themselves before you and then you lose more and more until you have lost sight of all. All truths are gone; you see no more of the Word, and it is as if you had never heard it. This is not to sanctify God's name. You should treasure up the Word as the richest treasure that may be.

Another sort to be rebuked are those who are so far from falling down before the Lord to receive the Word with meekness that they can bless themselves in their wicked ways, notwithstanding the Word coming and meeting with them. I only name this because of that notable Scripture we have in Deuteronomy 29:18–19 where Moses said to them, "Take heed, lest there should be among you a root that beareth gall and wormwood." What is that root that bears gall and wormwood? "And it come to pass when he heareth the words of this curse, that he bless himself in his heart, saying, 'I shall have peace, though I walk in the imagination of my heart.'"

Take heed that there is not among you a root that bears gall and wormwood. This is a bitter root in men's hearts when they can rise against the Word of God and have their hearts rise against it, and think to themselves that there is no such matter, that these are but mere words, but mere winds. "Let the minister say what he will and talk as long as he will, I will go on in my way. I will do well enough. What he says is only his opinion."

I say, when men can bless themselves thus in their way, and when there is such tumultuous gall and wormwood, take heed of it. It will quickly bring forth bitter fruit one day. But I should be quickly prevented if I should launch into this argument to reprove the several ways of sinning against God in the hearing of His Word. And therefore I leave those and come to show what a fearful thing it is for men and women not to sanctify the name of God in hearing His Word, so that you may see that God will have His name sanctified upon them.

THE DANGERS OF NOT SANCTIFYING THE NAME OF GOD IN HEARING HIS WORD

1. You who do not sanctify God's name in hearing His Word in those ways that have been opened to you lose the greatest and happiest opportunity for good that ever creatures had for an outward opportunity. Indeed, when God moves by His Spirit, if that is neglected, that opportunity is more than merely hearing

the Word but otherwise, unless it is at such a time when God adds His Spirit together with His Word, I say, you who are cast by the providence of God in such a place where the Word of the gospel is preached to you, applied and urged upon you, if you do not sanctify the name of God to hear as you ought, and profit by it, you lose the greatest opportunity for good that there is in the world! Oh, what have you lost who have lived many years under the ministry of the gospel and yet have not been acquainted with this mystery of godliness in sanctifying God's name in the Word!

There are many thousands of souls who are and shall be blessing God to all eternity for what of God they have met with in the Word; but you have sat under it stupid as a block, dead and barren, and no good has been done. "Wherefore is there a prize in the hand of a fool, and he hath no heart to get wisdom?" The loss of such an opportunity will lie heavily upon you one day.

2. Know that this Word that is appointed by God for the conveyance of so much mercy to His elect will prove to be the greatest aggravation of your sin that can be. "This is the condemnation, that light is come into the world and men love the darkness rather than the light." This is *the* condemnation. If that light had not come among you, then the condemnation would not have been so great. Your sin would not have been so great and your punishment would not have been so great. Matthew 10:14–15 says, speaking of those who enjoyed the Word and yet did not sanctify God's name in it, "Whosoever shall not receive you nor hear your words, when ye depart out of that house or city, shake the dust off your feet. Verily I say unto you, it shall be more tolerable for the land of Sodom and Gomorrah in the day of judgment than for that city."

It is a most dreadful Scripture. Their very dust must be shaken off in token of indignation, and it shall be more easy for the land of Sodom and Gomorrah that was consumed by fire from heaven, and that now suffers the vengeance of eternal fire (Jude 7). Certainly they shall not be so deep in judgments as those who live under the ministry of the Word and do not sanctify the name of God in it. Your sin is of a deeper dye than the sins of the heathens, yes, and in some respects than the sin of the devils. They never had the Word of the gospel sent to be preached to them. And therefore this will aggravate your sin not only beyond heathens, but beyond devils. Look to it, then, that God's name is sanctified in the hearing of His Word.

3.   Know that as much as the Word is rejected, Jesus Christ is rejected. Luke 10:16: "He that despiseth you despiseth Me, and he that despiseth Me despiseth Him that sent Me." It is Christ Himself who is rejected when the Word is rejected. You do not have to do with man as much as with Jesus Christ in the hearing of the Word. And the power of Jesus Christ is to be put forth either to do good by the Word or to avenge your neglect of the Word. Therefore, in Matthew 28:18–19, when Christ sends His disciples forth to preach, He makes this preface: "All power is given unto Me in heaven and earth; go ye therefore and teach."

It is as if He should say, "I, having received all power in heaven and earth through the power I received, send you to preach; and I'll be with you to the end of the world." That is, all power in heaven and earth shall go along with you to assist your ministry, either for the good of those who shall embrace it or for the misery of those who shall reject it. So that whoever stands out against the ministry of the Word stands out against all the power in heaven and earth that is given to Christ. Do not think that you resist a poor, weak, mortal man. You are resisting all the power in heaven and earth. And is this not a dreadful thing, then, to be guilty of not sanctifying God's name?

4. It argues an extreme hardness of heart not to be worked upon by the Word. Luke 16:31: "If they hear not Moses and the prophets, neither will they be persuaded though one rose from the dead." Certainly, that man or woman who shall not be worked upon by the Word so as to sanctify God's name in it, I say to such, if one should rise from the dead, they would not have their hearts worked upon; and therefore they are much less likely to be worked upon by afflictions. It may be that some of you think that you will repent when you are on your sick beds. No, surely, if that which is the great ordinance to bring men to God shall not work upon you so that God shall be honored in it, you cannot expect that sickness and affliction should do it. No, if one should come from the dead to tell you of all the miseries that were there, certainly if the Word does not work upon you, that will not do it.

But you will say, "One would think that there should be more power to work upon the heart."

Truly no, because that is not as great an ordinance appointed by God for working such great works upon the hearts and consciences of men as the Word is. It is true, the Word is but a weak thing in itself, but here lies the strength, that it is an ordinance of God appointed to work upon the hearts of men. Therefore, if this does not work upon you to give God glory in hearing it, there is no other means likely to do it.

5. When the Word does not work upon men it is a dreadful sign of reprobation. "If our gospel be hid," said the apostle, "it is hid to those that are lost." It is a dreadful argument that here is a lost creature, one to whom God intends no good. One the Lord

works upon, perhaps He lets another pass; one in a family and not in another. Now where it is so that the Word does not work, I say, there is no such dreadful brand of reprobation as this. It is true that we cannot give any certain sign of reprobation, therefore I cannot say of any man that he now has such a mark upon him that evidently proves that he is a reprobate. We cannot tell that because we do not know what God may do afterwards, but we may say this, it is as dreadful a sign as any.

There are no more dreadful signs than these two. First, for a man to be suffered to prosper in a final course, for God to let men go on and have their heart's desire satisfied in an ungodly way. And then, second, for the Lord to leave them to themselves so that the ministry of the Word shall not work upon them, that they shall be, by God's providence, so disposed of as to live under a faithful and powerful ministry and that it should not work upon them. These are the two blackest signs of reprobation; and therefore it is a most dreadful thing to sit under the ministry of the Word and not to sanctify God's name in it.

6. Surely there can be nothing sanctified to you who do not sanctify God's name in His Word. The Scripture says that everything is sanctified by the Word and prayer. How can you expect that the Word should sanctify anything unto you, seeing that you do not make conscience of sanctifying God's name in the Word? The godly think thusly: "'Tis the Word that must sanctify all things to my soul; and I need, then, to sanctify God's name in that from which I expect the sanctified use of all blessings." You, therefore, who can sit under it and not make conscience of sanctifying God's name in it, I say you cannot expect the sanctified use of anything that you have in this world.

7. Such as do not sanctify God's name in the Word are very

nigh to a curse. There is a notable Scripture for this in Hebrews 6:7–8, where the apostle compares the Word to the rain that falls upon the ground: "For the earth that drinketh in the rain that cometh oft upon it, and bringeth forth herbs meet for them by whom it is dressed receiveth blessing from God: but that which beareth thorns and briers is rejected and is nigh unto cursing, whose end is to be burned."

The meaning is plainly this: the rain here is the Word, and the good hearers are like the ground that receives the rain, brings forth fruit, and receives a blessing. But ill hearers who do not sanctify God's name in His Word are like the ground that receives the rain as much as the other, hears as many sermons as the other, but they bring forth nothing but thorns and briars. And mark what a dreadful expression is against that ground. First, it is rejected; second, it is nigh to cursing; and, third, its end is to be burned.

You reject the Word, do you? The Lord rejects your soul. If you have no need of the Word, the Word has no need of you. It is a dreadful thing to be rejected by God, and then you are "nigh unto cursing" (Hebrews 6:8). It may be that the Lord, for a time, will withdraw Himself from the soul and manifest that it is, as it were, rejected; but yet the soul does not have the curse of God upon it where God says, "Well, let this soul perish forever!"

But there are some who are under an actual curse, and God says, "Well, My Word shall never do good to this soul. Such a one has sat under it this long and has rejected it. My Word shall never do good to him."

It is like the place in Luke 14 where those made excuses when they were invited to the supper. The text says that "the master of the feast was angry," which was God Himself who invited them by the gospel to partake of His Son; and when men would not come in, but made excuses and refused the offer of the gospel, "Verily none of those men that were bidden shall taste of My supper." They shall never partake of any good of the gospel. This is a dreadful curse. May the Lord deliver you from having this curse pronounced against you; but I beseech you to tremble at this Scripture in Hebrews, "they are nigh to cursing."

Who knows how nigh some soul in this place may be to this curse, for God has to say, "This soul has often been invited, and yet has made excuses and put everything off. He shall never taste of My supper, of the good things in Jesus Christ. The Word that has been so rejected shall never do them good again."

It would be better that you had never been born than to have this curse actually upon you. Oh, fear and tremble lest your condition be such as to be nigh to cursing! Who knows what a day, a week may bring forth? It may be that the Lord may spare and be willing to pass by the neglect of former sermons. But who knows what the next actual rebellion against the Lord in His Word may do to bring the curse upon you? And then, if so, the next part of the verse will prove to be your portion: "Whose end is to be burned." Oh! It is a dreadful thing to sin against the Word. God stands much upon it.

8.   Know that if God's name is not sanctified in it, the end that God has appointed it for will be turned quite contrary to you. The proper end that God has appointed His Word for is to save souls, but now, where God's name is not sanctified, it is turned quite contrary. So the apostle says in 2 Corinthians 2:16, "To the one we are the savor of death unto death, and to the other the savor of life unto life." It is a dreadful thing that the good Word of God, in which there are such treasures of God's mercy, wherein the counsels of God concerning man's eternal estate

come to be revealed, should prove to be the savor of death unto death to your soul; that is, to have such an efficacy in it as to kill them by the very scent of it, as it were, as some things have such a poison in them that the very scent is enough to poison someone.

So, the apostle says, to some our word has that efficacy, being turned quite to the contrary end. Some souls are saved, and are and shall be blessing God to all eternity for the Word; and your soul is damned by the Word so that you will hereafter curse the time that you ever came to hear it. That will be a dreadful thing, that the same Word that others shall be blessing God eternally in heaven for, you shall be cursing eternally in hell for. It will be turned quite to the contrary end. If it does not work in the right way, it will work the other. The truth is, it hardens men's hearts if it does not bring them to God.

There is nothing that hardens the hearts of men more than the ministry of the Word—yet by accident, not by itself. There are no men in the world who have such hard hearts as those who are wicked under the ministry of the Word. It is not only an argument that their hearts are hard, but they are hardened by it. That Scripture in Isaiah 6:9–10 is remarkable for this, particularly because I find it so often quoted by Christ. I think it is quoted three or four times in the gospels. "And He said, 'Go and tell this people, "Hear ye indeed, but understand not; and see ye indeed, but perceive not." Make the heart of this people fat, and make their eyes heavy, and shut their eyes, lest they see with their eyes, and hear with their ears, and understand with their heart, and convert and be healed.' "

This is a strange Scripture. What, must a prophet go to them to make their hearts fat and to shut their eyes? Why, the Word is appointed to open men's eyes. But here the prophet is sent to shut their eyes that they may not be converted. This is dreadful; this is for the punishment of some former neglect of the Word of God sent unto His people. Above all judgments, you should be afraid of this. It is not so bad that a fire should be upon your houses as that God should make His Word to be a means to harden your hearts.

In Ezekiel 14:4 we have a dreadful expression to this purpose by the prophet, where the Lord said that the people came to inquire of Him with their idols in their hearts. But God said, "I will answer them according to their idol." If men come to the ministry of the Word with their beloved sins, and resolve that they will not part with them, the Lord, many times, in His just judgment, suffers some things in the Word to be accidentally a means to harden them in that sin of theirs. "I will answer them according to their idol." Those men are in a dreadful estate whose hearts come to be hardened by the Word.

9. If you do not sanctify God's name in hearing the Word, what comfort can you ever have by the Word in the day of your affliction? Certainly, when the day of your affliction comes, then there is nothing that can comfort you but the Word. "Unless Thy law had been my delight," said David, "I should then have perished in mine affliction." But you, having been exercised in the Word so much and God's name not sanctified, must not expect to have your soul comforted in the day of your affliction. It is no marvel, then, that though the Word has been applied again and again to your hearts, nothing would stick.

I remember an expression of one who was in a great deal of terror of conscience. Many came to apply comfortable Scriptures to him; and he, for a while, took those Scriptures and laid them upon his heart to pacify his troubled conscience. But a little before he died, he cried out with a most fearful terror, "There is a plaster made, but it will not stick on, it will not stick on." And so he died despairing.

So there is in the Word such a plaster as may help a wounded and troubled conscience. But can you expect, who have not sanctified God's name in your lifetime, that it shall stick upon your soul in the day of your affliction? Never expect it, for the Lord has said otherwise in Proverbs 1, "Because when I cried and called ye would not hear, you shall cry and call and I will not hear."

The Lord in His Word cries to you, "O you sinful souls who are going on in the ways of sin and eternal destruction, return, return. That is the way that will bring you to eternal miseries; but here is the way that will bring you to life and eternal salvation." Thus the Lord cries and calls today and you stop your ear. Oh, how just it is with God to stop His ear from your crying and calling in the day of affliction.

10. Further, know, you who do not sanctify the name of God in His Word, that all the Word of God will be made good one day unto you. God has His time to magnify His Law and to make it honorable (Isaiah 42:21). You slight God's law, you slight His Word and despise it, but God will magnify it and make it honorable. There is not any sentence that you have heard in the Word but it shall be made good, whatever becomes of your soul. You think that God is a merciful God and He will not damn you; but though God is merciful and has regard to His creatures, yet the Lord has ten thousand times more regard to His Word than to all the souls of men and women in the world—and God will stand to make that good. He will not have such regard to that wretched, vile, sinful soul of yours so as not to honor His Word. He will honor His Word whatever becomes of you; and all that you have heard and rejected shall be made good upon you one day.

11. Again, the Word that you reject and sin against shall be the Word that shall judge you (John 12:48). Look to it as well as you will. This Book of God out of which we preach, and those truths that we delivered to you from this Word, must be called over again at the great day to judge your souls by. The sentence of every one of your eternal estates must be tried out of this book. Oh, look upon it as the Word that must judge your souls at the last day, and then you will see it to be a dreadful thing not to sanctify God's name in it. And then when the Word judges you, you shall obey it whether you want to or not. Now the Word convinces you and you will not obey it, but when God comes to judge you by the Word, then you shall obey it. Then when God comes to read that sentence out of the Word, "Go ye cursed into everlasting fire," then, I say, you shall be forced to obey it.

12. There is yet one more thing (that I should have mentioned before) that is very remarkable. Those men who do not sanctify God's name in His Word will be cursed, even here while they live. Their parts and common gifts that they have will be cursed, wither, and come to nothing. We find ordinarily that many who are young and had very good beginnings, very good parts, who were very hopeful and would speak favorably when they came afterwards, began by degrees to neglect the Word, and the Lord has cursed them. Their gifts have withered; the common gifts of the Spirit have been taken from them.

I will give you one text for that in Luke 8:18: "Take heed therefore how ye hear." (It is an exhortation that follows upon the Parable of the Sower who went out to sow.) It is so that when the Word is sown as seed, there is so little of it that prospers, and most hearers do not sanctify God's name in it. Therefore, look to yourselves. Why? "For whosoever hath, to him shall be given; and whosoever hath not, from him shall be taken even that which he seemeth to have." You need to look to yourselves how you hear, for, the truth is, all depends upon it under God.

Have you got any common gifts of the Spirit of God, or any abilities to do any service for God? Do not be proud of them, neither be jolly, nor think that you are able to do better than others, and that those are but ordinary things that the minister speaks while you are in a higher frame. Look to yourselves. Take heed that you do not come to the Word with a proud spirit. Do not be offended at the plainness of the Word. Take heed how you hear, for if you do not, that which you seem to have shall be taken from you, Christ says.

You seem to have excellent gifts, yes. You seem to have grace, too. But take heed how you hear for all this. Whatever parts you have, though you are highly esteemed in the company where you come and are able to do things more than others, yet take heed how you hear; for otherwise that which you have will be taken away from you. Have we not seen this in our own experience? It is apparent that some among us began to be withered and to be cursed by neglecting the Word. And therefore I beseech you to look to this, that you sanctify the name of God in His Word and let your hearts bow unto it as the ordinance of God, and wait upon it in the ministry of it lest you wither and be cursed and come to nothing.

USE OF EXHORTATION. I shall be very brief here. Oh, that the Lord by this would cause something to stick upon your hearts. That which has been preached in this point may be made useful for many sermons afterwards! May it be said of you in this place as was said of them in Acts 13:48, "When the Gentiles heard this they were glad, and glorified the Word of the Lord, and as many as were ordained to eternal life believed!" Oh, that God would make every one of you to be a means to glorify the Word of God! That should be our care, that the Word of God may be glorified by us.

We come to hear the Word, but take heed that the Word of God is not dishonored by us. In 2 Thessalonians 3:1: "Finally, brethren, pray for us that the Word of the Lord may have free course and be glorified, even as it is with you." Oh, that we were able to say so! And yet, through God's mercy, in some degree we hope we can say so, and I could heartily pray that the Word of God might be glorified in all places as it has been with many of you.

But yet go on in this and labor, every one of you, that it may be more glorified, that you may manifest the power of the Word in your conduct, that all who behold you may glorify the Word and say, "Oh, what has the Lord wrought in such a place, in such families, families that were wretched, vile, carnal, and lived without God in the world, profane, swearers, foul-mouthed, unclean. Now since they have attended upon the Word, how has it worked upon them! What a change is there in such men and women!"

I pray that the carnal husband may say, "Since such time as my wife has attended upon the Word, I have seen such a beauty in her conduct. She is more holy, more gentle and meek, and my servant is more submissive and faithful, my children more obedient than before." Oh, that the Word may thus be glorified.

Take heed, I beseech you, that the Word is not blasphemed by any of you. In Titus 2:5, the apostle gives divers exhortations to wives and to servants: "To be discreet, chaste, keepers at home, good, obedient to their own husbands, that the Word of God may not be blasphemed." You must perform your duties unto your husbands. And why? That the Word of God may not be blasphemed, that is, that neither your husbands nor any of your friends may blaspheme the Word and say, "What, do you get this by going to sermons?" Oh, it should pierce your hearts when your consciences tell you that you may have given cause whereby the Word of God would be blasphemed. And so the apostle exhorts servants and others, and all in the strength of this argument, "that the Word of God be not blasphemed." You get up early in the morning to hear the Word. That's good, but take heed that you give no occasion that the Word be blasphemed.

Now I shall show what an excellent thing it is to sanctify God's name in the hearing of His Word so as to honor it, and how God will sanctify His own name in mercy to you.

1. First, all the good in the Word is yours if you sanctify God's name. There is an abundance of good in this Word that we preach. It is the Word of the gospel, and to have all the good in that to be yours must be an excellent thing. You will say, "Sometimes I read and hear such things in the Word that, if I were but sure that these things were my portion, how happy I would be!"

Here's one sign by which you may be assured that they are all your portion. Is it your unfeigned care to sanctify God's name in hearing His Word? Oh, peace be to you! All the good in the Word is yours. And here we might fall into a commendation of the Word of the gospel, and, if I should give way to that, a great deal of time would quickly be gone. I will only give you one Scripture to encourage you to sanctify God's name in hearing His Word by way of commendation of it. It is Romans 10:5 (a place I am afraid you have not had the sweetness of for lack of understanding it), and it is quoted out of Deuteronomy: "For Moses describeth the righteousness which is of the Law, that the man which doth these things shall live by them. But the righteousness which is of faith speaketh on this wise, 'Say not in thine heart who shall ascend into heaven, that is, to bring Christ down from above, or who shall descend into the deep, that is, to bring Christ again from the dead?' But what saith it? 'The word is nigh thee, even in thy mouth and in thy heart, that is the word of faith which we preach.' "

The text has some difficulty and yet is exceedingly sweet to us to know it. I confess that if the Apostle Paul had not quoted this place out of Deuteronomy and thus interpreted it, who could have ever thought in reading Deuteronomy that by the one was meant the word of the Law, and by the other the word of the gospel? Therefore, the meaning is this: here is a comparison between the word of the Law and the word of the gospel. Concerning the word of the Law there are two things wherein it comes short of the word of the gospel:

First, it is not so nigh unto you.

Second, it is not so certain to assure your soul what shall become of you to all eternity. "The word of the Law saith, 'Who shall ascend into heaven.' " But the word of the gospel "is nigh thee even in thy mouth and in thy heart."

QUESTION. You will say, "Why is not the word of the Law as nigh to one as the word of the gospel?"

ANSWER. The word of the Law you hear in your ears, but it is not written in the heart as the word of the gospel is. The Law cannot work savingly upon the heart of a man to bring salvation. Those who are merely legal can hear the duties that are required, but that word has no power to write in their hearts what they hear. But when you come to hear the word of the gospel that is near to you, even in your very hearts as well as in your ears, God speaks in it; and it comes into your hearts and there it works efficaciously, which the Law cannot do.

The Law is but a dead letter in comparison to the word of the gospel. If you come merely to the Law to hear the Law preached, and not in an evangelical way, you may hear it a hundred times and it will never be written in your hearts. But when you come to hear the gospel in an evangelical way, that will come to be written in your hearts, so that the word of the gospel is nigh unto you.

QUESTION. But what is the meaning of the other, "Say not, who shall ascend up into heaven?"

ANSWER. The meaning is this. It is as if the apostle should say, "The truth is, while you have no other but the righteousness of the Law, you are at an infinite uncertainty about your eternal estates. The Law says, 'Do this and live,' but you can never know when you have done enough to be certain that you are well for eternity. It says, 'Who shall ascend into heaven' to know the mind of God concerning me, whether He will accept me and the obedience I tender up to Him? 'Who shall go down into the deep?' In other words, who shall go down to hell to know whether that place is prepared for him or not?" It is a phrase that only expresses an uncertainty that one cannot be satisfied about his eternal estate unless he could go to heaven and there see and read God's Book, and so discover God's mind concerning him, or go down to hell and so know whether that place is appointed for him or not. Unless I can do one of these, I cannot tell (merely by the Law) whether I shall go to heaven or hell.

You who are merchants and dealers abroad, you have a great deal of uncertainty as to what shall become of your estates. Indeed, if I could send one over to the Indies to tell me how my ship was prospering, then I could be certain; then I could hear whether I was a rich man or not—but unless I can do such a thing, I am uncertain.

This is the expression here. It is as if a poor soul should say, "I would gladly be saved, and I am loath to perish eternally." But all the while the soul remains under the Law, it remains in an uncertain condition. But now, says Paul, the word of the gospel is nigh unto you, even in your heart. And this is the word that we preach, the word that says in Romans 10:9, "If thou shalt confess with thy mouth the Lord Jesus, and shalt believe in thine heart that God hath raised Him from the dead, thou shalt be saved."

It is as if Paul should say, "This word of the gospel that has come into your heart assures your soul of your eternal estate, so that though you cannot go up to heaven nor go down to hell, yet you have that in your heart which assures you that you shall be eternally saved, as if you were able to go up to the highest heavens and fetch news from there."

Oh, how we should prize the good word of the gospel and keep it in our hearts! For that in our hearts will assure us of our salvation to all eternity, and of God's eternal purpose to do the good in heaven. You would account it a great happiness if there could be any way to send abroad to the Straits or other places to know how things fare with you. But if you have the word of the gospel within you, if that prevails in your soul, you always have something in your heart that will tell you how things are with you in heaven and what shall become of you for all eternity. Oh, who would not sanctify the name of God in hearing His Word, seeing it is such a blessed Word wherein the gospel is opened with more clarity than it has been to many of our forefathers?

2. It is certain evidence of your election. We read in 2 Thessalonians 1:3–5: "Remembering without ceasing your work of faith, and labor of love, and patience of hope in our Lord Jesus Christ, in the sight of God and our Father, knowing brethren,

beloved, your election of God," Why? "For our gospel came not to you in word only, but also in power, and in the Holy Ghost, and in much assurance."

This excellency there is in sanctifying God's name in hearing the Word. I beseech you, mark it. It is a more blessed thing than if you bore Jesus Christ in your wombs. You who are women, would you not have accounted it a great happiness if Christ had been borne in your wombs? Now if you come to the hearing of the Word and sanctify God's name in it, you are in a better condition, and have a greater blessing upon you, than if you had borne Jesus Christ in your womb. Luke 11:27–28: "And it came to pass as He spake these things, that a certain woman of the company lifted up her voice and said unto Him, 'Blessed is the womb that bare Thee, and the paps which Thou hast sucked.'"

Seeing Christ and what gracious things came from Him, she spoke this way. But He said, "Yea, rather blessed are they that hear the Word of God and keep it." That is, "Labor to sanctify My name." That woman is blessed who does so more than the woman who bore Christ.

I think this one Scripture should be such a Scripture for women to cause them to sanctify God's name in hearing the Word more than a hundred Scriptures. Certainly, you may be so blessed if you will believe the Word that comes from Christ's mouth.

3. Do you sanctify the name of God in the Word? That will sanctify you. By that your souls come to be sanctified. It will comfort you in the last day of your affliction and it will save you at last.

4. You who sanctify God's name in hearing His Word will be

the glory of the ministers of God at the great day of judgment. You will be an honor to them before the Lord, His saints, and His angels. Philippians 2:6 speaks of "holding forth the Word of life." That is the duty of all the hearers of the Word: they must hold forth the Word of life. When you go home, you must hold forth the power of the Word you hear. Well, what will become of that? "That I may rejoice in the day of Christ, that I have not run in vain, neither labored in vain."

Let that be one motive among the rest, says the apostle. "This will be such a glory to me that in the day of Jesus Christ I shall rejoice that I have not labored in vain. I shall bless God for all my studies and care, and all my pains that I have ever taken, and for venturing myself for this people. I shall bless God in the day of Jesus Christ."

Would it not be a comfortable thing to you that all the ministers of God who come to preach the Word faithfully to you, if at the day of Jesus Christ you should hear them blessing God that ever He sent them to preach the gospel in such a place, and you should hear them say, "O Lord, it may be had I been sent to another place I would have spent all my strength in vain, but, through Thy mercy I was sent to a teachable people who were ready to embrace Thy Word. Oh, this is my crown and glory!"

Would it not do good to any whose hearts are faithful to think this, that their holding forth the Word of life will not only be a glory to God, which is chief, but it will be a glory to the ministers, to recompense all their labors, that you shall not only be saved yourselves in the day of Jesus Christ, but you shall add to the glory of His faithful ministers likewise when they appear before Christ?

5. I shall add one more particular. There is a time coming

when God shall magnify His Word before men and angels. In Isaiah 22:21, He will magnify His Law and make it honorable. What a joy it shall be to you when the Lord, before men and angels, shall come to magnify His Word and make it honorable, and for you to think, "This is the Word that spoke to my heart at such and such a time. This is the Word that I reverenced, that I obeyed, that I loved, that I made to be the joy of my heart."

This Word the Lord now magnifies and makes to be honorable. This will be comfortable to your soul.

SERMON XI

Sanctifying the Name of God in Receiving the Sacrament

"I will be sanctified in them that come nigh Me."

LEVITICUS 10:3

ow first for the word "sacrament." I confess that we do not have that word in all the Scripture. Neither do we have the word "Trinity," or divers other words that ministers make use of to set forth the mysteries of religion by. Yet it is useful to consider the meaning why ministers in the church have given this name unto those signs and seals that the church receives. "Sacrament" is to hallow a thing or to dedicate, because in the sacraments there are outward things that are made holy, for holy and spiritual ends. We ourselves, as it were, hallow or dedicate ourselves unto God in the use of these ordinances. That's one reason from hence it has the name.

Others have it *sacramentum,* because it is to be received *sacramente,* with a holy mind; and therefore it is called the sacrament. The churches have used it for a long time. In Tertullian's time, which was more than fourteen hundred years ago, he was the first we have found who used this word; and most who would open the word unto us say that it was taken from the

213

practice of soldiers who, when they came and enlisted, bound themselves in a solemn oath to be faithful to their captain and the cause they were to undertake. The oath they took they were accustomed to calling *sacramentum*, a sacrament.

Now in that regard, when Christians come to this ordinance, they come to seal a covenant with God; and though they do not formally and explicitly take an oath, yet they bind themselves in a holy covenant that has the strength of an oath in it (for a solemn promise to the high God has the strength of an oath in it), and from this they were called by this name, "sacraments." That is for the word so that you may understand it. But the word the Scripture uses to set out this sacrament I am now speaking of is the communion of the body and blood of Christ. So you have it in 1 Corinthians 10:16: "The cup of blessing which we bless, is it not the communion of the blood of Christ? The bread which we break, is it not the communion of the body of Christ?" I say, we are now treating this point as to how we are to sanctify the name of God in that which the Scripture calls the communion of the body and blood of Christ. And for the opening of that, first, we must know that this is a part of the worship of God and we draw nigh to God in this. Otherwise it will not come up to our point. Second, we shall show that God is to be sanctified in this duty of worship; and then, third, how we sanctify Him in this duty.

1. First, in this we draw nigh to God, we worship God. For when we are coming to receive these holy signs and seals, we come to present ourselves before God; and we have to deal with God Himself in a service that He Himself requires of us, a holy, divine service. We come to present ourselves to God for a blessing, for the communication of some higher good to us than possibly the creatures we have to deal with are able of themselves to

convey to us. We come for a higher good than to taste a piece of bread or drink a draught of wine. We come to present ourselves to God so that we might have communion with Him, and that we might have the blessing of the covenant of grace conveyed to us through these things. Certainly this is a drawing nigh to God, for to present ourselves for the conveyance of the blessing of the covenant of grace through these creatures, yea, that we might have communion with God Himself in them, this is drawing nigh to Him. When we come to His table, therefore, we draw nigh to God.

Had God not instituted and appointed these creatures, bread and wine, and the actions about them, to be the means of conveying a blessing to us, it would have been will-worship for us to have expected any further presence of God in such creatures than there is in the nature of them. It is true, God is present with every creature. When we eat and drink at our tables, God is present there; but we cannot be said to draw nigh to God and worship there, for we look for no further presence of God with us in them to convey further good than the Lord has put in to the nature of those things.

Only when godly people take them and receive them as blessings sanctified by the Word do they take them as the blessings of God that come out of love for them. But when we come to receive that which is called the communion, there we expect things that are beyond the nature of these creatures to convey that which is, by an institution of God, set apart for supernatural uses and ends—not to convey in any supernatural way such and such things, but in a supernatural way through the institution of God, and so it comes to be worship.

If we did not have a command for this, it would be superstition and idolatry for us to make use of such creatures for such ends. If any man in the world would have appointed a piece of bread or a draught of wine to have signified and sealed the body and blood of Christ, it would have been superstition and will-worship, and it would have been sinful and abominable to you; but we are to look upon God setting apart these creatures for such holy and solemn ends. And, therefore, when we come to be exercised in them, we come to worship God. And we come likewise to tender up our homage to God when we come to attend upon Him in such ordinances as these are, to tender up that homage that is due from us poor creatures unto such an infinite and glorious God—and therefore we draw nigh to Him in these.

2. We must sanctify God's name in drawing nigh to Him. Whatever we do, whether we eat or drink, we must do all to the glory of God. Now if in our common eating and drinking we must do all to the glory of God, then certainly in this spiritual eating and drinking there must be some special thing done for the glory of God in this.

One reason is because there is so much of God in it, for here there is presented before us the great, yea, the greatest mysteries of salvation and the deep counsels of God concerning eternal life. These are presented before us in these outward elements of the bread and wine and the action thereof. Now when we come to eat and to drink those things that are appointed to set forth the greatest mysteries of salvation, and the deepest of the counsels of God concerning man's eternal good in which God will especially glorify Himself, we need there to sanctify the name of God, for the things are very great and glorious that are presented unto us.

This ordinance of the Lord's Supper, or communion, is an ordinance that Christ has left to His Church out of the abundance of His love. Therefore you shall find, if you read the institution of it in Matthew 25, that the same night wherein Christ was betrayed He took bread and broke it. Though Christ was to die the next day, and to encounter the wrath of God (yes, that very night He was to be in agony and to sweat great drops of blood, and the next day to die and have these trials of wrath poured upon Him so as to put Him to cry out, "My God, My God, why hast Thou forsaken Me?"), yet He busied His thoughts that very night to institute this supper. Surely it must be a great ordinance, and there is a great deal of the love of Christ in it.

Christ saw that His church had need of it, that He should, that night when He was betrayed, have His thoughts busied about such a thing as this is. One would think that at this time He had enough to take up His thoughts concerning Himself, having to encounter the Law and the wrath of God for man's sin, but for all that great work Christ had to encounter, yet His thoughts were busied about this great ordinance of the institution of the supper; and therefore there was great love in it. Christ saw that it was a matter of great importance. Now if it is so, then there is great cause why we should sanctify God's name in such an ordinance as this is, and not to account it a common and ordinary thing.

We must sanctify God's name in this because it is the sacrament of our communion with Christ wherein we come to have such a near union and communion with Him so as to eat His flesh, drink His blood, and to sit at His table. We come to have communion with Christ in all our senses. Christ coming so fully to us calls upon us to sanctify His name when we come before Him.

In this, the covenant of grace is sealed. The covenant of grace comes to be sealed in both parts of it. Now when we come to have to deal with God in the way of the covenant of grace, both to have the seal on His part and the seal on ours, surely this must call for a sanctified use of such a thing as is so holy as this. And that's the reason why we are to sanctify God's name in this, because if we must do this in ordinary eating and drinking, then we must do so in this, where there is so much of God, where the mysteries of godliness are set out before us, where there is so much of the love of Christ, where we are to have close communion with Jesus Christ, and where the covenant of grace comes to be sealed on both sides. There needs, therefore, to be a sanctifying of God's name in the use of it.

Consider that there is no duty in all the Book of God that I know of that is urged with more strength and severity than this. That place in 1 Corinthians 11 shows where you have it required of everyone who comes to receive the bread and wine in the Lord's Supper that they should "examine themselves and so eat." And you have the most dreadful expressions against those who do not do so that I know are mentioned against the neglect of any duty in all the Book of God. There the Holy Ghost says that "whosoever eats and drinks unworthily," first "he is guilty of the body and blood of Christ," and then seconds, "he eats and drinks his own damnation." These two expressions have as much dreadfulness in them as can be imagined, and we do not find an exhortation to a duty backed with two such severe expressions, in case we should neglect our duty, as this exhortation.

What if we do not sanctify God's name in this duty? We come to be guilty of the body and blood of Christ! Blood-guiltiness is a terrible thing. You know that David cried out, "Lord deliver me from blood-guiltiness." To have but the blood of an ordinary man to lie upon one, to shed the blood of the most vile rogue who lives in a murderous way, would lie upon the conscience and be very terrible. It is impossible that such a man can be quiet all his days though he never has such a seared conscience. A heathen could not be at peace if he had the guilt of blood upon him; but to be guilty of the blood of Christ, whose blood is ten thousand times more worthy than the blood of all the men who ever lived upon the face of the earth, must be a most dreadful thing. It is a fearful expression, "guilty of the body and blood of Christ." That is, he offers such an indignity to the body and blood of Christ that the Lord will charge him of being guilty of it, guilty of abusing the body and blood of Jesus Christ.

And then, "he doth eat and drink his own damnation." But we shall speak more to that when we come to show how God will sanctify His name in those who do not sanctify it here in this holy ordinance. I will not therefore spend further time in those Scriptures, for I bring them now only to show that there is a necessity that we sanctify the name of God in this ordinance.

There is nothing that strikes more upon a man's conscience. We find it by experience, even upon wicked men's consciences, and especially upon such as begin to be enlightened in the holiness of this ordinance. God has put much honor upon it. I confess that some men may use it superstitiously, even though it is an ordinance of the church, yet God has put a great deal of honor upon this ordinance while men who are very wicked do otherwise. Yet their consciences tell them that when they come to this ordinance then they must be good, then they must not sin but have good thoughts and good prayers at that time. And many times they dare not come if their consciences tell them that they live in sin.

I myself once knew one who was to be executed, and he had never received this ordinance in all his life, though he was about forty years of age. And being asked the reason why, he confessed that he lived in some sin that he was loath to leave, and therefore would never come to that ordinance in all his life, though herein the devil beguiled and deceived him. But I mention it to show what a power there is in the consciences of men about this ordinance. This, ordinarily, is one of the first things that strikes upon the souls of men when they come to have their consciences awakened. "Oh, how have I profaned the name of God in the ordinance of the holy communion, and have not sanctified His name in it!"

That God should be sanctified in this ordinance is clear enough, but now the great work is (which is the third thing I promised to show) how we should sanctify God's name in this ordinance. Certainly the name of God has been taken in vain a great deal. There has been a great deal of pollution in the use of this ordinance, and in men's spirits, when they have been exercising themselves in such a holy ordinance as this is. Therefore I will open this to you and shall not be very large in it, only to show you the main and principal things that may serve to direct us that the name of God may not be so taken in vain and dishonored as heretofore. And I shall cast what I intend to speak of into these particulars.

First, those who come must be holy themselves. This is not an ordinance appointed for conversion, to make holy. Others who are not converted may come to the Word because the Word is appointed to work conversion. It is appointed to work grace, to work the first grace. "Faith cometh by hearing." We do not find in all the Scripture that this is appointed for conversion, but it supposes conversion. None are to come to receive this sacrament but men and women who before are converted by the Word.

The Word, therefore, is first to be preached to men for their conversion, and then this is an ordinance appointed to seal them. Therefore, in the primitive times, they let all come to the hearing of the Word, and then when the sermon was done, there was an officer who stepped up and cried, "Holy things for holy men." Then all others were to go out, and therefore it was called *missa*, though the Papists corrupted it and so called it the mass afterwards by mixing their own inventions instead of the Supper of the Lord. But it had that name at first. I say, this holy communion was called by the name of *missa* because all others were sent away and only such as were of the church and accounted godly stayed. "Holy things to holy men."

And this must be so because the nature of it, being the seal of the covenant of grace, requires it. It must be supposed that all who come hither must be in covenant with God. They must be such as have been brought to submit to the condition of the covenant. Now the condition of the covenant is, "believe and be saved." It is therefore appointed for believers. And as the nature of it, being a seal, supposes a covenant, so none can have this covenant sealed to them but those who first submit to it and are brought into covenant. When you make an indenture and put the seal to it, certainly the seal belongs only to those who have their names in the indenture. Now it is true that though men's names are not mentioned in the Word, yet the condition is to those who are brought in to believe in Jesus Christ. God says, "I come now to seal all my mercies in Christ to their souls." We abuse God when we come to take the seal to a blank. It is to make this ordinance a ridiculous thing. Therefore, there must be some transaction between God and your souls before you come to the seal.

If a man should say to you, "Come, set your seal to such a thing," and there were never any kind of transactions between this man and you before this, you would account it ridiculous. After there have been agreements between you, then you will seal. So it must be here.

I would appeal to many of your consciences, you who have come to the Lord's Supper. What transactions have there been between God and your souls? Can you say, "The Lord has been pleased to reveal Himself to me, to make known to me my wretched condition and the way of grace and salvation, and has showed me that upon my coming in to receive His Son He would be merciful to me and pardon my sins. And I have found the Spirit of God working my heart to Jesus Christ, the Lord speaking to me from heaven, and I sending answer to heaven again. How willing my soul was to accept the covenant that the Lord has made with poor creatures in the Word of His gospel!"

Can you say this in the uprightness of your heart? If not, know that this seal does not belong to you until the Lord has, by His Word, subdued your heart to this agreement with Him.

Second, this ordinance is the ordinance of spiritual nourishment, of eating the flesh of Christ and drinking His blood in a spiritual way. Now it must suppose that there must first be life before there can be any nourishment received. If it is appointed to nourish and increase grace, then surely there must be grace before. What nourishment can a dead child take? The very first thing that is to be done is nourishment here. The Word has power to convey life and then to nourish, but we read of no such thing here. But that which is to be done here is presently to feed, to eat, and to drink. That's the end of the sacrament. Therefore it must be supposed that you must have spiritual life. There must come no dead soul to this ordinance, but those who are quickened by the Spirit of Jesus Christ. They must come for nourishment.

Third, the act required here notes that only those who are holy and godly can receive this sacrament. We are required by the apostle to examine ourselves. To examine ourselves of what? It must be of our godliness. Examine what work of God has been upon the soul, how God has brought the soul to Himself and what graces of the Spirit of God are there, and how we have been brought into covenant with God. Now if only these can receive worthily, and if only these are to come who first examine themselves, then certainly only such as are godly are to come, for they alone can perform those acts that are required.

Fourth, it's a sacrament of communion with God and communion with the saints. Now "what communion hath light and darkness? Or what fellowship hath Christ with Belial?" If it is a sacrament of communion, of coming to the table of God, will God have His enemies to come to His table? You will not invite any enemies to your tables, but your children and friends. So they must be the children of God and the friends of God, those who are reconciled to God in the blood of His Son, and those who are His children may sit at His table. Therefore they must be holy.

Now this may suffice for that first thing, that this is not an ordinance for all sorts of people, but such as have submitted to the condition of the covenant before. Such as have grace and ability to examine themselves of their graces, and such as are children and are reconciled to God, are fit to sit at the table of God and enjoy communion with Him and with His Son, and with the saints; for we are one body sacramentally when we come to this holy ordinance. All others, therefore, are certainly to be kept from this sacrament but such.

2. It is not enough that we be holy ourselves. And so all ignorant, profane, and scandalous, yea, all who are merely civil, who cannot make out any work of godliness upon their hearts in bringing them to Christ are excluded. But it is to be done in a holy communion, and this is clear from 1 Corinthians 10:16–17:

"The cup of blessing which we bless, is it not the communion of the blood of Christ? The bread which we break, is it not the communion of the body of Christ?" And then the apostle says in verse 17, "for we being many are one bread and one body."

Therefore, all who come to receive the sacrament must so come as one body, one spiritual corporation. This very consideration, that those with whom we receive the sacrament are one body with us, has a great deal in it to help us to sanctify God's name. This ordinance is to be received only in a holy communion. One Christian cannot receive the sacrament alone. There must be a communion wherever it is administered. It is not enough that there is one godly man there, but there must be a communion of saints, and in that communion it is to be received.

QUESTION. You will say, "Must it be received in a communion of saints? What if wicked men come there? Will that hinder us from sanctifying God's name in partaking of the sacrament with them? Do we not find in Scripture that the church always had wicked men among them? There are always tares growing up with the wheat. If you read in Corinthians you shall find that there were some in the church that were wicked, yea, and it is thought that Judas himself received the sacrament, too. Therefore, if wicked men are there, does that hinder?"

ANSWER. It is true that in the church of God there have been wicked men to the end of the world, but wherever there is a right communion of saints, there ought to be the power of Christ exercised to cast out those wicked men, or at least to withdraw from them. This is the law of Christ, that if there are any who have communion with you, if any of them appear to be wicked, you are bound in conscience to go and tell them. If they do not reform, you are bound to take two or three; and if they do not yet reform, then you are bound to tell the church, to tell the assembly of the saints when they meet together, for so the word "church" signifies.

We find in 1 Corinthians 5 that when there was an incestuous person to be cast out, it was done in the presence of the congregation. Thus far you are bound to do, otherwise you cannot say that it is nothing to you if wicked men are there, for you have not discharged your conscience. And so you come to be defiled and you do not sanctify God's name in this ordinance because you have not done to the uttermost your duty for the casting out of those wicked men.

Mark that in 2 Corinthians 5:7, the apostle, writing to the church, bids them that they should purge out the old leaven. He says, "Know ye not that a little leaven leaveneth the whole lump?" The apostle is not speaking here of sin, but of the wicked, incestuous person. He says, "You must look to it that this man is purged out from you or else you are all leavened by it." That is, the whole church would be leavened by it if there was not care taken to purge out that one man.

You will say, "Shall we be the worse for one wicked man's coming?"

No, if we are no way faulty of it then we cannot be said to be worse, and it cannot leaven us. But when it is our duty to purge him out and we do not do it (as in all communion of saints there is a duty, and there is not anyone but may do something towards it), thus far every communicant in every communion must go. If there is a wicked man there, if you come to know it and you do not go thus far as I have spoken, you are defiled.

You are defiled by him. You are not defiled by the mere presence of wicked men, for that's a mere deceit and gall that some would put upon men who differ from them otherwise. But you are defiled by their presence if you do not do your duty and the uttermost you are able to do to purge them out. Yes, then the whole congregation is defiled if they do not do their duty.

It is the duty of everyone in the congregation to tell their brother, or to take two or three, and after that to tell the church and so come to profess against them. Or if the church will not do their duty as they ought, then to free your own souls your duty is to profess that here is one who is so and so guilty and may be proven to be. And so for your part, to free your own soul, you must profess that this man or woman ought not to have communion here. Thus you have come to free your own souls; and when you have done this, though wicked men are there, you may eat and drink and not be defiled by their presence for you cannot be said to eat with them now, not to have communion with them, any more than if a dog should come and jump upon the table and take a piece of bread. You cannot have communion with him because he takes it any more than you have with those wicked men once you have dealt this far with them.

You have professed against them that you cannot have communion with them. This is not to eat with them. The apostle says in 1 Corinthians 5:11 that "if any man that is called a brother be a fornicator, or covetous, or an idolater, or a railer, or a drunkard, or an extortioner, with such a one no not to eat, for what have I to do to judge them also that are without?" That is, the heathens and those who were in no communion with them, I have nothing to do to judge them, "but do not ye judge them that are within?" When we have so far freed ourselves as professing against their sin, then we cannot be said to have communion with them; and then we withdraw from those who walk disorderly when we do our duty thus far.

1 Thessalonians 3:14: "If any man obey not our word by this epistle, note that man, and have no company with him, that

he may be ashamed." And in the sixth verse of that chapter he commands them in the name of our Lord Jesus Christ that "they should withdraw themselves from every brother that walketh disorderly." So that until we do our duty we come to be defiled. But if we do our duty, then it is not the mixture of a congregation that is enough to hinder any from receiving the sacrament there, and this will tend much to satisfy men about receiving in mixed congregations where any are cast into them and are actual members there.

But now on the other side, if we are in a place where either this congregation will not take upon them any such power to cast out unworthy ones, or are not convinced of this power, then there is no rule that Christ has set that we must be forced all our days to continue to be in such a congregation as denies one of the ordinances of Jesus Christ. If so be there are any who are wicked and we do first what we can to have them cast out, and we wait with patience in such a congregation to have them cast out, and yet we see that either the congregation does not understand that they have any such power or denies such a power as they do have, and so upon that all the people are left in a mixed way, then I say there is no rule in all the Book of God that should force men to continue to be members of such a communion where they cannot enjoy one ordinance of Jesus Christ, which is the ordinance of separating the precious from the vile, the ordinance of casting out the wicked and ungodly. It would be a very diseased body, and in danger quickly of the loss of life, to take everything into it and to have no expulsive faculty to purge anything out again. So a congregation that is altogether without such an ordinance as that is of expelling such as are wicked and ungodly, I say, I find no Scripture that forces people and requires them as bound in conscience to continue there where they may not enjoy all the ordinances of Jesus Christ. The right understanding of what I say now will help us to answer all those Scriptures that are brought.

If the issue of Judas is raised, first it is hard to make out clearly whether it was the Lord's Supper that he received or not. But suppose it is granted that he did. Yet I make no question but such as Judas was, who shall continue to make such an outward profession as he did and could not be discovered in the church way, that we may receive with such as are close hypocrites.

You will say, "Jesus Christ knew him to be faulty, and He told John who lay in His bosom what he was." But though He knew him as God, yet He dealt with him in His ministerial way. And He had appointed before that none were to be cast out, but were to be dealt with in such a ministerial way.

So it is not enough, though I know by revelation from God that such a man was a hypocrite. Suppose God should reveal from heaven to me that such a man was a hypocrite. I think I might communicate with him still when he does not so far reveal himself that I can by witnesses prove his evil. Therefore, though men are wicked, yet it does not defile the communion where they are if they use the way that Christ has appointed to be observed in His church. And when that is done, then I am to withdraw from him and to profess against communion with him, so that it's enough to answer the case.

We read likewise that there were divers wicked men among the Corinthians, and of tares that grew in the wheat. It's true, there were wicked men among them, but they were enjoined by the apostle to cast out those wicked men; and if they did not do it, it was their sin and they were defiled by it.

And for tares that were among the wheat, take it that this is meant concerning the church. Suppose it were, and yet Christ said plainly that the field is the world and 'tis the godly and the wicked living together in the world, and so I find many interpreters take it. But however you take it that is meant of the church communion, yet this much is clear, it was through the fault of the officers that there should be any tares among the wheat, for so the text says plainly that while the servants slept there, tares sprung up. Therefore there should have been none.

Also, they were not tares as would spoil the wheat, but, as Jerome said, in those countries the tares grew much like wheat all the while it was in the blade, so it was hard to distinguish, though some that were of more understanding were able to discern them from the wheat. Therefore, though such as grow up like the wheat may be suffered, and yet in this case only, that is, in case that it will prejudice the wheat, that is, when they are so close to the wheat that there will be danger in plucking them up to pluck up the wheat, too, then they must be left alone.

Mark, first it was through the negligence of the officers. They should have been kept out. Second, if they do get in, yet while they grow so close to the wheat that there will be danger that when you pluck them out you pluck out the wheat, too, only in that case must it be forborne. But this gives no liberty that therefore all sorts may be let into the church, and there should be no kind of ordinance to cast out those venomous weeds that will do hurt and mischief.

But if you understand it, as many do, concerning the world, then the meaning is this: the preaching of the gospel comes to a place and there's only good seed sown, and that seed is a means of the conversion of many. But together with the conversion of some, there are others who hear the gospel preached; and the truth is that they, being mingled among the hearers of the Word, instead of bringing forth good fruit according to the Word, bring forth tares.

Now says the servant, "Lord, how does it come to pass that

we preach such excellent truths in this place and yet there are so many wicked men who bring forth such wicked fruit? Lord, is it Thy mind that we should be wholly separated from them and have nothing to do with them, that there should be a full separation while we live in this world?"

"No," says Christ, "not so." For if all godly men should wholly withdraw from wicked men and believe that they may not live among them, they could not live in the world. If you believed it were your duty to not so much as live near a wicked man nor to have anything to do in any kind of converse with him, there would be no wheat growing in this field of the world here. And therefore you must be content, when you live where the preaching of the gospel is, and the seed brings forth good fruit in some and in others it brings forth tares. You must not be offended by this, that here in this world God does not by some visible stroke of judgment come and strike them dead, or that God does not take some course that there should be a full separation here, but that they might live together until the day of judgment.

Here, I say, you shall not have such a full separation. So you see that it carries a very fair sense to take the field to be the world and the kingdom of heaven there to be the preaching of the gospel in any place. And so we must be content while we live in this world to be where wicked and ungodly men are. But it does not follow from this place that we are to have converse in the closest communion, in church communion, with wicked men, to be made one body by eating the same bread and drinking the same wine. It does not hold forth such close communion as this is. So there's little strength that can be taken from that place, but still it holds that wherever there is the sacrament of the Lord's Supper, there must be a holy communion of saints.

OBJECTION. The Scriptures only say, "Let us examine ourselves."

ANSWER. I grant, for the benefit of my own soul, I must look to examine myself more especially; but for another, I am but only so far bound to look to him as to keep myself clean. It is true, I am not bound to go and pry into his life and all his ways so as to force him to give an account of things that are secret, but I am bound to keep a watch; and if anything is done that offends me, then I am bound to go to him according to the former rule of Christ. And if he appears to be wicked, then I am bound to see him purged from the congregation. For take that other text in 1 Corinthians 5:6: "Know ye not that a little leaven leaveneth the whole lump?" If I do not do so much as concerns my duty, then I am defiled by it.

So you must not think that it is nothing to you how many wicked men come to the Lord's table, and that it belongs only to the ministers to look to it. The truth is that everyone in his place is to look to it, and everyone may be defiled if he does not perform this duty that God requires of him.

Do not say, "What have I to do with my brother? Am I my brother's keeper?" That was the speech of Cain. If you are of the same body, you are to have care for your brother. "Do ye not judge those that are within?" There is some kind of judgment that everyone may pass upon such as join them in the same body. Surely it concerns me much. What shall I do in such an action as to join with them to eat bread, whereby I must profess that I believe myself to be of the same body that this drunkard is of, that this whoremaster is of, that this swearer is of?

Whenever you receive the communion with any company, you profess yourselves to be of the same body with that company. Only in this case, if I have discovered any and can particularly profess against anyone, then I do not profess myself to be of the same body with him. But when I come in an ordinary way, and I know such to be wicked, vile, and profane, and I profess nothing against them nor take any course at all, then I, by partaking with them, profess myself to be of the same body that they are of. You do, as it were, openly declare, "Lord, here we come and profess that we are all of the body of Jesus Christ." Now when you know such and such are notoriously wicked and profane and do nothing in the world to help purge them out, do you not think that God's name is taken in vain? Is not God's name profaned here?

Therefore, it concerns us very much to look unto it that it is a holy communion that we receive the bread and wine in. I beseech you, therefore, understand things rightly that I have spoken of. I have labored to satisfy men that there is a way that we may partake of the sacrament though wicked men are mixed with us. But this is that which is required of you for your doing your duty, to keep yourselves clean so that you may not be an accessory in any way to any wicked man's coming to partake of this holy majesty of the body and blood of Christ.

There are divers other things further about this, and the special thing I thought of was to show you the holy qualifications that there ought to be; but this I conceived to be necessary, and I would not have had peace in my own conscience as being faithful to you in what I am speaking, of sanctifying the name of God in this ordinance, if I had not mentioned this.

Sermon XII

What is Required in Receiving the Sacrament?

"I will be sanctified in them that come nigh Me."

LEVITICUS 10:3

There's an error on both sides that I desire to meet with. One error concerns those who come hand over head and think it does not concern them at all with whom they come to the sacrament other than to look to their own hearts. And there's an error on the other side, that if they do what they can to keep wicked men away, and yet if they should be suffered to come, they may not come to partake of those things. Now it is very useful for us to know what we should do in this case.

If I were in a church where I could have but a piece of the sacrament, suppose they dealt with me as the papists do with their people; that is, they will give me the bread and not the wine. Certainly I would not be bound to stay with them then, but I would be bound to go where I might have the whole sacrament. So if a church will give me one ordinance and not another, I confess that as long as there is hope that I may enjoy it and that they are in the way for enjoyment, I think there should be a great forbearance to a church as well as to a particular person. I must not withdraw from a particular man when there is still hope of his reformation and that there may come good

233

from my forbearance; and towards a church much more.

But I say, if I cannot enjoy, neither does there appear any hope of the enjoyment of all ordinances, certainly it would be only a cruelty to force men to stay there when somewhere else they may enjoy all ordinances for the good of their souls. And this cannot be a schism to do so. Is the following example schism? Suppose a man were in a place and joined in such a communion for his outward benefit. He may remove his dwelling from one place to another if he can have better trading in another place. Then certainly if he may have more ordinances for the edification of his soul, he may as well remove from one to another, as he may remove if his trading is better in one place than another. Christ would have all His people look to the edification of their souls; and should I account that schism?

When a man or woman, merely out of tenderness and a desire to enjoy Jesus Christ in all His ordinances for the benefit of their souls, finds such want to their souls of all ordinances that, though they may have some in one place, yet if they cannot have all, their souls do not so thrive. Now if this is all the end why they remove, that they might have more edification to their souls, enjoying the ordinances of Christ more fully, God forbid that this should ever be accounted such a sin that the Scripture is to brand as schism. No, it is schism when there is a violent rending out of malice, for a want of love. For as apostasy is a rending from the head, so schism is a rending from the body, that is, when it is out of an evil spirit, from envy or malice, from want of love, or from any base, sinister ends and upon no just ground. But when it is merely out of love for Jesus Christ, that I might have more edification to my soul, and I still retain love to the saints that are in a communion, and as far as they have any thing good among them, I hold communion with them in that. Only I desire in humility and meekness that I may be in such a place where my soul may be most edified, where I may enjoy all those ordinances that Christ has appointed for His church.

Certainly the soul that can give this account to Jesus Christ for going from one place to another will be freed by Jesus Christ from such a sin as what the world calls "schism." But the truth is, this word is in men's mouths who do not understand what it means. And the devil will always have some word or other cast upon them that are good, for he has heretofore gained much by it, so he still takes account to gain much by words and terms. And therefore men should take heed of words and terms that they do not understand and what is held forth in those words. And so much for the point that it must be in a holy communion. Wherever there is the receiving of the Lord's Supper, it must be received in a holy communion.

Now we are to proceed to that which is the main thing, and that is what the holy qualifications or dispositions of the soul are together with the actings of it in receiving the Lord's Supper. What is required in the soul for the sanctifying of the name of God in this holy sacrament? There are many things required.

1. Knowledge is required. I must know what I do when I come to receive this holy sacrament, knowledge applied to the work that I am about. When some of you have come to receive this sacrament, if God should have spoken from heaven and said thus to you, "What are you doing now? What do you go for?" What account would you have been able to give Him? You must understand what you do when you come here.

You must be able to give this account to God: "Lord, I am now going to have represented to me, in a visible and sensible way, the greatest mysteries of godliness, those great and deep counsels of Thy will concerning my eternal estate, those great things that angels desire to pry into that shall be the matter of eternal praises of angels and saints in the highest heavens, that they may be set before my view. Lord, when I have come to Thy Word, I have had in my ear, sounding the great mysteries of godliness, the great things of the covenant of grace; and now I go to see them represented before my eyes in that ordinance of Thine that Thou hast appointed.

"Yes, Lord, I am now going to receive the seals of the blessed covenant of Thine, the second covenant, the new covenant, the seals of the testimony and will of Thine. I am going to have confirmed to my soul Thy everlasting love in Jesus Christ.

"Yes, Lord, I am going to that ordinance where I expect to have communion with Thee, and the communication of Thy chief mercies to my soul in Jesus Christ. I am going to feast with Thee, to feed upon the body and blood of Jesus Christ.

"Yes, I am now going to set the seal of the covenant on my part, to renew my covenant with Thee. I am going to have communion with Thy saints, to have the bond of communion with all Thy people to be confirmed to me so that there might be a stronger bond of union and love between me and Thy saints than ever. These are the ends that I go for, this is the work that I am now going about."

Thus you must come in understanding. You must know what you are going about. This is that which the apostle speaks of when he speaks of discerning the Lord's body. He rebukes the Corinthians for their sin and shows them that they were guilty of the body and blood of Christ because they did not discern the Lord's body. They looked only upon the outward elements, but did not discern what there was of Christ there. They did not see how Christ was under those elements, both represented and exhibited unto them. That's the first thing, there must be knowledge and understanding.

And now for the knowledge and understanding of the nature of the sacrament. There needs to be knowledge in other points of religion; for we can never come to understand the nature of this sacrament without knowing God and knowing ourselves, knowing in what estate we were by nature, knowing our fall, knowing the way of redemption, knowing what Jesus Christ was and what He has done in making an atonement, the necessity of Jesus Christ and what the way of the covenant is that God has appointed to bring men's souls to eternal life by. The main points of religion must be known, but especially that which concerns the nature of a sacrament.

Now this knowledge, likewise, must be actual, not merely habitual knowledge. But there must be a stirring up of this knowledge, that is, by meditation. I must be meditating, have actual thoughts and meditations of what I know. That ought to be the work of a Christian in coming to receive the sacrament, to quicken up his knowledge, to have a renewed work of his knowledge by actual thoughts and meditations of the main points of religion, and especially of the nature and the end of this holy institution. That is the first thing.

2. As we must come understandingly, without which we cannot sanctify God's name, so we must come with hearts suitable to the work that we are about. That is, because the great thing that is here is the breaking of Christ's body and the pouring forth of His blood. A suitable disposition to this is brokenness of heart, a sense of our sin, of that dreadful breach that sin has made between God and the soul. Our sin should be upon our hearts so as to break them, but this brokenness must be evangelical. It must be through the applying of the blood of Christ unto my soul. I must come sensible of my sin, but especially I must be sensible of it by what I see in the holy sacrament. That must

make me sensible of my sin. There are a great many things to make me sensible of my sins: the consideration of the great God that you have sinned against and the curse of the Law that's due to you, the wrath of God that is incensed against you for your sin, and those eternal flames that are prepared for sinners, those everlasting burnings.

But those are not the things that will break the heart in an evangelical way, in a gracious way. The main thing by which the soul must come to break its heart must be beholding the evil of sin in the red glass of the blood of Jesus Christ, beholding Him broken. And truly there is nothing in the world that has the power to break the heart for sin as beholding that which is to be beheld in the holy sacrament. That heart is a hard one that can see what is to be seen there and not break in the apprehension of sin. When I see here what my sin cost, what a price was paid for my soul; when I see the hatred of God against sin and the justice of God in not sparing His Son, but in breaking His Son for my sin, and in shedding the blood of His Son for my sins, I see here that making my peace with God cost more than ten thousand worlds is worth. I see that by my sin such a breach was made between God and my soul that all the angels in heaven and men in the world could never make up this breach. Only the Son of God, He who was God and man, who was thus broken by the burden of the wrath of His Father for my sins, could do this.

The truth is, when we come to this holy communion, we are to look upon Christ as if we saw Him hanging upon the cross. Suppose you had lived at the time when Christ was crucified and had understood as much concerning the death of Christ as you do now, and what Christ was. If you could have beheld Him in the garden, there sweating drops of blood and water, lying groveling upon the ground crying, "if it be possible, let this cup pass from Me," and if you could have followed Him to the cross and there had seen His hands and feet nailed, His side pierced and the blood trickling down, and had heard Him cry out, "My God, My God, why hast Thou forsaken Me?"—would not such a sight as this is have broken your heart for sin? The truth is, there is more. I won't say only so much, but I say there is more in this sacrament to break the heart for sin than such a sight as that could have done.

You will say that if you had seen Christ crucified again before your eyes, if you had seen the body of Christ hanging upon the cross and there beheld Him crucified, and heard Him cry out, "My God, My God why hast Thou forsaken Me," you would think that if your hearts did not break for sin then that they were desperately hard. Know that every time you have come to receive the sacrament, you came to see such a sight; and is it not as great an aggravation of the hardness of your heart if it has not broken at this sight as it would be if it should not break at that sight?

We read in Galatians 3:1 of Paul's speaking of the preaching of the gospel. He says that Christ was crucified before those who heard the Word; and "foolish Galatians, who has bewitched you that you should not obey the truth, before whose eyes Jesus Christ has been evidently set forth, crucified among you?" He does not mean that Christ was crucified in Galatia, but that where the Word was preached, He was evidently set forth and crucified among them. But now, my brethren, the crucifying of Christ in the Word is not such a real, evident, and sensible setting forth of Christ crucified as when He is set forth in this sacrament; and 'tis that which works with more efficacy to break the heart than that other sight. The reason I give is this: because you do not find that God set that apart as an ordinance, an institution appointed to the end that they should come to look upon that for the breaking of their hearts. There was indeed a naturalness in it, that if they beheld Christ it might break their hearts, but it was not such an ordinance. It was not a sacrament as this is. Now this being in a sacramental way, in the use of an ordinance appointed by Jesus Christ to set forth His sufferings and all the riches of the covenant of grace to the soul, there may be expected here a further blessing than in the other, though it is true that the other might work mightily upon the heart. But yet this being a great ordinance of Christ in the church, a great institution of Jesus Christ for the setting out of His sufferings, it has a more special blessing that goes along with it.

Every ordinance has a promise and a more special blessing than any other thing that is not an ordinance. So when you come here to behold Christ crucified before you, you cannot see Christ naturally crucified as upon the cross; but you have Christ crucified before you in the way of the sacrament, in the way of a solemn institution of Jesus Christ that has a special blessing which goes along with it. Therefore, if the heart is not broken here, there is an aggravation of the hardness of the heart as great as if we should behold Jesus Christ upon the cross and our hearts not be broken there. And indeed, this is a special reason why those are said to be guilty of the body and blood of Christ who receive it unworthily.

It is as if a man had been alive and had been before the cross, and there had seen how the blood of Jesus Christ was shed for sin, and should not have been affected with it but should have accounted it as a common thing. This man, in some regard, might have been said to be guilty of His death, that is, to have joined and consented with those who crucified Him; for if a man sees another commit a sin, if he is not affected with that sin, and if it does not stir up his heart, he may come to be a partaker of his sin. So those who come to see Jesus Christ crucified and do not have their hearts at all stirred with the crucifying of Jesus Christ are, in some regard, truly said to be guilty of the body and blood of Jesus Christ. And that's the second thing, brokenness of spirit is suitable to the light of a broken Christ.

3. The third thing that is here to be done in the sanctifying of God's name is the purging and cleansing of the heart from sin, and actual cleansing and purging of the heart from sin there ought to be. The Jews in their Passover were to cast out all leaven, and those who write of the custom of the Jews say that they were in the habit of doing three things in casting out their leaven.

First, they made diligent search for leaven. They lit candles to look into every corner lest there should be any bit of leaven left in the house.

Second, when they found it, they cast it out.

Third, they used a curse. They cursed themselves if they should willingly keep any leaven in the house.

So, my brethren, when we come to partake of this holy ordinance, there should be a diligent inquisition for sin, for sin in Scripture is compared to leaven. You should make a diligent search to see what sin there is in your heart, in any of the faculties of your soul, what sin there is in your thoughts, what family sins, what personal sins. You should make a diligent search to see whether there is not some leaven, some evil in your heart; and, whatever sin you shall come to find in your heart, there must be a casting out of it. That is, your soul must be set against it to oppose it with all your might, whatever beloved sin, whatever gainful sin. Whatever becomes of you, your soul must renounce that sin of yours.

Yes, and in a kind of curse on yourself, you must say, "Lord, as ever I expect to receive any good by this body and blood of Christ that I now come to receive, so Lord, here I profess against every sin that I have found in my heart. I desire to find out all, and profess against all, and renounce all, and I would do to the uttermost what I am able for the delivering of my soul fully from every known or beloved sin. Oh, that there might not be any remaining sin in my heart."

This must be the disposition of the soul coming here, and it must be thus or else we cannot sanctify God's name, because there is nothing more suitable than this disposition unto the receiving of the sacrament. For we come here to profess that we acknowledge that sin cost as much as it did, that it cost the blood of the Son of God. Now this cannot help but cause the heart to renounce sin. If indeed I believe that sin has cost the blood of Christ, that it cost Him as dearly as it did, that it troubled heaven and earth, that there must be such a mighty, wonderful way of satisfaction to God for my sin committed against Him, certainly sin has a dreadful evil in it. Oh! Let me never have to do with such sin that was the cause of such sufferings to my Savior, who shed His blood.

If you saw the knife that cut the throat of your dearest child, would not your heart rise against that knife? Suppose you came to a table and there is a knife laid at your plate, and it was told to you that this is the knife that cut the throat of your child. Fathers, if you could still use that knife like any other knife, would not someone say, "There was but little love to your child?" So when a temptation comes to commit any sin, this is the knife that cut the throat of Christ, that pierced His sides, that was the cause of all His suffering, that made Christ to be a curse. Now will you not look upon that as a cursed thing that made Christ to be a curse? Oh, with what detestation would a man or woman fling away such a knife! And with the like detestation it is required that you should renounce sin, for that was the cause of the death of Christ.

I remember that it was reported of Anthony, that when Caesar was slain, he came to stir up the people against those who had slain Caesar. And he took the clothes that were bloody and held them forth to the people and said, "Here is the blood of your emperor." And upon that the people were enraged against those who had slain him and went and pulled down their houses upon them. So when you come to this sacrament, you see the blood of Christ gushing out for your sin if ever your sin is pardoned. Either your soul must be eternally damned for your sin, or else your sin cost the gushing out of the blood of Christ.

Now when you see this, this should cause a holy rage in your soul against the sin that caused this. Surely the putting away of sin, the risings of the heart against sin, must be a disposition suitable to such an ordinance as this is. And that's the third thing required in the sanctifying of God's name in this ordinance, the purging out of sin and risings of the heart against it.

4. The fourth thing to be done for the sanctifying of God's name here is the hungering and thirsting of the soul after Jesus Christ. Whoever comes here comes to a feast, and the Lord expects that all His guests should come with stomachs unto this feast, come with a hungering and a longing for Jesus Christ. This should be the disposition of the soul, "Oh, that my soul might enjoy communion with Jesus Christ. Now this is the end that I am come for. Oh, the Lord, who knows the workings of my heart, knows that this is the great desire of my soul, that I might enjoy communion with Jesus Christ. Oh, that I might have more of Christ, that I might meet with Christ, that I might have some further manifestation of Jesus Christ, that I might have my soul further united to the Lord Christ, and so have further influence of Christ to my soul. I come thirsting after the

Lord Christ, knowing my infinite need of Him and the infinite excellency that there is in Jesus Christ. My soul famishes and perishes forever without Christ—but in the enjoyment of Christ there is a fullness for the satisfying of my soul. I have had that of Christ sometimes in the Word and sometimes in prayer, but I expect a further communion of Christ here, for this is the grand ordinance for communion with Jesus Christ."

Indeed, the Word, in this respect, is beyond this ordinance. That is, it is not only for the increase of grace, but for the begetting of it. This is only for the increase of grace and not appointed for the begetting of it. Now in that respect; the Word is above the sacrament, but the sacrament is a more full ordinance for communion with Jesus Christ. This is the communion of the body of Jesus Christ and of His blood, and therefore there ought to be hungering and thirsting desires of the soul after Jesus Christ. Therefore you must take heed you do not come with your stomachs full of trash, as children do when they can get plums and pears and fill their stomachs with them when they come to your tables. Though there is never so much wholesome diet, they have no mind to it at all.

So it is with men of the world. They fill their hearts with the trash of this world, with sensual delights; and hence it is that when they come to such a great ordinance to enjoy communion with Jesus Christ, they feel no want at all of Christ. They only come and take a little piece of bread and a draught of wine, but for any strong, pausing desires to meet with Jesus Christ there in the ordinance, to come so as they know not how to live without Christ, even as a man who is hungry cannot live without his meat and drink, and so for the soul to have such a disposition after Christ is a rare thing. But you know that God's name is not sanctified unless you come in such a way unto this holy sacrament. That's the fourth thing, hungry and thirsty desires after Christ from a deep sense of the need of Him and the apprehension of the excellency in Him.

5. There must be an exercise of faith for the sanctifying of God's name here. Faith is both the hand and the mouth for taking this spiritual meat and spiritual drink. When you come to the feast of the Lord, faith is first the eye, and then the hand and the mouth. It is the eye of the soul to give a real sight of what there is here. You are not able to discern the body of the Lord but by the eye of faith. If you come only with bodily eyes to look upon what is here, you see nothing but a little bread and wine. But where the eye of faith is, there is a real appearance of Jesus Christ to the soul, as if Christ were bodily present. And we do not need to have the bread turned into His body, for faith can see the body of Christ through the bread and the blood of Christ gushing in the wine. It is a mighty thing to have Christ and such spiritual things made real, and not to be fancy.

If one looked upon a painting of a fire, he could not heat himself in cold weather with that. He would need a fire that is really burning upon the hearth. So it is with those who come to receive the sacrament and do not come with faith, who have only the eye of their bodies. They only see, as it were, a painted Christ. They do not see Christ really. His body and blood and those great mysteries of the gospel are not presented as real things to their souls, and hence it is that they go away and get nothing. But when the soul comes with the eye of faith, the soul sees the wonderful things of God. It is the most glorious sight in the world. All the glory of God in the heavens and earth is not like this sight of Jesus Christ, and the mysteries of the gospel that appear to the eye of faith.

Therefore you may know by this whether you have come with faith to the sacrament or not, whether you have seen the most glorious sight that ever your eyes beheld, alas, with our natural eyes. We behold a minister coming with a piece of bread and a little wine, but when the eye of faith is opened, then we behold the glorious things of the gospel. Many times when you come to hear the Word your hearts burn within you, as they who went to Emmaus. But when you are breaking bread, the eye of faith must look upon Jesus Christ; and in this sense those who have pierced Christ must look upon Him. That Scripture is fulfilled from Zechariah 12:10: "They shall look on Him whom they have pierced by their sins, and then mourn and lament." This eye of faith will cause mourning and lamenting for sin.

And then as faith is the eye to make what is here real, so faith is the hand to take it. When you come to a feast, you must have something to take the meat to you. That is what Christ says. He broke bread and gave it to His disciples saying, "Take, eat this." Take it? How shall we take it? By reaching out the hand. If you sanctify God's name in this ordinance, as you reach out your hand to take the bread and wine, so there must be an actual reaching out of the soul by faith, putting forth an act of faith to receive Jesus Christ into the soul, to apply the Lord Jesus Christ to your soul with all His merits and good things that He has purchased.

When the minister gives out that ordinance, you should look upon God the Father giving out His Son as if this were your condition: "I am now in the presence of the eternal Father who now actually gives out His Son to my soul and says, 'Soul, here receive anew this day My Son with all that He has purchased for your good.' "

Now when the soul acts upon this and, by stirring up an act of faith, comes and closes with this gift of the Father and casts itself upon Jesus Christ and says, as it were, "AMEN," to what the Father gives, it is really saying, "O Lord, here I come and embrace Thy Son as my life, as my Savior, as the Fountain of all my good in whom I expect all the good I am likely to have, either here or to all eternity." So there must be a stirring up of the act of faith in an actual taking of Christ if you are a believer.

Can you remember what you did when you first took Jesus Christ, when the Lord, in the preaching of His Word, revealed Jesus Christ to your soul? What did your soul do then? How did your soul work in closing with Christ? As your soul did then in closing with Christ, so it must now renew the work. There must be a renewal of the work at that time. So when you come to the sacrament, you must not think that it is then a time to listen to doubts, fears, and scruples; no, but it is a time that God calls for the exercise of faith, the casting of the soul upon Christ and His merits for life and salvation, or else the name of God is not sanctified as it ought to be. You do not sanctify God's name when you are busying your soul in doubts and scruples in your receiving of the sacrament.

And then faith is the mouth. When you come to eat and drink, how can you if you do not have a mouth? You have a bodily mouth to take in bread and wine, but know that without faith your soul cannot take in Christ. Faith is, as it were, the mouth. That is, by the act of faith the soul opens itself for Jesus Christ, and not only opens itself, but takes in Christ to the soul and makes Christ and the soul as one. As our bread and wine is made one with our body, so faith takes in Christ and makes Him one with you and turns Christ into the nourishment of your soul. And you and Christ, by faith, are made truly one as the bread and wine that is put into your body is made one with your body. This is the work of faith without which we cannot sanctify the name of God.

6. There must be spiritual joy. That must be exercised here for

it is a feast. Here we come to sit with Christ at His table. We come as children to our Father's table and to sit there with Jesus Christ, our elder brother. Now a father does not love to have his child sitting in a sullen and dogged way at his table or to be crying, but would rather have the child sitting in comfort with a holy cheerfulness, with a holy freedom of spirit; not in a sullen way, but as a child in the presence of his father, and not as a servant with the master.

OBJECTION. You told us before that there should be a brokenness of spirit and a sense of our sin.

ANSWER. That may be and joy, too. We rejoice with trembling. Therefore, that brokenness of spirit that I meant must not be slavish horror and fear, but a kindly melting of the soul from the apprehension of the love of God unto it in Jesus Christ, who was willing to be at so great a cost to purchase the pardon of sin. It must be such a gracious mourning as may stand with joy! The truth is that sorrow for sin in the sacrament that is not mixed with joy is a sorrow that does not sanctify God's name. Godly sorrow and evangelical joy may stand together very well.

And therefore know that this is not the time to give liberty to have your hearts sink. No, there must be no sinking sorrow of heart, but such a sorrow of heart as in the midst of it you may be able to look upon God as a reconciled Father to you, and have a cheerfulness of spirit as in the presence of God. You must look upon yourselves as God's guest, to be merry at His table. Now this is a great mystery of godliness, that there should be at the same time the sight of Christ crucified and a spiritual cheerfulness in the assurance of the love of God in Jesus Christ. I say it is a mystery, and only those who are believers are able to understand this mystery, how to have their hearts break and yet how to rejoice at the same time in that unspeakable love of God that is here presented unto them in this sacrament.

7. There must be thankfulness. Therefore it is called the "eucharist." And where one of the Evangelists says, "Christ blessed the bread," another one says, "Christ gave thanks." When Christ instituted this sacrament He gave thanks. He gave thanks? For what? He gave thanks to God the Father that He was pleased to send Him into the world to die for poor souls. Now shall Jesus Christ give thanks unto the Father for that which cost Him His life? "Yes," said Christ, "I see that here is a way to save souls, and let it cost Me My life if it will, yet I bless Thee, O Father, if souls may come to be saved, though it costs Me My life."

Christ rejoiced in His Spirit in thanking His Father for this. Then how should our hearts be enlarged with thankfulness when we come to this which the ancients used to call the "eucharist," that is "a thanksgiving?" We are to give God thanks for every mercy.

You will not eat your own bread without giving thanks, but when we come to have this bread, this bread of life, here is a matter of thankfulness; here is a matter of enlargement of soul. You who have the deadest and dullest soul and straightest spirit, yet when you come here and understand what you are doing, here you cannot but see matter for the enlargement of your heart, and wish that you had ten thousand times more strength to express the praises of the Lord. Here is a thing that must be the subject of the "Hallelujahs" and "Doxologies" that angels and saints must forever sound out in the highest heavens.

Do you know what the Lord presents to you here? It is more than if the Lord should say, "I will make ten thousand worlds for the sake of this creature, and give all these worlds to him." You would think that you were bound to bless Him then.

Only when God, in the bread and wine, reaches out to give you the body and blood of His Son, here is more matter of praise than if ten thousand thousand worlds were given to you. And therefore, God expects that you should say to your soul, as in Psalm 103:1–3, "My soul, praise thou the Lord, and all that is within me praise His holy name; bless the Lord, O my soul, and forget not all His benefits; who forgiveth all thine iniquities, who healeth all thy diseases."

O poor soul, here is the foundation of all mercies. Do you praise God for justification? For sanctification? Here is a glorious application of the mercy of God to the souls of sinners; and therefore, if ever you were thankful, be thankful here. The Sabbath, my brethren, is appointed to be the constant day of thanksgiving for the great mercies of God in Christ, and there are other days for national mercies. Now a special work of the Lord's Day is the celebration of this holy sacrament. The Christians in former times used to do it every Lord's Day because that's the day appointed by God to be the day of thanksgiving for that great mercy, the Lord Jesus Christ. And that's the reason why the Sabbath was changed. The last day of the week was the Jewish Sabbath, and that was to celebrate the memorial of the creation of the world. And the first day now is to be the day of thanksgiving for all the work of God in man's redemption.

8. If you would sanctify God's name, you must be willing to renew your covenant; that's the end of it. There must be an actual renewing of your covenant with God. "I come to receive this bread and this wine, and this is to be as the seal of the covenant on God's part. Now this will be implied in the nature of the thing that, if I take the seals of the covenant, I must be willing to set my seal to it too, to renew the covenant that God

calls me to."

Now know, all men and women who are saved are saved by the virtue of the covenant of grace; and there God, on His part, promises and makes a covenant that He will bestow His Son, life, and salvation through Him; and you must likewise come in on your part and believe in His Son and repent, which is the tenor of the gospel.

Now every time you come to receive this sacrament, you come to renew this covenant. It is as if you should say, "Lord, Thou hast been pleased to make a covenant of grace. As the first covenant was broken and all men were cast by that covenant, now Thou hast made a covenant of grace and called Thy servants whom Thou intendest to save, that they should renew their covenant with Thee in this sacrament of Thine. Lord, here I come; and Lord, here I renew it and set my seal to it, to promise and covenant with Thee that as ever I expect to receive any good from Christ, so Lord, here I will be Thine. I will give myself forever up to Thee as Thou hast given the body and blood of Christ for my salvation. So Lord, here I consecrate my body and blood to Thee, the last drop of my heart's blood shall be given up to Thee. And so my strength, and estate, and name, and whatever I am or have shall be Thine."

Have you done thusly when you have come to receive the sacrament? Have you actually renewed your covenant with God? You who have taken the body of Christ, have you given up your body to Christ? What's the reason, then, that you sin so much with your bodies? That you abuse your body with uncleanness? And drunkenness? And other wickedness afterwards? Oh, you profane the name of God and the very body and blood of Christ in this unless you give up your body and soul to God in this way of covenant.

9. For sanctifying God's name there is required a renewing of love, coming with lovely dispositions and the renewing of the grace of love, not only towards God, but towards our brethren. For it is the feast of the Lord, and it is an act of communion; communion not only with Christ, but with His churches, with His saints. And as I have told you that there is a profession of ourselves to be of the same body with Jesus Christ, then the Lord requires that His children should not fall out who come to His table, but that there should be love and peace. There's a mighty bond upon you when you come to the sacrament, and therefore, first all heart-burnings and heart-grudges must be laid aside. Second, you must come with a willingness to pass by all infirmities in your brethren.

Here I have the seal of God's willingness to pass by all my sins; and therefore I must be willing to pass by all infirmities in my brethren. I must now cast out all ill wishes towards others and come with a desire of all good unto them, with a heart ready to embrace any opportunity to do good. You lie to God unless you come with such a heart as this: "Lord, Thou knowest that I am willing to take all opportunities to do good to those with whom I now communicate, for it is the nearest communion that can possibly be in this world between one creature and another." And this is the reason why there should be that ordinance of Christ set up everywhere to cast out those who are unworthy, because it is the greatest union and communion that can possibly be. They are the same members of Christ.

Now, if you do not think such a one to be a member of Christ, why do you not do what you can to have him cast out? But as long as you have done nothing in private to him, or in telling the church, you own him to be a member of Jesus Christ. If you do so, take heed how your heart is estranged from him; take heed how you behave yourself to them. Take heed how you lie in a disputing and contentious way with them and hold them off at stave's end, or walk at a distance from them. Though they are never so poor and mean, know that you profane this holy ordinance every time you come to it when you come with such a heart as this.

If you do not find this renewed love say, "Lord, then there has begun a strangeness between me and those who have communicated with me; but, Lord, Thou art pleased to condescend to us to come once more to this ordinance that shall unite our hearts together more than ever they were. I will study to do what good I possibly can to my brother so that, as we join here to the feast of the Lord with comfort, we may live together in peace and love as becomes the saints of God and the members of the body of Jesus Christ." Oh, how far are people from any such work of God as this is. The Lord expects that this should be in you every time you come to the holy communion.

So nine particulars have been mentioned for sanctifying the name of God when we come to partake of the sacrament. But, O Lord, what cause have we to lay our hands upon our hearts! For if this is to sanctify Thy name, then it has been a riddle, a mystery to us.

Certainly, my brethren, these things are the truth of God that have been delivered; and so far as you have been wanting in any of these, know just so far you have taken God's name in vain in this holy ordinance. You have not been worthy receivers of this sacrament. You have cause to look back to your former ways and spend humiliation for your sin therein, and not to be greedy of it as some are. They must have the communion, but I put it to your consciences, have you repented for the profaning of God's name? And that's what we should have spoken further of, that God will be sanctified. That's thus: if we do not sanctify

God's name, it will turn quite to the contrary. It is the proper end of the sacrament to seal up our salvation, but if we do not sanctify God's name it will seal up our condemnation. If it has not been your endeavor to sanctify the name of God, as many times as you have received the sacrament, so many seals have you upon you for the sealing up of your condemnation. Many men's or women's condemnations are sealed with three or four hundred seals, it may be.

But yet for your comfort, while you are alive, it is possible that these seals may be broken open. As we read in Revelation, John saw the Book that had seven seals on it and none could be found who was able to open it. At length the Lamb that was slain was found worthy to open the Book. So I say, your condemnation is sealed up with many seals, and there is no creature who is able to cancel these seals, only the Lamb, Jesus Christ. Yes, the Christ whose blood you have shed and been guilty of, only He is worthy. And He is willing to open these seals, for as it was with those who crucified Christ, yet they are saved by the same blood that they had shed, as in Acts 2.

So though you have been guilty of shedding the blood of Christ again and again by this profane coming to the sacrament, yet know, seeing there is life in you and the day of grace is continued, that it is possible that your soul may be saved by that blood that you have crucified. Oh, how many are cut off who have thus profaned the name of God in this sacrament and have never come to understand this danger! They are cut off and now are undone forever. Why, bless God that you are alive to hear more about this sacrament and how God's name should be sanctified, that you are alive and have time to repent of this great evil of profaning the name of God in this holy sacrament.

SERMON XIII

Keep to the Institution of the Sacrament

"I will be sanctified in them that come nigh Me."

LEVITICUS 10:3

*T*here is one thing more about sanctifying the name of God in the sacrament which clearly concerns us, and that is to keep to the institution of the sacrament; for this is such a worship of God as depends merely upon institution, that is, upon a positive law, upon the will of God. There are some duties of worship that are natural, that we may know by the light of nature that they are due to God; but the sacrament is a duty of worship that is only by institution, and if God had not revealed it we would not have been bound to it. Therefore, in these duties of institution, God stands very punctual upon them. We must be very exact, neither to err on the right hand nor the left, to make any alteration in the points of instruction.

1. Now, therefore, for the institution of this sacrament, we find it in divers of the Evangelists. In Matthew 26:26 you find that Christ and His disciples eat the sacrament together; this was the way it was done. They were together sitting at the same table, so it is called the table of the Lord sometimes in Scripture. Therefore, that's the first thing that is according to

the institution, that those who communicate must come to the table as near as they can, as many as can sit about it, and all to come as near as they can. Otherwise you will not be able to attain to the end why God would have you come to receive.

The end is to remember the death of Christ. Now unless you are able to see the sight, to see what is done, to have your eye as well as your ear exercised, you do not fully accomplish the end that is appointed; for this is a sacrament that presents to our eyes the death of Christ and the great mysteries of salvation, and therefore it is according to the institution that every communicant must be where he may behold what is done. He must be where he may see the breaking of the bread and the pouring forth of the wine. Certainly it has been a disorderly way, therefore, for people to sit up and down in their pews everywhere in the congregation, and for the minister to go up and down after them so that they could see nothing nor scarcely hear anything.

There is much for the attaining to the end of the institution for all communicants to look upon the breaking of the bread and the pouring forth of the wine in the sacrament; and therefore all should come together and there as many as can sit at His table, or, for those who cannot, near to it. And the rather because this is not only from the example of Christ, that He did so, though that's significant, but because it has a spiritual significance in it, and that's the reason that it should be done.

We find in Luke 22:26 the institution of the sacrament. Now upon their coming and being with Christ at the table, He says in verses 29–30, "And I appoint unto you a kingdom as My Father hath appointed unto Me, that you may eat and drink at My table in My kingdom, and sit on thrones judging the twelve tribes of Israel." He spoke it upon the occasion of the disciples sitting with Him at the table when they ate bread and took the cup. Upon that occasion Christ spoke to His disciples and said, "I appoint to you a kingdom, that you may eat and drink at My table in the kingdom and so sit on thrones judging the twelve tribes of Israel."

It is as if Christ should say, "You can sit with Me at My table here, and know that this sitting with Me at My table is but a prelude, a fore-signification of the communion that you shall have with Me in My kingdom. You shall have that familiar communion with Me when I come unto My kingdom, there to sit, as it were, with Me, to join with Me in My kingdom judging the twelve tribes of Israel, even as you do now in that holy fellowship join with Me sitting at My table."

This is the measure of Christ, so that the gesture in the sacrament is not a mere indifferent thing. Heretofore it has been thought unreasonable to contend for what gesture we should use.

Now that which has been the institution of Christ and has a spiritual significance in it is not indifferent, for not only the eating of the bread and drinking of the wine is significant, but so is the gesture whereby we have fellowship with Jesus Christ here, to signify that fellowship we shall have with Him in the kingdom of heaven. So that the people of God would be deprived of a great deal of comfort, and of one special benefit of this holy sacrament, whereas they might not receive it sitting.

When Christ said that your sitting with Me here is a signifying of your sitting with Me when I come into the kingdom of heaven, some say they must kneel because they may receive it with more reverence. Certainly, if it were a thing indifferent, as some say, it would be another matter, but to say it is not reverent to sit is to accuse Christ Himself of a lack of reverence, as if He would appoint a way, or would have His disciples use any such way, as was not reverent.

Christ says, "I intend, by your gesture, to have this signified unto you, that though you are poor, wretched worms, yet even such is My love to you as you shall sit with Me when I come to My kingdom, and you shall judge the twelve tribes of Israel." And every time you come to His table and there sit at it or about it, then you should be put in mind that there is a time, that though you are poor, unworthy creatures, worthy to be among the dogs, yet the mercy of God is such unto us that He has appointed us to have a familiar fellowship with the Lord Jesus Christ when we come into His kingdom to sit with Him, and even to judge the twelve tribes of Israel, yea, to judge the whole world. So says the Scriptures, "Shall not the saints judge the world?" Now this hinders spiritual meditation and comfort that the saints have. Therefore we are to look to the institution and follow it. That's the first thing in sitting with Christ at His table.

2. The bread being taken by the minister is to be blessed, broken, and then to be given. Christ took it, He blessed it and broke it, and gave it; and the people there are to look upon all this, to look upon the minister's taking, blessing, breaking, and giving, and then the cup by itself. We find Christ in Matthew 26:27 first blessing the bread, and then He blessed the cup distinctly by itself saying, "This is My blood of the New Testament which is shed for many, for the remission of sins."

And you shall observe that the text says, "He drank it, and said, 'Drink ye all of it.' " So it is not according to the institution for a minister to go up and down and to give it into every man's hand. Certainly this was not so from the beginning. This is a way of man's own devising, for the bread and the cup to be given into everybody's hand by the minister. Christ gave it once, He gave it to them all and said, "Drink ye all of this." So it was done.

QUESTION. But you will say, "Is it not better for it to be given into everyone's hand?"

ANSWER. No, because giving it once for all signifies more fully the fellowship and communion that they have together. At a table, it would be a strange thing if every bit of meat were given to one particularly. No, the dishes must be set before them and they must take it themselves. Indeed, if they are children, you cut every piece of meat and give it into their hands or mouths. But it's suitable to a fellowship at table and communion to have the meat set before them, being blessed, and then for all to partake of it.

And besides this, giving it into everyone's hand certainly came to us from a popish and superstitious conceit of the papists; for the papists will give it into their mouths because the people will not defile it with their hands. And it was to bring more reverence to the sacrament. Now there's a great deal of danger in bringing in men's devices to cause more reverence. We are to look to the ordinance of Christ. He gave it once and said, "Drink ye all of it," generally to them all, and so the ministers should do.

And besides, there is this in it. One would wonder that ministers should give it in particular and not in general to the church, for by this means ministers might abundantly ease themselves of a great deal of charge and guilt. For upon this ground it will appear that a minister, though an eminent officer, is to look to the congregation that they be fit; yet, the truth is, it concerns the church as well to look who comes there, and likewise the minister, I say, to look about him so that he does not say, "The body of the Lord Jesus Christ was given to you," when he knows they are profane and wicked.

It concerns the minister to look that he does not tell a lie; but when the minister gives it generally to the church and says, "Take, eat," and "Take, drink," he gives it particularly to no one. Now, then, his charge is divided to the church, and if there is anyone who is unworthy, let the church look to it as well as he. Though he is an eminent officer, it's more especially in particular his duty than any others. Heretofore the charge would lie much upon the minister, but the minister, according to the institution, should give the sacrament to no particular person, but in general to the church. And therefore, if there were any particular person whom the minister, upon a particular knowledge, knew to be wicked, he might in great part discharge himself as professing against this or that particular man—for it is not in his power alone to keep any from the sacrament. But if it is that he shall profess against such and such men, the church must join with him to labor to keep them from the sacrament. And that is the next thing for the institution: Christ did not give it into any particular man's hands, but He gave it to all, saying, "Drink, and eat ye all of it."

3. A third thing that is to be observed for the institution of this is that all the while the communicants are taking, eating, and drinking the bread and wine, they should all have their thoughts exercised about the death of Jesus Christ, for that's the institution: "Do this in remembrance of Me." There should be no action intermingled in the time of the receiving of the sacrament, nothing but minding the work that you are about, which is to remember the death of Jesus Christ and to discern the body of the Lord. Not only when you take the bread and wine to yourselves, but when you see the bread and wine broken or poured forth, and you see others taking the bread and wine, all that while you should be thinking of the death of Christ and discerning the Lord's body.

And consider that these outward elements signify and

seal the great benefit of the covenant of grace. Therefore, it is not according to the institution to be singing psalms in the meantime while the sacrament is being received, and so to have your thoughts about other things. Singing psalms in its due time is a good thing, but for you to do it at that time when the death of Christ is presented before you, and when Christ calls you to look upon His body and to think upon what He has done and suffered, this is no seasonable time for singing. If you read the institution, you shall find that Christ, after all was done, had them sing a hymn. So according to that institution, it is after the action of eating and drinking is done that the church is to join together and sing a psalm in the praise of God.

And then they must all mind the same thing together, for that's the thing to be done in the sacrament. What one does, all must do together; for when one part sings and the other part waits for the bread and wine, this is not suitable to the holy table and that communion that God requires of us. Though the things in themselves are both good that are being done, yet when we are about this holy ordinance, being it is an ordinance for communion, all are to be doing the same thing at the same time. And so when all have finished eating and drinking, then all are to join together in singing to the praise of God.

Now it may be that this, at first, seems strange to many, yet observe this: Keep to the institution in the sacrament. Though you may think it a more mean way, yet you will find a greater beauty in this ordinance than you ever found in all your lives; for the more we keep to Christ's institution and mingle nothing of our own, the more glory and beauty and excellency appears in the ordinances of Jesus Christ. But when any man shall mix any of his own inventions, though he may do it to a good end and think to add to and put a greater luster upon the sacrament, the truth is that what he thinks to be a greater luster, reverence, or honor upon it rather takes off the luster and glory of the sacrament. Then are the institutions of Christ glorious when there is no mixture among them.

Thus we should sanctify the name of God in receiving this holy sacrament. You have had divers things propounded to you whereby you may come to know and easily see that there has been a great deal of dishonor done to this sacrament, and the beauty and glory of it has been darkened, and the sweet that the saints might otherwise have received in partaking it has been exceedingly hindered.

There is but one more thing that I shall propound to you, and that is the various things that we should meditate on in receiving the sacrament. The most concerning meditations are suggested in the holy communion that are in anything whatsoever, more concerning, more efficacious, more various meditations we have suggested here than in anything; and it is a great sign that men and women do not discern the Lord's body if their meditations are barren at that time. I will therefore suggest some meditations so that the ordinance of God may hold out very plainly and familiarly to every communicant for the buying of their thoughts all the time that action is being done.

MEDITATION 1. The way of salvation is by a Mediator. It is not only God's mercy, God saying that He is offended by sin but He will be content to pass it by; no, but it is through a Mediator. Now this meditation is suggested thus: When I see the bread and wine, if I discern what they signify, it will hold forth to me that the way of man's salvation is not merely from hence that God said, "Well, I will pardon them and no more," but there is a great work required of God to make an atonement between sinners and Himself. This sacrament holds forth this much unto us. Wherefore else we have bread and wine, but to signify that the way of our reconciliation must be through a Mediator.

MEDITATION 2. This Mediator who stands between God and us is verily and truly man. He has taken our nature upon Him. The bread puts us in mind of the body and blood of Christ, and the wine of His blood; and therefore we are to meditate on the human nature of Jesus Christ. And this is a meditation that has an abundance of might springing out of it. What, has the Son of God taken our nature upon Him? Oh, how has God honored human nature! Then let me not abuse my body to lust or to wickedness, seeing that Jesus Christ has taken the body of man upon Him, human nature upon Him. Let me honor human nature that is so nearly united to the divine nature.

MEDITATION 3. Here is presented to us what this Mediator has done to reconcile us to God. His body was broken. He has subjected Himself to the breaking of His body and to the pouring forth of His blood for our reconciling. It is not merely, as I said before, that God has said, "I'll pardon them," but it has cost Christ, undertaking to make peace between His Father and us, the breaking of His body and the pouring forth of His blood. This is a useful meditation. Oh, what should we be willing to suffer for Jesus Christ in our bodies, even to resist unto blood, seeing that Christ has been content to have His precious body broken and His blood shed for us!

MEDITATION 4. Here we have occasion to meditate on what the Scripture says, that we are saved by the blood of God. "They crucified the Lord of glory," that's the Scripture phrase. We should consider, when we see the wine poured out and are so put in mind of blood, whose body and blood is this. It is no other than the body and blood of Him who was truly God, the second Person in the Trinity. This is the great mystery of the gospel, and this is very needful for us to be thinking of when we see the body broken and the blood poured out.

What, will the breaking of the body and shedding of the blood of a mere creature be sufficient to make peace between God and man? Surely not. Therefore you must meditate on whose body this is. It is the body and blood of Him who was God. It's true, God has no body or blood, but the same person who was God had a body and blood. That body and blood was united unto the divine nature in a hypostatical union, and from thence it came to have an efficacy to satisfy God, for to reconcile God and us together is the great mystery of godliness.

MEDITATION 5. Another meditation is this when you see bread broken and wine poured out. Oh, the infinite dreadfulness of the justice of God. How dreadful is the justice of God that, coming upon His own Son and requiring satisfaction from Him, should thus bruise and break Him, that should have His blood, that should require such sufferings even from His Son! Dreadful is God's justice. The justice of God is to be feared and trembled at. Here we see what is required for the sin of man, and nothing would be abated to Jesus Christ Himself.

MEDITATION 6. Another meditation is this: Here I see presented to me what every soul that shall be saved cost. Whoever shall have his soul saved has it saved by a ransom, by a price paid that is more worthy than ten thousand thousand worlds. You slight your own soul; but if you prove to be saved, it cost more than if thousands of worlds had been given for you, even the shedding of the blood of Christ, every drop of which was more precious than ten thousand worlds.

MEDITATION 7. Again, from hence we see the evil of sin. How great is that which has made such a breach between God and my soul that only such a way and such a means could take away my sin. I must either have lain under the burden of my sin eternally or Jesus Christ, who is God and man, must suffer so much for it. Oh, what meditations are these to take up the hearts of men!

MEDITATION 8. Behold the infinite love of God to mankind and the love of Jesus Christ, that rather than God see the children of men to perish eternally, He would send His Son to take our nature upon Him and thus suffer such dreadful things. Herein God shows His love. It is not the love of God so much in giving you a good voyage and prospering you outwardly in the world, but "God so loved the world that He gave His only begotten Son." And it pleased the Father to break His Son and to pour out His blood. Here is the love of God and of Jesus Christ. Oh, what a powerful, mighty, drawing, efficacious meditation this should be unto us!

MEDITATION 9. Those who are believers shall be nourished to eternal life so that there is no fear that a believer should ever quite fall off from God and die in his sin. Why? Because the body and blood of Christ is given unto him for his spiritual nourishment. Though a believer is never so weak, yet seeing that God has appointed the body and blood of His Son for him to feed upon and to drink in a spiritual way, then surely the weakest in all the world will be strengthened to go through all the hazards and dangers that there are in the world. 'Tis that which strengthens believers to encounter all kinds of dangers. It's this that preserves the weakest grace in a believer, namely the spiritual nourishment that God the Father has appointed to them, even the feeding upon the body and drinking the very blood of His Son. This is meat indeed and drink indeed that will nourish to eternal life.

MEDITATION 10. The last meditation is this: when you come to see the bread broken and the wine poured out, you have an occasion to meditate on the whole New Covenant, the covenant of grace that God has made with sinners. For so the words of the institution are: "This is the cup of the New Testament." The New Testament, which is all one with the New Covenant, only differs in this particular: It contains the substance of the New Covenant, but it is called "testament" in this regard to show that the Lord does all in the New Covenant. That is, He not only promises such and such mercies upon condition of our believing and repenting, but He works believing and repenting, and works grace; and therefore the same thing that is sometimes called a covenant is called a testament. That is the will of God wherein the Lord bequeaths His rich legacies to His children, to those who shall be eternally saved, so that all the good things in the covenant of grace are bequeathed by way of testament as well as covenant. And this is a mighty comfortable situation to the saints.

Indeed, when they look upon the way of the gospel as in a way of covenant, then they think this: "This requires something to be done on our part, and indeed God will keep covenant on His part, but it may be that we shall not keep covenant on ours and so we may fail at last." But when you look upon all the good things in the gospel that are dispensed in the way of a testament, that is the will of God, the legacies that God bequeaths to His servants, this is a mighty comfort to the soul, that all the precious things of the gospel come to me in the way of a testament. And that's the meaning of the New Testament, that is, the mercies of God in Christ coming now in the way of another administration than they did before.

'Tis not only new in respect of the covenant of works that God made with Adam, but new in respect of the administration. Our forefathers, the patriarchs, had the same thing in substance, but administered in a different way, and there are many differences. But when we hear of the New Testament, there is presented unto us all the riches of the covenant of grace in the way of a legacy and in the administration of it with clarity and with a great deal of mercy and goodness from God, the terror and harshness of the old administration being taken away.

Now these are the meditations by which we should labor to sanctify our hearts when we are receiving the sacrament; and in working these meditations upon our hearts, we shall come to sanctify the name of God when we are drawing nigh to Him in that holy ordinance of His.

The next thing when we are there must be an actuating of these holy dispositions that we spoke of before. 'Tis not enough for a Christian to bring grace to the sacrament, but there must be a stirring of that grace at that time; otherwise the name of God is not sanctified in receiving the sacrament. And above all graces is the actuating of the grace of faith. 'Tis not enough that you are a believer, but your faith must act at that very instant.

First, when you hear the minister in the name of Christ say, "This is the body of Jesus Christ which was given for you. Take, eat," you should have your faith so acting upon the mercy of God in giving Jesus Christ for the nourishment of your soul to eternal life that it should be as if you heard a voice from heaven saying, "Here is the body of My Son given for you particularly. Take it and eat; apply it to yourself, and so make Christ one with you by faith as the bread is made one with your body when you eat it."

When you come to take hold of the bread, you are to put forth an act of faith, faith being the hand of the soul. And at that instant when you take the bread and put it into your mouth to eat, you should stir up the act of faith afresh, laying more hold upon Jesus Christ. Look as once you did in your first conversion when Christ was presented to you in the Word or in any other way. There was an act of faith drawn forth whereby your soul cast itself and rolled itself upon Jesus Christ. So should you renew it. Renew the same work of faith that you found in your very first conversion, and thereby you shall come to have renewed comfort in the renewing of that act.

I might name other graces and dispositions for you, how there should be a stirring and an acting of them, only remember that I leave all this point with this note: that grace is not enough for partaking of the sacrament of the Lord's Supper unless there is an acting and a stirring up of that grace. Many Christians are careful to prepare and examine beforehand whether they have grace or not, but at that time when they come to receive, then there is not a lively working and stirring up of that grace. And so they come to lose the comfort and benefit of that ordinance. This much shall suffice for the point of sanctifying God's name in receiving the holy communion.

Sanctifying the Name of God in Prayer

"I will be sanctified in them that come nigh Me."

LEVITICUS 10:3

I shall now come to the last point, which is the sanctifying of the name of God in prayer. This argument might take up many sermons, but upon occasion of the days of prayer and humiliation I have preached divers sermons about the point of prayer. Therefore I shall be brief and only reckon up together and set before your view the several things that are to be done for sanctifying the name of God in prayer.

First, in prayer we draw nigh to God, and it's a duty of God's worship. That, I suppose, all of you cannot but acknowledge, and it is a natural duty of worship. The other was instituted, but this is natural. It's natural for the creature to draw nigh to God in prayer, wherein the creature tenders up his homage to God, manifests his dependence upon God for all the good that he has, and acknowledges God as the Author of all good. Therefore this is worship, and it's a great part of worship.

Prayer is such a part of worship that sometimes in Scripture it's put for the whole of worship. "He that calls upon the name of God shall be saved," that is, he that worships God rightly. Jeremiah 10:25: "Pour out Thy wrath upon the heathen that

know Thee not, and on the families that call not on Thy name,"
who do not pray, that is, who do not worship Thee. There one
part of worship is put for the whole as being a principal part of
the worship of God.

Surely we must sanctify God's name in prayer, for it is that
which sanctifies all things to us. 1 Timothy 4:5: "Everything is
sanctified by the word of God and prayer." And if the argument
of Christ was right, as no doubt it was, that the temple was greater
than the gold upon the temple (because the temple sanctified
the gold) and the altar was greater than the offering that was
offered upon it (because it sanctified the offering), then prayer
must be a mighty great ordinance, a greater thing than any
other because it sanctifies all things. The Word sanctifies the
creature, but prayer sanctifies the very Word unto our use.
And therefore, when we read the Word, we are to pray for a
sanctified use of the Word.

Prayer is a great ordinance, a great duty of worship that
sanctifies all. Prayer has a casting voice in all the great works
of God in the world, the great affairs of the kingdom of Christ.
I say that prayer has a kind of casting voice, and orders under
God the great things of the world. They are according to the
prayers of the saints. They bring down blessings upon the godly;
they pour forth judgments on the wicked. The prayers of the
saints are the vials that are poured forth in a special manner
upon the heads of the wicked. Therefore God's name is to be
sanctified in prayer.

It is to be sanctified first in preparation. Psalm 10:17: "Thou
wilt prepare their heart. Thou wilt cause them to hear." It is the
Lord who prepares the heart, and then He causes his ears to
hear. Therefore, in 1 Peter 5:7, we are required to "watch unto
prayer." Men and women should keep a narrow watch over
their hearts and minds so that they may not be hindered in

their prayers, that they may always be in a fit posture to pray.

It's that which would help us against many temptations to evil. If I give way to such and such temptations, it will hinder my prayers. I shall not have that freedom and enlargement in prayer as otherwise I would if I give way to such and such things. Therefore let me take heed of this or it will hinder my prayers.

It is as if the apostle should say, "This should be the care of Christians. Then they are likely to sanctify the name of God in prayer if this is their great care, that there is nothing in the world that shall hinder their prayers."

Oh, let me take heed that I do nothing to hinder my prayers. If I go abroad into company and am merry and mirthful, and there game and drink and sport myself in company, will this not hinder my prayers? Will this not hinder the spirituality of my heart in communion with God in prayer when I come home at night? I appeal to you, have you had that freedom in prayer afterwards? Surely not; "therefore watch unto prayer."

Now, for the preparation of the heart unto prayer, we must understand first what is to be done in the course of one's life, and second, what is to be done just when one comes to prayer.

For the first, the course of one's life, labor to keep all things even and clear between God and your souls so that you may not come with shackles about your legs, with guilt upon your consciences. Men who have given way to any base, sinful way, when they come to prayer, the guilt of their heart sinks them. But those who can keep their peace with God in the course of their lives have other manner of freedom in prayer than you who walk loosely and contract guilt upon your spirits.

The second thing is to keep our hearts sensible of our continual dependence upon God, sensible how we depend upon God for whatever we are, whatever we have, whatever we do. The blessing of all is from God. The beams of the sun do not depend upon the sun as much as we do God. If He withdraws Himself ever so little from us, we all sink down to nothing and perish forever. That soul that every day and hour is sensible of the infinite dependence it has upon God for its present and eternal estate will be fit for prayer. And it should be our care to carry ourselves so that at any hour in the day, or minute in the hour, we might be fit to go to prayer.

That's one meaning of 1 Thessalonians 5:17: "pray continually." Not that every moment we should be praying, but that we should keep our hearts in a praying frame. Some of you, when you have let out your passions and are in a distemper, what, will you go to prayer now? Your conscience will tell you that you are not fit to go to prayer at that time. Certainly, if you are not fit to pray, you are not fit to live! You are in an ill condition anytime you are not fit to pray; and there can be no excuse whatsoever that can be sufficient to plead for yourself why you should not be fit to pray at any time.

There is that continual dependence upon God for all, and that need you have of the blessing of God for everything. That is the reason why you should be in a fit condition for praying at all times, but now when you come to prayer at the set time, then there should be a special preparation.

First, you should prepare yourselves by getting fresh and powerful apprehensions of the glory of God before whom you go. Prepare by meditations about the glory of that infinite God you are now addressing yourselves unto. Possess yourselves with thoughts and meditations of the glory of that great God. That's the first.

Second, labor to get your hearts sensible of what you are going for. I am now going to God. For what? For pardon of sin, or for assurance of His love, or for power against sin, or for such and such mercies. Let me by meditation work my heart to be sensible of these things that I am going to God for, to set a due price upon those mercies that I am praying for and to get my heart affected with them.

Third, labor to get your hearts separated from the world and from all things that are here below in the world. That should have been a third thing in the course of your lives. You should never let out your hearts to any creature, either to businesses or pleasures in the world, but that you may have command of your hearts to call them in when you will, to call them in to God in prayer. And then when you come to prayer, there should be an actual separation of your hearts from all things in the world, a dedicating of yourselves to God for this time as one who has nothing to do with the world, nothing to do with anything but this duty you are now about. This is the preparation of your hearts to prayer in the course of your lives.

Then, for the prayer itself, first we must consider the matter of prayer and, second, the manner of it.

As for the matter of it, we must look to it that it is according to God's will. 1 John 5:14: "This is the confidence that we have in Him, that if we ask anything according to His will He heareth us." Therefore, for the matter, we must be sure that what we pray for is good. It must be for the glory of God, for the good of ourselves, and for the good of our brethren.

1. The glory of God should be the chief matter we are to pray for. So Christ, when He teaches us to pray, begins the very first petition in Matthew 6:9–10, "Hallowed be Thy name. Thy kingdom come, Thy will be done." First begin with the glory of God. Mind that in the chief place above all other things. God gives you leave to pray for outward things, but first for the glory of God, minding that before your own benefit, before the pardon of sin and your daily bread. How few sanctify God's name in this?

People have little mind to pray unless they are in outward afflictions, or when they are upon their sick beds. Then they will pray. At sea or in storms, then they will pray. Then it seems that the main matter of your prayer is only for yourselves; but how has the matter of the glory of the great God and the good of the churches taken your hearts all this while? How have your hearts been affected with this, that the name of God has been so little sanctified in the world, that the kingdom of God has not come, and that the will of God has not been done? Have these things taken up your hearts in prayer, the matters of the glory of God and the good of churches, though you do not have any particular interest in them? If these things took up your hearts in prayer then, when you were at sea, you would remember the cause of the churches as much as yourselves.

The church is, as it were, in the midst of the sea, tossed up and down in a great storm. Why do you not pray as earnestly for the kingdom of Christ among His churches as for yourselves when you are in a storm at sea? Yea, and spiritual things should be the chief matter of your prayer, for they are nearest to the glory of God. Though God has His glory from other things, yet spiritual things are nearest the glory of God. Now in these days of prayer, many will come to pray that they might be freed from danger, that they might have outward peace. This is good, but spiritual things are the chief things; and therefore the strength of your spirits should be thus powered forth to God: "Oh, that I could get my heart to God and the assurance of the love of God! Oh, that I could get the shine of His face! Oh, that I could get power over such and such corruptions!"

I beseech you to observe this. Spiritual things may be prayed for absolutely, but outward things must be prayed for conditionally. I may pray (and never put any condition in at all) that the Lord would pardon my sins and help me against my corruptions, and so forth. But when I pray for the health of my body, I ought to pray, "if this according to Thy will, then restore to me the health of my body, or the health of my husband, or the health of my wife." But you may pray, "Lord, convert the soul of my husband or the soul of my wife" without any condition at all.

When your estates at sea are in danger, when you pray for them you must make conditions. "Lord, as Thou seest best for me, so deal with me." This shows the excellency that there is in spiritual things above outward things. Surely spiritual things are to be more desired, for they are to be prayed for absolutely, and the other to be prayed for only conditionally.

2. We are to pray for our own good. God gives us leave to do so, only here a question comes in at this point.

QUESTION. Is it sinful to pray for afflictions, as sometimes some will be ready to do?
ANSWER. We may not pray that God would afflict us, because affliction is, in itself materially, an evil thing and a fruit of the curse. Therefore we may not absolutely pray for it, but we may pray for afflictions disjunctively, conditionally, comparatively.

Disjunctively thus, "Lord, either grant unto me a sanctified use of such a mercy, or otherwise let me rather be without it. Let me have a sanctified use of my sickness, or otherwise let my sickness be continued unto me." Thus you may pray for continuing in sickness.

Conditionally thus: "Lord, if Thou seest that my heart is so vile and wretched that I will abuse (through my corruption) such and such mercies, Lord, rather take them from me and let me be without them. If Thou seest that there is no way to break this proud heart of mine but such a way, Lord, let that be

Thy way to break it, if Thou seest it according to Thy will as the most fitting way."

Comparatively thus: "Lord, rather let me have any affliction but sin. Rather let me suffer the loss of my estate than sin against Thee. Anything, Lord, rather than sin." Thus you may pray for afflictions, but not absolutely. You must not pray that God would send you afflictions, for you do not know your hearts. It may be that if afflictions should come your hearts may be as stubborn under your afflictions as they are now, for affliction has no power in itself to do us any good.

3. And for the good of others, Christ teaches us to pray, "Our Father." There comes in here a rebuke of the wicked practice of some in cursing, and then a question about it.

It is a wicked thing to use curses, but it's a most wicked thing to wish evil to others in a way of prayer. Yet how many do so? Though it may be that they do not think it, they speak to God and desire Him to bring such and such evils upon their neighbors, yea, sometimes parents upon their children. This is a wicked practice of men. Is it not wickedness enough for you to have any desire that there should be any evil to befall your brother, but will you dare to presume to call God to be an instrument of the execution of your base, sinful wrath? That God must be a laborer, as it were, to your wrath and to your passion is abominable wickedness!

Any of you who have ever been guilty of this sin of cursing others, wives, children, servants, or friends, the Lord rebuke you for this sin. How far have you been from sanctifying God's name in prayer? Whereas, instead of sanctifying the holy name of God, you have called God to be a servant and a slave to your passion. Oh, remember this, you who have been at sea and have been angry, and when things have not gone according to your mind you have fallen to cursing and wishing such and such evils might come upon those with whom you are angry. That's a kind of prayer, but it is a most fearful taking the name of God in vain in the highest degree; and certainly God will not hold him guiltless who shall so take His name in vain. Therefore be humbled for this sin.

OBJECTION. But you will say, "Do we not read in the book of the Psalms where many times the prophet David cursed the enemies of God and wished evil to come upon them?"
ANSWER. First, the prophets and those who penned the psalms had a prophetic spirit; and those places that you read that are in a way of cursing are rather prophetic predictions of evil than direful imprecations. They are rather foretelling what shall be in a way of prophecy than wishing what should be.

Second, if they are wishing what should be, then I answer that those who were endued with such a prophetic spirit did not know who were the implacable enemies of God and who were not, as David prayed against Judas so many hundreds of years before he was born. By a prophetic spirit, he knew that he was the child of perdition. Indeed, if we could certainly know that a man was to be a castaway eternally from God, that would be another matter. It was determined almost generally by the church in the time of Julian, because of his apostasy being so abominable, that he had committed the sin against the Holy Ghost, and upon that they cursed him. Now I say that those who had an extraordinary spirit, who knew who these were, might do it; but this is no example to us in an ordinary way to wish evil and curses upon others. But thus far we may do it with all the enemies of the church.

First, we may curse them conjunctively: "Lord, either take them out of the way or keep them so that they may not do mischief in the church."

Or thus conditionally: "If Thou seest, Lord, that they are implacable, Thou knowest them. If so, let Thy wrath and curse pursue them. Lord, Thou seest what evil they are set upon, and therefore, rather than they should attain their mischievous designs, let Thy wrath and curse pursue them."

So we may do, but not absolutely to curse anyone. Though they should do us never so much wrong, we are called to blessing. But in our zeal for God, take heed that we are not carried on in our own passion. But being sure it is in zeal to God, we may wish the curses of God to pursue those whom God knows to be implacable. This is but appealing to God, and not at all fastening it upon any particular persons whom we know, but leaving it unto God for the execution of it.

And so in a zeal to the glory of God we may do it, and we are warranted to do so by the second petition, "Thy kingdom come." For that petition that requires us to pray for the coming of the kingdom of Jesus Christ also requires that we should pray against all means that hinder the coming of the kingdom of Jesus Christ. So that every time the church prays, "Thy kingdom come," they as much as say, "O Lord, set Thyself against all the enemies of Thy kingdom. If they belong to Thy election, Lord, convert them; but otherwise confound them."

Now thus we see how we are to sanctify the name of God in prayer in regard of the matter of the prayer.

THE MANNER OF PRAYER

But as for the manner of prayer, the most things, I confess, are here.

1. When we come to prayer, we must be sure to pray with understanding. 1 Corinthians 14:15: "What is it then? I will pray

with the spirit, and will pray with understanding also." God does not love the sacrifice of fools. We must not come babbling to God in prayer to speak we know not what, and to multiply words we know not where; but God requires that those who come to prayer come with understanding, that they offer to God a rational, reasonable, and understanding sacrifice. God is a Spirit, and He will be worshipped in spirit and in truth. Now as it belongs to all other duties of worship, so especially in prayer, to know what we are doing when we pray, not to think to put God off with a mere empty sound.

2. We must give up all the faculties of our souls in it. I spoke to that in the worship of God in general. We shall now apply it particularly to prayer, giving up not only our understandings, but our wills, our thoughts, our affections, and our strength in prayer. In 2 Chronicles 20:3, it is said of Jehoshaphat that "he set himself to seek the Lord." He gave his whole self to seek the Lord. We are to give our whole self, and not to be divided in prayer.

That is an argument that indeed might well take up a whole sermon, showing the evil of the wandering of our spirits in prayer. We should take heed of the wandering of our spirits in hearing the Word and receiving the sacraments—so also in prayer. The people of God are much troubled with the wandering of their thoughts both in Word and in sacrament. It is their great burden and should be so. But I never hear any more complaints of the wandering of their spirits than in the time of prayer. The people of God are much pestered in their spirits with this evil. It is very grievous to them, and many of them go under, as it is a grievous burden all their days. The chief burden upon their spirits is their wandering in prayer, so that if God should speak to them as He spoke unto Solomon and asked him what He should give him, I verily believe there are many in this congregation who already have a good assurance of God's love in Christ (if they did not have that, that would be the main thing they would ask for). But, having attained that, if God would speak from heaven and say, "What shall I give you for yourselves?" if He should ask you in general, it may be you would ask something for the churches, but if it is for yourselves, you would put up this petition, "O Lord, that I may be delivered from a wandering spirit in holy duties, and especially in the duty of prayer, that I may thereby come to enjoy more holy communion with Thee than ever yet I enjoyed." And they would account this to be a greater mercy than if God should give them to be kings or queens over the whole world.

If God should put these two into balance, either the whole world to possess, or otherwise to have more free hearts in coming to God in prayer, and to be delivered from that which has so hindered their communion with God in prayer, they would despise and scorn the world in comparison to such a mercy as this is. Carnal hearts think little of it, but those who are the servants of God find it to be very grievous to them. But seeing that the time is past, I shall reserve that to speak of yet more largely for the help of those who are under the burden of it.

I'll only speak one thing further now, and that shall be to those who are wicked and vile, who not only have vain, wandering thoughts in prayer, but in the very duty of prayer many times have wicked and ungodly thoughts. How horrible are they! Unclean thoughts, murderous thoughts, it may be, and most abominable. I confess even those who are godly may sometimes have blasphemous thoughts cast into them, for the devil is never more busy than at the time of prayer. But they rather come from the devil than from the stream and corruption of their own hearts, which we may make out more clearly afterwards. But now I speak to such as have most wicked, abominable thoughts rising from the stream and corruption of their hearts, such thoughts as their hearts close with in prayer. And they can roll those thoughts about in their minds like a child will roll a piece of sugar in its mouth. This is the wickedness of men's and women's hearts.

Take this one note with you, that all those dreadful, vile, unclean, covetous thoughts of yours in prayer have been to God as if you had spoken them in words. Thoughts to God are all one with Him as words are to men; for God is a Spirit, and the spirit converses with God in thoughts as well as men converse with men in words. And what a woeful guiltiness would have been with you if you had spoken such vile and wicked things to men as have sometimes been in your minds when you are praying to God. How would the company have spit in your faces and kicked you away from them? None who have any face of godliness would have endured you in their company, and yet here's the evil of it: your hearts are not troubled, but you rise off your knees and away you go. You have a cauterized conscience, a seared conscience, that can entertain such vile thoughts at any time without having your spirit afflicted and going away with shame and confusion as if the greatest evil had befallen you. Therefore, take heed of this.

We are first to sanctify God's name in regard to the matter of our prayers, and, second, in regard to the manner. For the first, we made an end of it the last day and came unto the manner, and there were two things mentioned.

First, we must pray with understanding. Second, we must give up ourselves to prayer. Now in the close of the exercise we had occasion to fall upon that argument about the wandering of our thoughts in prayer, and by that we come to take God's name in vain instead of sanctifying His name. God expects that we should have our thoughts, will, and affections, our whole soul acting upon Him in the duty of prayer, or else we do not pray to God as unto a God.

Vain thoughts in prayer pick up the sacrifice like the birds that Abraham drove away from the sacrifice so that they would not peck it. Wicked lusts in men's hearts are like swine to take the meat and all to pull it in the dirt. So their prayers are filthy and dirty with their lusts. But those that are otherwise godly, yet by their vain thoughts the beauty and excellency of their prayers is taken away. As wine and beer that have the spirits of them gone, so the life and spirit of our duties are gone by our vain thoughts, and therefore vain thoughts deaden the heart a great deal.

So said David in the 119th Psalm, "Turn away mine eyes from beholding vanity, and quicken me in Thy Law." While our eyes look upon vanity, there will be no quickness in our hearts in any service that we tender up to God. Now many of God's people have experienced the evil of this and groan under the burden of this. And as I said the last time, if so be that the Lord should speak from heaven to them and ask them what they would have, already having the assurance of His love in Christ, they would ask for the deliverance of a vain spirit in the performance of holy duties.

"Bring Me no vain oblations," said God in Isaiah 1:13. Oh, what vain offerings do we bring by the vanity of our thoughts in prayer! 'Tis true, the best of all will have vain thoughts sometimes, but yet one compares the vain thoughts of men in prayer to a spaniel that goes out with a man. He walks perhaps but half a mile, but the spaniel will be running up and down, this way and that way, and if all the space of ground which the spaniel has gone over should be measured, it may be that while you are walking half a mile, the spaniel will have gone half a dozen miles. So our fancies are like a spaniel that will go this way and that in a thousand vain thoughts.

But it is different with a godly man. Even though a spaniel is running from his master, yet if he gives a call, he is able to bring the spaniel to him immediately. And it would be well if it were so with us. Though our fancies are wild, yet if we were able to call in our fancies and have them at our command, it would be well with us.

And I often find it that those who are newcomers complain much of the vanity of their thoughts. They used to pray before and never had such vain thoughts as they now have. The reason why there is so much vanity of thoughts, or at least so much taken notice of, is first because there is but a little grace in the midst of a great deal of corruption in young converts. I liken it to a spark of fire in the midst of a great deal of ashes. Now if there lies a heap of ashes and nothing else, you do not stir them. But if there are ashes and some fire, then you will stir them and blow those sparks to kindle another fire. Now when you come to make any motion, then the ashes will fly about whereas before they lay still. So it is here.

Before God worked upon your heart, there was nothing else but ashes upon your soul and they lay still. But God has kindled some sparks of grace in your heart, and God is blowing them up to a greater heat and is bringing them to a flame. Upon this motion that is in your heart and the stirring to kindle those sparks further in your heart, it is that the ashes of your corruption fly, as it were, about your ears. And that there are such stirrings of corruption more than there were before is not because there is more corruption than there was formerly, but that before, there being nothing else but corruption, it lay still. Now, because there is something else, that corruption so stirs.

And besides, you know that if a man who used to keep lewd company is turned by God, he will keep that company no more. At first he shall be more troubled with them than he was before, and they will knock at his door more often and labor to get him with them again. So it is here. When the soul, vanity, and lusts were friends together, there was no disturbance or taking notice of anything then. But when the soul casts out those sinful distempers and will have no more of them, they, for the present, will be more importunate, active, and stirring than they were before.

Besides, the Lord does this to humble your heart more so that thereby you may come to see the great corruption that was in your soul before. The working of your corruptions will reveal much evil in your heart that you did not think was there before. When the corruptions of men and women lie still, they think that there is no such thing in their souls. Take, for example, your civil men. What's the reason that they bless themselves and think they are in a good condition? It's because their corruptions lie still in them and do not stir. They would not be able to believe what an abundance of wickedness is in their hearts, if God should open the wickedness that there is in the hearts of men naturally. And so all unregenerate men would think you speak strange riddles when you tell them that they bless themselves. They bless God, and know of no such thing in their hearts.

Yes, there are such things, only they are not stirred, but lie quiet as mud in the bottom of a pond. It is there, yet you cannot see it until it is stirred. At first conversion, the Lord suffers your corruption to stir so that He may reveal to you what an evil heart you have, what an abundance of sin there is in your heart. And therefore some young converts look upon themselves as more loathsome and vile than they ever thought they had been.

Besides, the devil sees it is a vain thing to tempt a young convert to any gross act of sin. When conscience has life and power in it, he shall never prevail that way. But now he thinks he may prevail to disturb them with vain thoughts, and therefore he lays his strength most that way. Therefore, let not such be discouraged who find their spirits annoyed and pestered within them. If they make them to be the burden of their souls, notwithstanding much vanity of thoughts, the Lord will accept any desire that they have to sanctify His name in holy duties.

I shall give you these five rules to help you against these wandering and vain thoughts in holy duties, and especially in prayer.

RULE 1. When you go to prayer, account it to be a great work. Set a high price upon your prayer, not as having any excellency in it because it comes from you, but set a high price upon it as a great ordinance of God wherein there is communion with God to be enjoyed, and the influence of God to be conveyed through it. So set a high price on prayer every time you go to it.

"Lord, I am now setting upon a work that is of very great consequence, and much lies upon it. And I would account it to be a sore and a great evil to me if I should lose even this prayer." This would be a special means to compose your spirit, and to keep you from wandering, as was the case with Nehemiah in Nehemiah 6:3. This is a place that I have sometimes quoted upon such an occasion, when the enemies of Nehemiah, who would hinder the building of the temple, sent to him so that they might talk together. "No," he said, "I am doing a great work so that I cannot come down."

So when the devil and the vanity of your own heart would send you to parley and talk with you, give this answer: "I cannot stand parleying with these things. The work that I am about is a great work." There are very few people who account the work of prayer to be a great work. If you did, it would greatly help you against the vanity of your thoughts.

RULE 2. Every time you go to prayer, if you are most troubled with such vain thoughts, renew your resolutions against them. "I have been troubled with vain thought heretofore, and am afraid that if I do not look to it I shall lose this prayer also. Therefore, O Lord, here I renew my resolutions to set against them in this prayer with all my might."

There is a great deal that can be done by strong resolutions, for an old resolution begins to grow weak. A man who has resolved upon a thing a great while ago finds that it has little power over him. But when a man has resolved upon a thing just this morning, and just at the time when he is going about it he resolves upon it and sets himself upon it, and resolves through the grace of God that whatever difficulty he meets with, whatever it costs him, he will go through with this work.

I say that resolutions renewed have a great deal of power, and you cannot imagine what a great deal of power the renewing of resolutions against vain thoughts will have if they are renewed every time you go to prayer until you get power over your thoughts. Make trial of this. You have lost many a prayer by vain thoughts and you have been troubled for them, yet they come again. Do but try this all this week.

I said in the point of passion and anger that we should resolve with ourselves, "Well, whatever falls out this morning, I am resolved I will bear it." So remind yourself how many prayers you have lost by vain thoughts, and now renew your resolutions and covenant with God that for this prayer you will set yourself against them. Whatever pains it takes, you will be sure yet withal to look up to God's grace to assist you. You will be sure this prayer will keep your heart close to what you are about. And perhaps that will help you a little. Yet some vain thoughts will come for all that. Then the next night renew them again, and the next morning renew them again, and do that until you come to a habit of keeping your heart close to the duty. Though now you see your heart is so wild that you think it is impossible to bring it into order, certainly by such a means your heart will be brought into order.

RULE 3. Be sure to set the presence of God before you in prayer. Have a real sight of the infinite greatness, majesty, and glory of that one whom you present yourselves unto when you are calling on Him. If you can have a real sight of God in His glory, it will keep your heart close to the duty. If a man is looking about with his eyes and watching every feather, if the king or some great person came into the room, all his thoughts would be about the king or that great person who was coming in.

So if you would present the Lord in His glory and greatness, excellency, majesty, and power before you, what a merciful God He is to us in His Son, this would mightily compose our hearts. Certainly men and women are so wandering in their thoughts because their eyes are not open to look upon God in His glory. They are, as it were, dreaming, and do not apprehend that God stands and looks upon them and observes them, and that God takes notice of every wandering thought that comes from them. They do not consider that God converses with the thoughts of men as well as men do with the words of men.

RULE 4. Take heed that you are not deceived because those thoughts you have in prayer do not appear to be very evil in themselves. This is a great deceit, and hinders many in sanctifying God's name in prayer. Sometimes vain thoughts are darted in. Now because the thought has no great evil in itself, they think they may play with it, and their hearts close with it, and so run along with it as a fish does with bait. If the devil casts in a thought of blasphemy, that makes you quake and shake, but if your thoughts have no great evil in them but are slight things, matters of no importance one way or another, upon that your heart begins to be pampering and playing with them. Therefore remember this rule: in the time of prayer, whatever thoughts are in your mind that do not concern the present duty are sinful before God. Though the thoughts are never so good as far as the matter of them, yet you are to abandon them as sinful at that time. Therefore, never be deceived into thinking that these thoughts are not very sinful.

RULE 5. If God has ever helped you at any time in your prayer, so that your heart has been kept close to a duty and you have had communion with Him, bless God for that help. 'Tis a rule of very great use for us to get further assistance from God in anything, if our hearts are enlarged to bless God for any assistance we have had heretofore. And the reason why we gain and prosper so little in our Christian course is because we do not take notice of what God has done for us, to give God glory for mercies formerly received; and therefore God takes little or no delight in coming with further mercies to us.

Suppose you had a young nursery of trees and they began to thrive very well. But in came a company of caterpillars and spoiled almost all the young trees that were set; only two or three were kept from the caterpillars. If a man went into his orchard and looked upon his trees and saw that this one is spoiled and that one is spoiled, but he saw two or three that flourished fairly well and were full of buds, likely to come to something, he would rejoice mightily in those because they are saved when so many others are spoiled.

That is how you should view your prayers. Consider how many have been spoiled, as it were, by these caterpillars; for I compare wandering, vain thoughts in prayer to caterpillars that come upon trees. We see that when stormy weather comes, the caterpillars fall; and one would think that these blustering storms, and the hand of God that has been out against us, would have cleansed our thoughts and souls from these caterpillars that have been upon our duties. But many duties have been spoiled, yet you may say, "Through God's mercy, this morning in my closet the Lord has preserved a prayer for Himself, and I have gotten power over this vain heart of mine." Bless God for this, and so the Spirit of God will be more ready to come in and help you another time. But this much shall suffice to speak of this. That's the second thing, we must give up ourselves wholly to this duty.

3. There must be the breathings of the Spirit of God, otherwise God's name is not sanctified. That verse in Romans 8:26 is clear for this: "Likewise the Spirit also helpeth our infirmities, for we know not what we should pray for as we ought, but the Spirit itself maketh intercession for us with groanings which cannot be uttered."

If any of you should ask, "How can we sanctify God's name? We are poor and weak, we can do little." Mark it, it is said here that the Spirit helps our infirmities to pray. The word is exceedingly emphatic in the original. In your books it is but merely helping our infirmities, but the meaning of the word is that the Spirit helps us in these two things. Suppose a man is taking up a heavy piece of timber at one end, but he cannot get it up alone. Then another man comes along and takes it up at the other end and so helps him. The word signifies such a kind of helping as when a man takes a thing at the other end or on the other side, one standing one way, the other standing the other way; one taking up one end, the other taking up the other end.

That is the meaning of the phrase, "He helpeth our

infirmities." The poor soul is pulling and tugging with its own heart, and finds his heart heavy and dull like a log in a ditch. And have not many of you found your hearts so? But now then when you are tugging with your hearts and would gladly lift up your hearts to God in prayer, the Spirit of God comes in at the other end, takes the heaviest end of the burden, and helps you to lift it up. If a child were at the light end of the log and the other end was very heavy, if one comes and takes up the heavy end, a little strength will serve for the lighter end. So the Spirit comes and takes up the heavy end in duty and so helps our infirmities, helps together.

And the other word is "the Spirit." Together with the actings of the graces of the Spirit in our hearts, you must not say, "Alas, what can I do? It must be the Spirit of God that must do it all."

It is true, He does all. He gives converting and habitual grace as well as assisting and actuating grace. But when the Spirit has worked grace so as to convert the heart, and has given habitual grace in your heart, why, when the Spirit comes to assist it, do you expect that you should stir up all the gifts and graces of the Spirit and the very strength of your body? The Spirit of God expects that you should act to the uttermost that you are able. What power has been given you by God? And when you are acting, then the Spirit comes and helps together with us, noting that we are to put forth what strength we have.

Thus God's name will be sanctified when we put forth the graces of the Spirit in us, and the Spirit comes and helps. And what comes from us now comes from the breathings of the Holy Spirit in us; and then God, who knows the meaning of the Spirit, will know the meaning of our sighs and groans. Therefore, when you are going to prayer, you are to eye the Spirit of God. You are, by the eye of faith, to look upon the Spirit of God and to cast your soul upon the assistance of the Spirit of God. You are to look upon the Holy Ghost as appointed by the Father and the Son to that office to be a helper to His poor servants in the duties of worship, and especially in that great duty of prayer.

Now upon reading this text, and having opened it thus, this is one good help for you in prayer. Read this text and then exercise your faith upon it. "Lord, hast Thou not said that Thy Spirit helps our infirmities when we do not know what we pray for, nor how to pray for anything as we ought? But the Spirit will come, so now, Lord, make good this Word of Thine to my soul at this time and let me have the breathings of the Spirit of God in me. Alas, the breaths of men, if it comes from their gifts and parts, I know Thou wilt never regard unless there are the breathings of the Holy Ghost in me in prayer."

Now if you would know whether the Spirit of God comes in or not, you may know it by this: the Spirit of God carries us unto God and it makes the prayer sweet and delightful. As much of the Spirit of God is as there, it comes to the soul in the duty and leaves a savor behind it. A gracious savor is always left behind when the Spirit of God comes to breathe. Oh, the breath of the Spirit of God is a sweet breath, and it makes prayers sweet. It never comes in to the soul but after it has done any work it came for. It leaves a sweet scent. After that the souls finds a sweetness in that prayer.

Now many of you have been in prayer in the morning, but I appeal to you. What sweet savor of the Spirit of God is left behind? Certainly if the Spirit has been there, it is like perfume that has been put into a little box. Though you take out the perfume, there will be a sweet savor left behind. So though the Spirit of God, in respect to the present assistance, withdraws Himself, yet it leaves a sweet savor behind.

4. There must be purity of heart, pure hearts and hands

(Hebrews 10:22). Revelation 5:8: "having every one of them harps and golden vials full of odors which are the prayers of saints." Mark, the prayers of saints are odors in golden vials. The golden vials I may compare to the heart. The hearts of saints must be as golden vials, and then prayers will be as odors. In 1 Timothy 2:8, the Holy Ghost gives directions as to how we should pray, and it is with this qualification: "I will therefore that men pray everywhere lifting up holy hands without wrath and doubting."

5. The outward conversation must be pure and the heart must be pure. In Job 22:26, mark what's said concerning that holy man. There is a promise made to him for lifting up his face to God, putting away evil from his tabernacle. So by putting away evil from our tabernacles and from our hearts, we may be able to lift up our hearts with joy.

6. When we come to call upon God, we must call upon Him in truth. Psalm 145:18: "The Lord is nigh unto all, to all that call upon Him in truth."

QUESTION . "What's the meaning of that?"
ANSWER. First, there must be inward dispositions answerable to the expressions. For instance, when I come to express the greatness of the majesty of God, then I must have an inward disposition suitable to this expression. I must have a fear and reverence of the infinite majesty of God.

Second, when I come to confess my sin, to judge myself for my sin, there must be an inward disposition suitable to such a confession. Oh, how many men and women will come and speak great things against themselves for their sins, and judge themselves for their sins, and yet there is no such disposition in their hearts suitable to their words. You shall have some who, while praying with others, will be the means to break the hearts of others. They will list their sins and take such shame and confusion upon themselves for their sin, and yet God knows that their hearts are not stirred at all. And then they will call upon God for pardon of sin and for power against sin, and yet God knows that their hearts close with sin and are loath to part with sin in the meantime. This is falseness of heart when the inward disposition is not answerable to the outward expressions.

I beseech you, my brethren, consider the prayers you have made, and especially you who pray much with others. Look what expressions you have made and see whether there are answerable dispositions to the expressions you have made, and know that the Lord remembers every expression you have made.

Third, we must call upon God in truth. That is, we must conscionably perform the engagements of prayer. Prayer puts an engagement upon the heart. Now those who call upon Him in truth are conscionable to perform the engagements. For example, do I pray for any good thing? I am engaged to endeavor in the use of all means to attain that good thing. When you confess a sin, you are engaged by that means to endeavor with all your might against that sin. And when you pray for grace, you are engaged to make use of all means you can for attaining that grace.

And then, besides, in prayer there is much profession unto God for our sincerity and uprightness, and of our willingness to be at His disposal, to perform these engagements that we make to God in prayer. If God should present to us all our professions that we have made to Him in prayer, and tell us how we have come short of them, it would make us be in shame and confusion in our own thoughts.

Another thing in prayer must be said. Pray without doubting, as in the former Scripture. The prayer of faith prevails much (James 1:6–7). A man who wavers and doubts must not think to obtain anything from God. But I should have opened what that faith is that we should have in prayer. We must have faith to believe that the thing we do pleases God. Faith in God's promises as well as faith in God's providence should be exercised in the time of our prayers; and therefore, after we have done, we should go away believing. So did Hannah in 1 Samuel 1:18. We read that after she had been praying, she went away and looked sad no more. The text says this, noting that after we have been pouring forth our souls to God, we should believe and exercise faith, and not go on in as drooping a way as ever we did.

OBJECTION. You will say, "Yes, if we certainly knew that God will hear us."

ANSWER. The way to be assured that God will hear you is to be casting yourselves upon God. How can you know that He will hear but by resting upon Him? "I have been with God, and I have been doing the duty of a poor creature, and as for the success, I leave that to God." Therefore, it must be with faith.

QUESTION. "But I have so many sins mixed with my prayers, how can I believe?"

ANSWER. You have an excellent Scripture for that to help a soul to exercise faith in prayer, notwithstanding that there have been many infirmities. In Psalm 65:2–3 we read, "O Thou that hearest prayers, unto Thee all flesh shall come."

OBJECTION. "Aye, God hears prayers, but I have a great many sins that hinder."

ANSWER. No, mark what the verse says.

QUESTION. What if iniquity prevails against me. Will God still purge my transgressions away?"

ANSWER. Oh, make use of this Scripture though you do not remember other things. Yet you who have dejected hearts and are afraid that God will not hear your prayers, see what the text says," Thou hearest prayer, Lord."

QUESTION. "But will my sins hinder?"

ANSWER. No, says David, "iniquity prevails against me, as for our transgressions, Thou shalt purge them away." Exercise faith in this, and know that God does not hear your prayer because you are not sinful, because of your unworthiness, but merely because of His free grace.

Another holy disposition in prayer should be this. The soul should come with a holy freedom, with the spirit of adoption to God crying, "Abba, Father." If you come to God merely as a Judge (though it's true that those who do not know that God loves them are bound as creatures to pray) you can never sanctify the name of God until you have a child-like spirit, the spirit of adoption. The Lord loves to have His children come with freedom of spirit to Himself in prayer, to come as children, and not to come with dejected countenances and discouraged hearts. But come freely to open your heart to God as any child would open his heart to a gracious and loving father.

Another disposition is fervency in prayer. The effectual, fervent prayer of a righteous man avails much, and that will be a means to help against vain thoughts, too. When the honey is scalding hot, the flies will not come to it. If your heart were, as it were, scalding hot in prayer, you would not have such vain thoughts.

Next, there must be constancy in prayer (1 Thessalonians 5:17). By this I mean, never give over until we have that which we have prayed for, or something else in lieu of it. It may be that you have prayed and nothing has come of it. Do not be discouraged that you have to deal with a great God. Pray again and again and again, and pray with this resolution, "Well, let God do with me as He will, I will call upon Him as long as I live. And if God casts me away, He shall cast me away calling upon Him."

Take the poor woman of Canaan. When Christ called her a dog and discouraged her, yet she prayed, "Aye, but dogs have crumbs." That heart is in an ill condition in prayer because it does not get what it would, and therefore to think that we might as well not pray at all, take heed of any such thoughts.

Again, if you would pray to God indeed so as to sanctify His name in prayer, there should be humility in your hearts so as to be sensible of your own unworthiness. I spoke somewhat about being sensible of the distance between God and us when I spoke about sanctifying God's name in general.

The last thing that I shall speak of is this. When you have done all of this, these qualifications will not sanctify God's name unless it is all tendered up in the name of Jesus Christ and in the power of His merits. Let a man or woman pray with as much fervency, zeal, constancy, and purity as they can, in truth and sincerity, yet unless he puts up all in the name of Christ, I say he cannot be accepted. Our spiritual offerings must be tendered up in His name, but I have already preached much about that.

Now put all that has been said together, and this is what it is to pray. That is, when I pray understandingly, when I give myself to prayer, when there are the breathings of the Holy Ghost in my prayer, when there is purity of heart like a golden vial, when it is with sincerity, when it is in truth of heart, when it is in faith, when it comes from a spiritual adoption, when it is in fervency, when it is in constancy, reverence, humility, and all put up in the name of Jesus Christ, then a man prays.

As it was said of Saul, "Behold, he prayeth," so I may say of those who are instructed in this art, "Behold, they pray." You see now that prayer is more than to read something from a book, more than to say a few words. You see it is a very hard thing to pray, a work of great difficulty, and it is no wonder that we have lost so many of our prayers. We must not charge prayer and God with it, but look to ourselves. I mean we must not charge the ordinance of prayer, but the vileness of our carriage in our prayers.

Let us for the time come to know what a Christian life means. It is said of Christ in Luke 9:29, "as He was praying the fashion of His countenance was changed." Oh, that's an excellent thing, when we have been in our closets at prayer to come away with our faces shining. My brethren, could we but pray in such a manner as this is, the very fashion of our countenances would be changed, like Moses when he came from the presence of God upon the Mount, or as Christ, who had the fashion of His countenance changed. Prayer is the sweet ease of one's spirit; it's the help at a dead lift; it's the great ordinance of communion with God in this world; and therefore let us learn the art of sanctifying God's name in prayer.

I shall conclude all this you have heard of the mystery of sanctifying the name of God in worshipping God. Now I beseech you, you who have been a long time in the school of Christ, who are, as it were, apprentices to Christ, to learn Christianity; be ashamed that you have understood so little of this art in sanctifying the name of God in prayer. It is an art and a mystery that you must be instructed in, and you are not Christians until you are instructed in this as in an art and mystery. And that man or woman who shall be instructed truly in this art and mystery of sanctifying God's name in worshipping Him, such a man or woman shall be to all eternity sanctifying the name of God in praising Him. There is a time coming when all the saints must be in the presence of God and be always praising Him, and they shall then sanctify God's name forever. Let us now learn this art of sanctifying God's name in praying so that we may eternally sanctify His name in praising Him.

FINIS

A Summary of The Gospel

by Jeremiah Burroughs
From Gospel Conversation (1657)
and reprinted by Soli Deo Gloria Publications

The gospel of Christ in general is this: It is the good tidings that God has revealed concerning Christ. More largely it is this: As all mankind was lost in Adam and became the children of wrath, put under the sentence of death, God, though He left His fallen angels and has reserved them in the chains of eternal darkness, yet He has thought upon the children of men and has provided a way of atonement to reconcile them to Himself again.

Namely, the second Person in the Trinity takes man's nature upon Himself, and becomes the Head of a second covenant, standing charged with sin. He answers for it by suffering what the law and divine justice required, and by making satisfaction for keeping the law perfectly, which satisfaction and righteousness He tenders up to the Father as a sweet savor of rest for the souls that are given to Him.

And now this mediation of Christ is, by the appointment of the Father, preached to the children of men, of whatever nation or rank, freely offering this atonement unto sinners for atonement, requiring them to believe in Him and, upon believing, promising not only a discharge of all their former sins, but that they shall not enter into condemnation, that none of their sins or unworthiness shall ever hinder the peace of God with them, but that they shall through Him be received into the number of those who shall have the image of God again to be renewed unto them, and that they shall be kept by the power of God through faith unto salvation.